THE RUSSIAN INTELLIGENTSIA

Makers of the
Revolutionary State

The Russian Intelligentsia

Makers of the Revolutionary State

STUART RAMSAY TOMPKINS

NORMAN: UNIVERSITY OF OKLAHOMA PRESS

By Stuart Ramsay Tompkins

The Russian Intelligentsia: Makers of the Revolutionary State
(Norman, 1957)
The Russian Mind (Norman, 1953)
Alaska: Promyshlennik and Sourdough (Norman, 1945)
Russia Through the Ages (New York, 1940)

The publication of this volume has been aided by a grant from
The Ford Foundation.

To Edna

Preface

IN presenting a second volume of a series on the intellectual movements in modern Russia, the writer feels that certain explanations are in order. In the volume, *The Russian Mind*, published in 1953, an effort was made to follow the development of various phases of intellectual progress down to the terminal point of 1855. However, in presenting the story of the period from 1855 to 1917, it began to appear that by far the most significant development was the growth of a class called the *intelligentsia*, which was responsible for the various phases of the revolutionary movement. I have, therefore, concentrated on this development which has been so epoch-making in the history of Russia and of the world and have left untouched other movements of great importance but secondary to the main issue. Some of these are Russian historiography, education, literature, the women's movement, and Pan-Slavism. However, in a number of cases monographs have appeared dealing with one or another of these subjects, which seems to be justification for neglecting them. Considerations of space have also had some influence. But to emphasize what was said at the beginning, I believe that it is of the utmost importance for the English-speaking readers to understand and appreciate in its true value this very unique development.

I wish to express my gratitude to Mr. Johan G. Ohsol of New York and Professor Hans Schmitt, a former colleague in the Department of History of the University of Oklahoma. Both of these men have read the manuscript and have offered invaluable suggestions. Indeed, Mr. Ohsol placed his thorough knowledge of and experience with the revolutionary movements at my disposal. I wish to pay tribute to this extraordinarily useful assistance.

Stuart Ramsay Tompkins

Edmonton, Alberta, Canada
October 1, 1957

Contents

Contents

tion" and the Program of Terror; Domestic and Foreign Complications; Policy of the Social Revolutionary Party; "Bloody Sunday" and Its Results; Count Witte; Soviet Workers' Deputies; Widespread Strikes; Appeal for a General Rising; Activities of the "Fighting Organization"; Azeff the Spy; Martin Sauer; Pinkerton.

Illustrations

THE RUSSIAN INTELLIGENTSIA

Makers of the
Revolutionary State

1. The Reforms

THE loss of Sevastopol in 1855 left the Russian public stunned and paralyzed. After the signing of the Peace of Paris, the surge of patriotism which had pervaded all classes and had sustained the Russian Army suddenly collapsed, to be succeeded by a wave of disillusionment and near despair that swept over the country. There seemed to be no way out of the collapse for Russia except by a far-reaching organization of the state. The young monarch, Alexander II, felt that only heroic measures could lead Russia out of the morass of corruption, inefficiency, and torpor which had succeeded to the exalted spirit of war. Since he was young, it was easy for him to turn his back on the recent peace and to allow himself to be carried along by the general sweep of public opinion which was demanding a radical program of reform.

The difficulties of the monarch were not with the public but with his own government officials, most of whom were bureaucrats who had grown old in the service, were accustomed to the old ways, and could not envisage a state or an administration run on other lines than those of the past. His first measures, therefore, were in themselves, or because of the reluctant collaboration he received, halting and indecisive. But as time went on and he began to feel the pressure of public opinion behind

3

him, he gathered confidence and was prepared to press for those reforms which seemed most urgent, resorting even to methods that did not stop short of coercion to overbear the resistance of his own subordinates.

The problem of reforms had been before the Russian public vaguely for a century. The lofty aspirations of Catherine had come to nought; the generous plans of Alexander I had been frustrated largely by the Napoleonic wars and had allowed little more than superficial changes in the administration.

Liberation of serfs and distribution of land among them had been advocated most eloquently earlier by the Petersburg merchant Timofei Torgovanov.[1] In his essay entitled "Open Gate to the Temple of Happiness," he urged the apportionment of land to prevent idleness among the agriculturists and barrenness of the soil. He suggested, as had Pososhkov in the eighteenth century, that all services and dues of peasants be commuted into fixed money payments due on definite dates to government institutions so that dissatisfied landowners could not burden their underlings with undue demands. He offered to submit details on all points of his project, which he transmitted in 1810 to M. M. Speransky, to General Dibich in 1825, and also to the Tsar's General on duty, Potapov.

Though Torgovanov got no official reply to his offer, and the general question of emancipation was to remain in abeyance for half a century, the issue was put to a sort of exploratory test by the Emperor himself in the Baltic states. During his visit to Livonia in 1802, Alexander I had received the grievances of the peasants of that country who had been smarting for six centuries (since 1201) under the yoke and oppression of German invaders—the Knights of the Sword, militant armed monks and bishops sponsored by the pope, and eventually the Baltic barons, the Polish *shlyakhta*, and the Russian conquerors. Alexander issued a decree in 1804 patterned after the Swedish agrarian code whereby the Livonian peasants were granted tenure of their holdings, which were to be resurveyed, revaluated,

[1] Yakovleva etc. izd., *Velikaya Reforma, Sbornik Statei*, 55.

4

and then assessed according to their yields.[2] The peasants were granted the right to sue in courts; they were protected from willful seizure of their movable property. Breeding cattle, seed, and implements could not be seized for debts. A peasant could not be dispossessed of his holdings otherwise than by a court order.

This liberal decree aroused the Livonian barons, and they obtained its repeal. In 1819 a new decree liberated the Livonian peasants from serfdom without land, which remained the property of the landlords, who also retained complete control over police, courts, churches, inns, and markets. A similar liberation decree had been issued in 1817 for Kurland and in 1816 for Estonia.[3]

The Estonian decree contained two very odious provisions inserted through the influence of the landlords. One clause forbade the peasants to move to towns before the number of the peasant male population reached 120,000 and to go to another province before this figure reached 140,000. The law was to come into full effect only after fourteen years. The cruelty of these provisions is obvious, if we remember that not until 1854 did the peasant male population of Estonia reach the first of these figures.

After the Decembrist Revolt of 1825, the question of internal reform in Russia had been complicated by revolutionary outbursts in Europe which had generally acted as a brake. Not that Nicholas himself had been hostile to all reforms, but he still held to the old-fashioned idea that it was not possible for the autocrat to divest himself of his absolutism without endangering the tranquillity of the country. His efforts in this direction had been largely a failure. He had expressed himself, it is true, in no uncertain terms on the need for the emancipation of the serfs. "I do not understand," he is reported to have said, "how a man has become a chattel. I cannot explain this in any other way except through guile and deceit on the one hand and igno-

[2] *Latvijas Enciklopedya*, Book 7, 577.
[3] Yakovleva etc. izd., *Velikaya Reforma, Sbornik Statei*, 65.

rance on the other. We must put an end to it. Serfdom is the reason why we have neither trade nor industry among us."[4]

In his manifesto on the conclusion of the Paris peace treaty, Alexander II had promised to all his people the opportunity to "enjoy the fruits of their toil." This phrase had created a stir of disquiet among the nobility, who had interpreted these words as a threat to deprive them of the services of their serfs. The marshal of the Moscow nobility, Count Zakrevsky, urged the Tsar to allay the fears of the nobility on the occasion of his visit to Moscow. Alexander spoke to the noble lords gathered to felicitate him on the conclusion of peace:

> Gentlemen, I have heard that rumors are being circulated among you that I intend to abolish serfdom. To obviate the spread of groundless rumors on such an important matter, I deem it necessary to declare that I do not intend to do it now; but, of course, gentlemen, you can know yourselves that the existing system of ownership of souls cannot remain unchanged. It is better to abolish serfdom from above than to wait until it will begin to abolish itself from below. I beg you, gentlemen, to consider how to accomplish this. Please convey my words to the nobility for its consideration.[5]

Following this up, early in 1857, the Emperor Alexander named a nonofficial committee, the most important members of which were the minister of the interior, Lanskoy, his deputy, Milyutin, and the adjutant general, Rostovtsev. At this stage the word "emancipation" was not used, and the official language merely spoke of "the improvement of the peasant's lot." The rescript which called for the committee laid down certain guiding principles which were to be followed. First, the rights of ownership to the land should rest with the landlord, but the peasant was to be guaranteed the possession of his *usadba* and his strips in the common fields.[6] Second, the peasants were to be

---

[4] O. Kaidanova, *Ocherki po istorii narodnogo obrazovaniya v Rossii i S. S. S. R.*, II, 4.
[5] Yakovleva etc. izd., *Velikaya Reforma, Sbornik Statei*, 95.

grouped in communes under the police supervision of the landlords. Third, provision was to be made to insure collection of
all state and local taxes through the commune.

This was followed by a later document (an *otnoshenie*) of
the Minister of the Interior which spoke vaguely of a period
of transition for the peasants from serfdom to freedom. It also
listed two questions that remained to be settled. First, was the
peasant bound to redeem his *usadba* even if he showed reluctance to do so? Second, was the landlord bound to assign the
peasant his strip in the common field, and was the rent he was
required to pay to be temporary or permanent?

This document seems to have been occasioned by the petition
of the nobility of the provinces of Vilna, Grodno, and Kovno;
in reply to which Alexander had recommended the appointment of a special committee in each province to consider the
above issues. Later, in 1858, the nobility of the wealthy province
of St. Petersburg also submitted a petition and named a provincial committee; this example was followed by a number of
less important provinces. Gradually, all the provinces had
named committees, and the government met this initiative halfway and turned the nonofficial committee into a general committee on the peasant question. However, the latter, wishing
to restrict its conferences to broad general issues, recommended
that there be a special "editing commission" to receive the reports from the provinces and to sift them with a view to em-
bodying them in the necessary legislation.[7]

Thus was the great reform launched on its way. The main
committee had little to do during the year 1858 while the provincial committees were at work, and Rostovtsev, on whom
fell the bulk of the labor, went abroad to study the program

---

[6] *Usadba*, a name applied to the house and kitchen garden of the peasant
in the communal village.

[7] This material follows an article of E. I. Vishnyakov, "Khod krest'yanskoi
reformy: Nachalo zakonodatel'nykh rabot," *Velikaya Reforma*, IV, 144–45.
Much the same material can be found in S. Tatishchev, *Imperator Aleksandr
Vtoroi; Ego Zhizn i Tsarstvovanie*, I, 199–385. For some time there actually
were two editing commissions which were finally merged into one.

at his leisure and to be relieved of other duties. Towards the end of the year, the recommendations of the provincial committees began to come in, accompanied in some cases by minority reports, and were submitted to examination by the editing commission. When the latter had finally harmonized them and reduced them to legal language, the general principles of the emancipation issues began to stand out more clearly; but it required the intervention of the Emperor to overbear the opposition of the conservatives who wished to keep the reform within the narrowest limits possible.

Eventually, towards the end of 1860, the project began to take shape. Unfortunately, three of the pillars of the reforming element were removed before it appeared in its final form. Rostovtsev died in 1860, and in 1861, Lanskoy, minister of the interior, and his subordinate, Milyutin, were removed.[8] Lanskoy was succeeded by Count V. N. Panin, who was known for his conservative leanings; therefore, his appointment, even at a late stage of negotiations, had the effect of putting the brakes on the reforming movement. However, by the beginning of 1861, emancipation had reached the definitive stage, and the proclamation setting in motion the process was finally issued on February 19, 1861.

The proclamation did not attempt to legislate in detail with regard to serfdom throughout the empire or in any of its parts, but merely laid down some leading principles as basic for emancipation. First, all relations of personal servitude were terminated without compensation to the former serf's owner for the loss of such service. Second, the peasant, if he had up until this time enjoyed the *usufruct* of strips in the common field and the possession of a house and the attached structures and garden (*usadba*), was to retain these, all labor obligations being commuted for rental (*obrok*). The ownership remained with the landlord, except that the peasant's *usadba* was to be his own. Third, it was contemplated that the peasant would ultimately

8 Probably in deference to conservative opposition and because of outbreaks of student disorder. Consult Dzhanshiev's *Epokha Velikykh Reform*, 192.

8

become the owner through a process of long-term redemption, provided this could be arranged between landlord and peasants. The peasant did not become actually an individual with the right to own and to till his land as he saw fit, but he was to be a member of the commune which was collectively responsible for the payment of dues as well as the prevention of crime, for which purpose the peasants were given the right to govern themselves and to administer justice.

The above provisions covered the peasants of individual landlords. Those of the state were to be treated in general on the same principle, while household peasants, who were also subject to special treatment, were given nothing more than their freedom.

The original proclamation was followed up by a series of edicts, each of which dealt with special areas of the empire or special categories of peasants. In the final analysis the peasant might expect to receive an allotment of land lying somewhere between a minimum and a maximum for the particular area in which he resided. Later provisions provided that peasants might receive final settlement of all claims against the landlord if they would accept one-fourth of the land they had formerly tilled. To settle disputes between peasants and their landlords, special arbitrators were appointed to arrange compromises. A period of transition was provided to allow the peasants to pass from one status to another. This period varied up to twelve years.

In the beginning there was legislation to furnish a basis for the redemption of the land by the peasants, but this could only go into effect if the landlord was willing and if the peasants could furnish one-fifth of the purchase price. The voluntary nature of the provision, however, did not encourage the process; and after endless bickering and confusion, the government in 1881 insisted that the purchase should be compulsory for both parties. The landlord, under these conditions, had to forego the 20 per cent that he would earlier have received from the peasants.

9

There was, undoubtedly, injustice. One of the frequent complaints was that the landlords managed largely to secure pasture lands, woodlands, fishing rights, and other privileges formerly enjoyed by the peasants. The most serious complaint, however, was one that was difficult to resolve. The land was to be priced at its actual cash value; but in most cases probably the price was raised enough to compensate the owner, at least in part, for the labor of the peasants of whose services he was deprived. The change affected some twenty million peasants and could not but have tremendous repercussions on Russian life. Many of the difficulties were due less to the injustice than to the rigidity of the settlement, which did not allow for redistribution of population but kept the peasant chained to the commune through his redemption dues.

Hardly had the emancipation got under way when a serious revolt broke out in the Polish provinces. During the early part of 1863, the government was forced to deal with this uprising. It did not, however, seriously retard progressive reform, and it was decided to extend the emancipation to Poland. In the case of Poland, however, the peasants were given far-reaching advantages at the landlords' expense.

The second great reform was the abolition of what had long been a serious blot on Russian life and Russian justice—namely, corporal punishment. Early visitors to Russia had been horrified by the severity with which crimes and misdemeanors of all kinds were punished in the courts, in the military services, and in the schools. Moreover, peasants were liable to be punished this way by their landlords while, theoretically at any rate, even nobles had been subject to this degradation. A *ukaz* of April 17, 1863, on the birthday of the monarch, did away with the following penalties: women were exempted (this is qualified by the fact that women exiles continued to be subject to this indignity until 1893); the running of the gantlet was done away with in the army; the cat-o'-nine-tails was done away with in the navy; and the use of the whip for civil service was abolished. One form, however, that of the birch rod, was maintained for the courts of the justice of the peace, but only until adequate prisons could be provided.

In 1864 came the reform of the courts, perhaps in some respects the most far-reaching reform of all. The court system was reorganized on modern lines, the empire being divided for judicial purposes into territorial units (into which the old districts were absorbed) which contained the courts of the first instance for civil and criminal cases. Then came the *Sudebnye Palaty* (those of the second instance), to which appeal could be carried, but which also were courts of the first instance for important civil and criminal cases. The Administrative Senate acted as a supreme court of cassation.

The most significant part of this, however, was the complete separation of police and judicial powers; though preliminary hearings remained secret, the justices were to be independent and irremovable. Trials were to be open to the public, and evidence was to be given orally instead of in written depositions as formerly. The theory of formal proof was abolished, and evidence was to be evaluated as in the Western countries. The practice of law was entirely separated from the official bureaucracy; lawyers, whether prosecution or defense attorneys, henceforth formed a corporate body with certain rights of self-government. The most radical change was the introduction of trial by jury. This caused a great deal of heart-searching, for a very considerable body of the Russian people believed that the system could not be applied in Russia, owing to the disposition of the Russians to regard the criminal as more sinned against than sinning. Peasant justice, as formerly, was dispensed by the peasants in their own courts in which they applied their own standards. For unimportant cases the government decided to make the experiment with justices of the peace, but this system was discontinued in 1889.[9]

The third great reform was the restoration of autonomy to

[9] A full account of these changes is contained in Samuel Kucherov, *Courts, Lawyers, and Trials Under the Last Three Tsars*, chapter 1. The book also contains an extensive bibliography.

the universities. The universities in Russia had been formed on the German model, with a considerable degree of self-government. This had been seriously abridged by Nicholas I in the period from 1835 to 1849. Freedom of thought had a precarious existence in Russia and had been subject to the whim of autocracy. Various student disturbances in 1861 were evidence that academic circles were chafing under these restraints. The government, however, went only part way in its concessions. While the rights of self-government of the faculty were restored in 1864, student self-government was curtailed.

On April 6, 1865, after ten years of vacillation on the part of the government, during which various temporary measures had been enacted, it was finally decided to replace the old form of censorship (*predvaritel'naya*), by which all books and periodicals had to submit to preliminary examination by the censor, with a new one (*karatel'naya*). Henceforth, the press was to be free from interference, subject only to the full severity of the law when it offended against law, morality, and the like. The law provided for a series of warnings, on the third of which the paper could be suspended or suppressed.

In 1865 came the reform of local government. This was organized on both a provincial (*guberniya*) and a county (*uyezd*) basis. Both *zemstva* consisted of two parts, the administrative and the legislative branches. The second of these, the so-called assembly of the county *zemstva*, consisted of delegates elected by the village communes, by the towns, and by the nobles on a class franchise. The provincial assembly consisted of delegates from the county assemblies. In general the fields of activity of the two types were not clearly differentiated. Both were to provide for local needs such as schools, hospitals, public health, roads, and bridges and were authorized to engage in general activities to promote the welfare of the population. Between 1865 and 1867 *zemstva* were organized in the greater part of European Russia—Poland, the Caucasus, and Asiatic Russia being excepted. The *zemstva*, in addition to raising money for their own needs, were required to collect taxes

12

levied by the government. There was some complaint that the demands made by the government were so heavy that it was impossible for the *zemstva* to raise adequate sums for local needs. Nevertheless, the *zemstva* were regarded as a bright spot in Russian history, and gave the population for the first time a wide field of activity for local initiative.

The next important reform was the introduction of municipal self-government in the cities, which took place June 16, 1870. This was in reality an amplification of the reforms of 1785 inaugurated by the Empress Catherine. It provided for the town assembly (of all the *ratepayers*), a council elected by the citizens, and a mayor (or *golova*). For the first time in the history of Russia, there emerged some measure of urban self-government.

The last of the great reforms was that providing for universal military service, introduced on January 1, 1874. The legislation terminated the old system inaugurated by Peter, under which military service was an obligation of two classes of the community only, the peasants and the *myeshchane*. Under this system military service fell on persons selected by the landlord, or by a government official in the case of the state peasants. Since only a proportion of the population was liable, it resulted in the selection of the most unfit physically and mentally. This service, which was of twenty-five years' duration, was shunned by all who were able to avoid it. The army, therefore, was made up of the dregs of humanity, and the measures of discipline and the conditions of life were almost intolerable. This reform, however, was not dictated by humanitarian motives entirely, but was rendered necessary by the striking victory of the Prussians in the Franco-Prussian War. Russia, like all other countries, had to follow the example of Germany to keep up in the race of armaments. Since all persons were now liable to military service, it removed any stigma heretofore attached to the service.

The original impulse to reform must have been extremely powerful to have carried the Emperor and his officials along for almost twenty years, and by any test was nothing less than epoch-making. It is true that after 1861 public interest fell and enthusiasm flagged, but, despite the Polish revolt, Alexander persisted in his efforts. The attempt of Karakozov on Alexander's life in 1866 is often alleged to have put an end to the reforms, but actually two important pieces of legislation followed it some years later.

The reforms were received with coldness and some disappointment. The emancipation of the peasants left them still chained to the commune and incapable of holding land in their own names. Moreover, they were subject in all things to the authority of the commune. In the commune, however, each peasant had the right to express his views and take part in its deliberations. Moreover, the new courts of the justice of the peace were little more than peasant's courts presided over by a *starosta*, who was also a peasant and who tried his cases according to peasant law. There were claims of injustice in the distribution of the lands by the commune; the peasants generally lost out in the amounts they received and in the payments required of them either as rental or as redemption dues when the scheme of compulsory purchase was inaugurated. This is all true, and yet in the light of Russia's past the reforms mark a step forward. It is probable that the most serious criticism leveled at the emancipation concerned the inadequate amount of land assigned and the tying of the peasants to the land by making them members of the commune, from which it was almost impossible to separate themselves. As the population increased, recourse was had to continual division and redivision of the allotments to provide for the descendants of the original proprietors, and the passport requirements to which all were subject in Russia did not allow the peasants to move to unsettled areas, even should he persuade the commune to release him. Moreover, the redemption dues weighed heavily on the peasants, and the result was that the increased population, without any corresponding increase in the amount of land or in the productivity of that land, meant that each generation had

14

a harder time than the preceding one. The most striking proof of the inadequacy of the emancipation settlement was the disastrous famines through which Russia passed in 1891–92 and 1897–98. It is no wonder that General Kuropatkin reported in 1900 that the peasants called up for military service were showing alarming signs of malnutrition.

The reforms of Alexander II were in some respects a complete break with Russian tradition in that they for the first time seemed to associate the representatives of the people in the tasks of government; the judicial system, as well as certain other matters, brought Russia into line with Western Europe. They constituted, however, more or less of an experiment by the autocracy to establish how far the principles of absolutism could be combined with those of popular participation in government. It will be instructive to examine to what extent this gesture inviting the people to participate in their own government was successful.

It is difficult at this distance, when the reforms have long since been wiped out, to make anything like an accurate and convincing appraisal of their effectiveness. Together they would, in any country and in any age, constitute an impressive achievement; they certainly stand out as little less than revolutionary in a country where Peter had long since set the pattern for clean breaks with tradition. But, like Peter's reforms, those of Alexander II have provided a fertile field for speculation and theory, and those who entered on it have often taken diametrically opposed points of view. It will be instructive perhaps to examine these.

At best, the program of emancipation represented a compromise. It pleased neither the extreme conservatives, who would have none of it, nor the extreme radicals, who would have accompanied the grant of individual freedom with a grant of land. The latter, being the more vocal element, quickly gained the ear of the public with their contention that a great wrong had been done. But there was another more serious defect. Emancipation came at a time when the economic theories of the Man-

15

chester school in England were everywhere in the ascendant and Alexander and his entourage had been persuaded of the advantages of a system of *laissez faire*. When, therefore, the emancipation settlement stopped short of making the peasant a free agent in his economic relations and put a curb on individual initiative and enterprise, there was involved a serious contradiction between two opposing principles. This grave weakness was not immediately apparent, but as the century drew to a close, the widespread famines pointed up in a manner that could not fail to be understood the complete bankruptcy of the whole emancipation program.

Perhaps in one sense the reform of the courts represented the most beneficial of all the reforms and marked the most radical departure from tradition. But here again its later history is befogged by propaganda. The revolutionaries were determined to find nothing good in any of the reforms, as we see in this characteristic blast from one of their underground organs:

The autocracy [after the Crimean War] was forced to have recourse to liberal reforms. The people were given freedom but the *knut* was ready to strike everywhere the enthusiastic citizen, when in his faint-hearted disbelief in the sincerity of the aims of the autocracy, he incontinently took the fictitious freedom for real. The brilliantly colored curtain of liberal reforms, the announcement of "self-government," and *habeas corpus* were quickly assessed at their real value. The bitter disillusionment of the intelligent strata of society; the agitation among the peasants in the various parts of Russia on the occasion of the "half-emancipation" from the bonds of serfdom, only to pass into the bonds of indenture to the same lords; the kindling among the people of a conscious longing for self-education; the active spread of socialist propaganda, foreign to the old European tradition; all marks of ferment testifying in the opinion of today's bureaucrat to the immaturity and incapacity of society to adapt the benevolent reforms of the "peace-loving Tsar-emancipator," frightened in no humorous way, the imperial government. It required no sharp spur from without to exploit the opportunity against the discontented disturbers of the peace. With a movement so deep-

16

seated and grave, the attempt of Karakozov was not needed to
spur the autocratic government, to make it abandon its program
of reform, to substitute one of criminal police adapted to curb
the rising popular clamor. Following the secret trial of Karakozov in the torture chamber, the so-called rescript of the Emperor to Gagarin, full of patriotic fury against the false teaching seeping down to the people, summoned the administration
to exercise vigilance over the political temper of the people. The
native administration awoke from sleep and put the question
bluntly: Can the autocracy, after abolishing serfdom, count on
the people? To the question raised, history has already answered
in the negative. With the dissembled retort of Ivan Groznyi at
the place of execution, the bonds linking the Tsar to his people
were snapped, the confused picture of the Tsar, combined with
the hope of freedom from the violent rule of the boyars, flashes
on the people.[10]

Dostoyevskii, in a brilliant chapter in his *Diary* written in
1873, took an unfavorable view of the new courts and particularly of the jury system. In discussing one of his favorite topics,
the tendency which he ascribed to the Russian people to regard
the criminal as the unfortunate victim of circumstances, he
claimed that the consequence was an epidemic of acquittals by
the juries when the new courts were established.

And now, it is well known that they seldom find a man guilty
but invariably acquit him. . . .
Quite recently I have been living abroad for a number of
years. When I left Russia the new courts had just begun to function. How eagerly I read everything in the Russian newspapers
that had to do with the Russian courts. . . . But sometimes when
I left the reading room, I almost felt envious of *émigrés* and emigration. My heart felt a stab of pain. You read that they acquitted
a wife who had killed her husband. The guilt was clear, having
been proved beyond a shadow of doubt; she admitted it. "Yet

[10] *Nachalo*, April, 1878, "Narod i Gosudarstvo," *Revolyutsionnaya Zhurnalistika Semidesyatykh Godov*, 70–71. According to Kluge, *Nachalo* was not
the organ of any one party but represented the anarchism (of Bakunin), with
its peasant cult. See Kluge, *Die Russische Revolutionäre Presse*, 97.

17

she is innocent." "Here is a young man who has broken open a safe and stolen money. He was madly in love, of course, and needed money to gratify his mistress." And though all these incidents are justified by compassion or pity, yet the fact is that I could not grasp the grounds for acquittal. A vague feeling, almost a shameful one, struck me. In these moments I saw Russia as some kind of slough, or a morass, in which someone was planning to build a palace. To look at it, you would think it firm and smooth, and yet it is something like the surface of a pot of jelly. Venture a step and you will sink down out of sight. I often upbraided myself for my meanness of spirit; I took some comfort, however, [from the thought] that from a distance I might see things wrongly; that in spite of everything I was for the time being an *émigré;* I did not see things at close range. . . .[11]

It is highly questionable whether Dostoyevskii was justified in his strictures on the jury system in Russia. He had a passionate interest in courts and lawyers, and his *Diary* as well as his books are generously sprinkled with passages dealing with this subject. But his judgment, written in 1873 on the basis of what he had read in the papers, was delivered a bare nine years after the courts had come into existence (1864). Later judgments on the basis of longer experience cast a serious doubt on the propensity of the Russian juries to acquit in the ordinary criminal case. While opinions are by no means unanimous concerning the merits of the jury system, a recent work makes the following claim:

The fifty years in which trials with jury existed in Russia have brilliantly proved all the futility of the objections presented against this institution in Russia and of the criticism formulated against its functioning after it had been introduced. The bold experiment of turning over jurisdiction concerning the most important and complicated criminal cases to a people emancipated

[11] F. M. Dostoyevskii, *Dnevnik Pisatelya, za 1873 god.* The first citation is from 194, the second from 203. Both are taken from a discussion of *Sreda* (environment). From his unfavorable comparison of the operation of the jury system in Russia with its functioning in England, one would judge he thought the Russian people not mature enough to make the proper use of it.

from serfdom "almost yesterday" proved a success. This was a fact which the government had to acknowledge after several decades of the most furious attacks against the jury on the part of the rightist press, which, of course, in that case as in all others, expressed views completely or almost completely inspired by the government.[12]

The truth is that it was the acquittal of political prisoners with which the government was concerned. The most notorious of these cases was the acquittal and discharge of Vera Zasulich in 1879 by a jury that tried the case against her for having fired on and wounded General Trepov, governor-general of St. Petersburg. As a result of this and other incidents, these cases were withdrawn from juries.[13]

The worst that can be said of the new judicial system is that Russia was probably not prepared for it and that it had no native roots. The same applies to the introduction of the *zemstva*, though these were perhaps a revival of older institutions of local self-government that had been destroyed during the process of centralization of the autocracy.[14] There was no tradition to buttress any of the new institutions, no organized groups to rally to their support, and they were rooted not in the habits of a people but in an autocratic *ukaz* which could take away what it had given. The fact is that the revolutionaries attacked the reforms because they had not gone far enough;

[12] Samuel Kucherov, *Courts, Lawyers, and Trials Under the Last Three Tsars*, 82. Kucherov supports his claims with impressive citations from many authors. D. A. Rovinskii, the jurist who helped prepare the judicial reform, similarly dismissed these arguments, somewhat scornfully. See Dzhanshiev, *Epokha Velikykh Reform*, 508–509.

[13] *Ibid.*, 83.

[14] For a discussion of this problem see V. D. Kuzmin-Karatayev, "Krest'-yanstvo i Zemstvo," in *Velikaya Reforma*. For the origin of the *zemstvo*, Kuzmin-Karatayev goes back to the dyarchy established by Ivan IV in 1564, which consisted of two distinct parts—the *zemshchina*, embracing local authorities, and the *oprichnina*, representing the central authority. He implies that local self-government was no longer needed under serfdom when the landlord acted as the agent of the government, which was endeavoring to increase centralization at this time, but that its reintroduction in 1864 was rendered imperative by the emancipation of the peasants.

19

the bureaucracy and the conservatives, because they had gone too far. The worst aspect of the introduction of reforms in Russia is that they were regarded as a sign of weakness and an excuse for demanding more. Reform based on a compromise between two extremes did not recommend itself to either side. The struggle between the government and the revolutionaries was regarded by both as a trial of strength, and the results were always considered from the partisan points of view of the extremists.

During the last forty years of the nineteenth century, the country made considerable economic progress. At this time, when the principles of the Manchester school were everywhere in the ascendant in Europe, it was taken for granted that relaxation of protective tariffs and of government controls were indispensable to sound economic development, and that if the government permitted private initiative to function, progress would take place naturally, as it had done in the countries of Western Europe.

In Russia, however, progress was disappointingly slow except in one field. The exception was the building of railroads, for which the government relied on private enterprise stimulated by the policy of guaranteeing loans floated by the individual companies. This seems to have encouraged the progress of railway expansion, which can be characterized by no other words than an orgy of speculation.[15] Most persons promoting the companies were concerned only with amassing private fortunes and not with the operation of the railways. By the end of the reign of Alexander II, about seventeen thousand *versts* had been constructed, largely through government loans. Even-

[15] A good account of the speculation is given in Tatishchev, *Imperator Aleksandr Vtoroi*. This matter is discussed at great length in Witte, *Vospominiya*, III, Chapter VII. There is some parallel with the period of western railroad expansion in the United States, except that the Russian government was unable to give the companies of the prospective railways grants of land, and was forced to resort to the policy of guarantee of loans. Sometimes the capital costs only were guaranteed, sometimes the interest also was guaranteed, and in a few cases operation costs as well. But the "Railroad Kings," who rose in this way to sudden wealth, were detested in Russia, as Witte explains.

tually, the confusion in the passenger-freight tariffs and the chaotic services forced the government to purchase the railroads back, a project which was begun under Vyshnegradskii (minister of finance, 1887–92). In 1891 the government proceeded with the construction, at government expense, of the trans-Siberian railway, which was completed in 1905.

Some expansion occurred in other lines. The textile industry, largely operated by free labor, was modernized by the importation of English machinery and skilled English operators, and began to assume considerable proportions. Indeed, by 1885 this industry was already having its labor troubles. The iron and steel industries suffered from the emancipation. The mines and mills in the Urals had been largely manned with serf labor, and after emancipation it was impossible to hold the peasants there. The difficulty of securing a free labor supply in the Urals led to the transfer of the metallurgy industries from the Urals to the Donets Basin, where both coke and iron could be readily obtained. Eventually, however, the transition from serf to free labor was completed. By 1890, industry as a whole had adjusted itself to a new social and economic order, and under the stimulus of increased railroad building, a protective tariff, and the introduction of the gold standard (which meant more favorable conditions for inviting foreign capital), Russia entered on an industrial boom that some have called a revolution and which went a long way towards rendering Russia relatively independent of other industrial countries.

However, there were breakers ahead. In 1891–92 and 1897–98, the wheat-producing areas of Russia passed through disastrous famines which pointed up the backwardness of Russian agriculture; when an industrial depression followed after 1899, the country was in the throes of an economic crisis of the first magnitude. This crisis was complicated by the Russo-Japanese War, which served to heighten the tension and increase the confusion, with the result that Russia passed through a revolutionary upheaval from which emerged the constitution of October 17, 1905.

Many persons observing the rapid transformation of Russia that was occurring in the nineties were confident that she had embarked on the course followed by the countries of Western Europe, and would shortly be assimilated to their ways of life. In Russia itself, however, the situation was viewed differently. There was a sense of frustration in the incompleteness of the reforms and the inadequate progress that was being made. The temper of the country, therefore, was not optimistic; and when the industrial and agricultural crisis arose, there was an almost irresistible tendency to believe that the reforms of 1861–74 should be replaced by far more drastic measures which would mean nothing more nor less than a complete revolution in Russian life.

2. Public Opinion

IT might be assumed that the reforms of Alexander II which ushered in the period of economic development, somewhat slow in the early decades but gathering speed as the century drew to a close, would have been accepted by the Russian public as a normal and welcome change from the sloth and stagnation of the previous century and a half. There were, of course, those who acquiesced or who wholeheartedly approved this change and believed that Russia was about to be assimilated to the pattern of Western Europe. This opinion, however, was not general, and there was to be observed a curious phenomenon: while the government was urging the country in one direction, many of its writers were urging that this direction was the opposite of what Russia should follow. This disagreement is so striking that a careful search is required for the reasons that led to it. Our first task, however, should be to narrate the developments as they occurred and leave aside, for the present, speculation about the reasons for them.

When Alexander II came to the throne on the death of his father in March of 1855, there was almost universal relief, with the dawning hope that now the country could escape from the straitjacket in which it had been held from 1848 to 1855. This optimism, it is true, was dimmed by the defeat at Sevastopol

23

which occurred in September of 1855, but the general yearning for peace was so great and Russian military effort so exhausted that Alexander swallowed his pride and his anger at the defection of Austria and agreed to meet the Allies at Paris. The conclusion of peace cleared the way for the reforms, talk of which was everywhere. The various steps in the inauguration of sweeping changes in government and society have been recorded in the previous chapter. We will now pick up the thread of the development of public opinion during the early years of Alexander's reign.

It appears that the first joy at relief from the horrors of war, and the expectation that the country was in for a period of relaxation of autocratic discipline and changes in the government to meet the expectations of the new age, were almost universal. This optimism was especially seen in censorship, which generally began to enjoy a period of comparative freedom, not on account of any change in the law but merely because of the relaxation of administrative pressures. Another symptom was the executive order of the Tsar that made the peasant question the order of the day and indicated his intention to emancipate the peasants. In the field of education the new trend was marked by the withdrawal of the restrictive measures which had curbed the activities of the students and faculty and by preparations for drawing up a new code. One indication of a new deal was the favor extended to Dr. N. I. Pirogov. Dr. Pirogov had had charge of the medical services at Sevastopol and had gained a high reputation for his ability as an organizer and his devotion to duty, which caught the Russian imagination. He already had some reputation for his work in the field of philosophy as well as medicine, having displayed great boldness and originality in both. He was known to have novel ideas in the field of education, and the government recognized his ability by giving him several positions, the most notable being that of curator of schools of the educational district of Kiev, a position which he held until 1861. The ban on private schools and *pensions* in the capital was raised.[1] By 1857 the reforms were in full swing. In 1859 came the organization of the first Sunday schools, whose formation was encouraged by the government with the view to eradicating illiteracy. However, official favor was soon withdrawn, and they were suspended in 1862.[2]

It must not be supposed that these changes were due to the initiative of the government alone. Change was in the air, and the government could only respond to the altered atmosphere. In the words of one writer:

> After the Crimean campaign, Russia seemed to wake as from a heavy sleep. She saw herself on the brink of an abyss. Confidence in the power of the government gave way. The country was in danger. Everyone was talking of the necessity of reform. Political activity became all of a sudden the pressing need of the moment. Literature could not be irresponsive. The political press seemed created perforce. I say "perforce" for Alexander's government was by no means disposed to put up with its appearance. But the intelligentsia felt it was already strong enough to act alone.[3]

One phase of the general stirring in the popular mind was the peasant unrest that attended the ending of the war. Given below is a citation on this, unfortunately not documented by the author:

> The threat of a peasant rising became especially dangerous during and after the Crimean War. In the years 1855–60, there were 474 serious peasant disturbances. Peasant disturbances in connection with the *ukaz* of April 3, 1854, with reference to naval forces and the manifest of January 29, 1855, with reference to full mobilization of the people, set in motion a mass exodus of the peasants from their landlords with the intention of enlisting in the armed forces and receiving their freedom. Rumors of the possibility of escaping from serfdom by that method were

---

[1] O. V. Kaidanova, *Ocherki po istorii narodnogo obrazovaniya v Rossii i S. S. S. R. na osnove lichnogo opyta i nablyudeniya*, I, 109.
[2] *Ibid.*, I, 288.
[3] Lev Tikhomirov, *Russia, Political and Social*, II, 83.

not justified. Serfs who appeared voluntarily to enlist were beaten with rods for leaving their estates of their own free will and sent off. In the stubborn refusal (of the peasants) to obey their masters, serious disturbances took place in the provinces of Ryazan, Vladimir, Nizhni Novgorod, Tambov, Penza, Saratov, Simbirsk, Voronezh, and Kiev.

The disturbances were repressed. The instigators were made to run the gantlet, they were beaten with *spitzruten*. This did not stop the movement. Violent peasant risings were growing into a revolution. The "secret committee" called into life by order of Alexander for considering measures for regulating the life of the peasants, at its first meeting on January 3, 1857, resolved to proceed with the abolition of serfdom.[4]

Other moves, such as the abolition of the famous Committee of April 2, which took place on December 6, 1855, unsettled the public mind and prepared it for the relaxation of restrictions, although many of these relaxations were years in coming.

The new era in censorship inaugurated in 1855 is attested to by Nikitenko in his diary,[5] and in 1857 the Minister of Public Instruction was directed to review censorship regulations.[6] It appears, therefore, that for the years following the accession of Alexander, there was an almost universal movement towards freedom in public life and in publishing. Nekrasov hailed the new regime in a short poem:

> *My favorite idea*
> *That the Petersburg climate is terrible,*
> *I can now insert*
> *In every article without fear.*
> *(Probably, I could not formerly put in every article without*
> *fear).*
> *But having undergone the blows of fate,*
> *At length in old age I have attained happiness.*
> *I have smoked cigars on the street.*
> *And written without censorship.*[7]

[4] A. M. Pankratova, Introduction to N. A. Alekseyev *Protsess N. G. Chernyshevskogo; arkhivnye dokumenty.*

This relative freedom from censorship seems to have reached its highest point in 1858.[8] There followed a period of vacillation on account of the uncertainty in the government as to how far this relaxation should go,[9] and until 1861 there was a period of tightening up of censorship through police supervision.

The year 1859 is generally taken as the point of rupture between the government and the public over the question of reforms. It is said that the writer Chernyshevskii definitely joined the opponents of the government on the question of emancipation after having for four years used his periodical *Sovremennik* as a mouthpiece for suggestions concerning the course this measure should take. Thereafter, he refused to discuss the project directly, and his views on the matter only revealed in articles expressed in "Aesopian language," were definitely inflammatory. Even Herzen, who had greeted the Tsar's original announcement of the approaching emancipation, was becoming critical of the government and of the various committees created to bring it about. By 1861 the coldness towards the government that had set in two years earlier had turned to open hostility, and the tension between the administration and the public flared into violent disorder that swept the universities. These uprisings led to a shake-up in the government, which resulted in the replacement of Lanskoy as minister of the interior by Valuev and the naming of Admiral Putyatin as minister of education.[10]

It was presumed by 1861 that emancipation had finally been worked out, but the government's solution of the problem did not please the peasants and generally had a bad press. The student disorders of 1861 were taken as an indication of widespread opposition to the emancipation settlement. These inci-

[5] N. A. Engelhardt, *Ocherki istorii Russkoi Tsenzury v Sviazi s Razvitiem Pechati, 1703–1903*, 222.
[6] Mikhail Lemke, *Epokha tsenzurnykh reform, 1859–65*, 15.
[7] Engelhardt, *Ocherki*, 202–203.
[8] *Ibid.*, 233.
[9] *Ibid.*, 227.
[10] Lemke, *Epokha*, 39–41.

dents were shortly followed by a number of surprising events, including the distribution of a series of pamphlets calculated to inflame the minds of the people and to urge action against the government. These proclamations included "To the Young Generation," "Young Russia," "To the Landlords' Peasants," and others. It was evident that there was taking shape an underground organization, probably with contacts abroad that were directing these activities.[11]

The following year saw an epidemic of incendiary fires in the capital which were ascribed to the activity of revolutionary groups. Opinion hostile to the government began to take form with the organization of groups such as *Velikoruss* (with a periodical of the same name), and *Zemlya i Volya*, a somewhat ephemeral group which took up the cause of the peasant. But in the spring of 1861, *Sovremennik*, regarded rightly or wrongly as the center of the anti-governmental movement, was suspended, and Chernyshevskii went back to his native Samara to await the verdict of the government on the fate of the journal. Two things occurred at this time to show to what lengths Chernyshevskii and his followers would go and how deep was the government's distrust of them.

The first was the "Letters Without Address," addressed by Chernyshevskii to the monarch (but suppressed by the censors); the second was an offer transmitted from Herzen in London to Chernyshevskii to undertake the publication of *Sovremennik*, should the government refuse its resumption. This offer was conveyed in a letter entrusted to Vyetoshnikov by Herzen. A telegram from some *agent provocateur* in the circle of revolutionary exiles betrayed the news to the government. The courier was stopped at the frontier and the letter confiscated. This seems to have had a good deal to do with sealing the fate of Chernyshevskii, against whom the government now proceeded in deadly earnest.[12]

[11] The smuggling of one of these proclamations, "To the Younger Generation," into Russia involved Mikhailov and led to his arrest and exile. See Pankratova in Introduction to N. A. Alekseyev, *Protsess Chernyshevskogo*, X.

28

For some time the Third Section had been paying special attention to Chernyshevskii. From October of 1861 until his arrest, he was under constant observation, with no less than 113 separate reports being turned in on him by agents. But until the summer of 1862 no incriminating evidence had been found.

In the meantime, information from an entirely different source was put in the hands of the police as a weapon against the writer. A young officer in a uhlan regiment by the name of Vsevolod Kostomarov—a nephew of the well-known historian who was at that time a professor of history at the University of Moscow—had established relations with a number of the radicals, including Chernyshevskii, and had secured a private press on which he printed at least one proclamation, "To the Landlords' Peasants."[13]

Kostomarov's brother, Nikolai, suspected him of complicity and denounced him to the police, whom he provided with copies of two incriminating proclamations, "To the Russian Soldiers" and "To the Landlords' Peasants," the second of which he ascribed to Chernyshevskii. Meantime the proclamation, "To the Younger Generation," published in London, had been brought back to Russia by Mikhailov, who was included in the denunciation of Nikolai Kostomarov.

Vsevolod Kostomarov was taken into custody and incriminated Mikhailov, who was arrested, tried, and sentenced to fifteen years of hard labor (reduced by the Tsar to seven years). During his confinement, Kostomarov was apparently approached by the police with the view of bringing up a case against Chernyshevskii. Kostomarov's own complicity in the revolutionary movement was apparently used to bring pressure on him, but he was shrewd enough not to give the police what they wanted until he was assured of relative immunity for himself.

At this point we perhaps ought to recapitulate the activities of

---

[12] I. Novich, *Zhizn'Chernyshevskogo*, 235.
[13] Lemke, *Politicheskie Protsessy v Rossii 1860-kh govov*, 325, 367–68.

Chernyshevskii in order to explain why he came to be associated by the government with this and succeeding outbreaks of revolutionary violence.

Sovremennik, of which he was editor-in-chief, after 1859 adopted a critical, and even hostile, tone towards emancipation. Although this attitude was veiled by Aesopian language and by other means of circumventing the censors, it was sufficiently pronounced to draw the attention of well-wishers of the government and of those who urged a policy of reserve while emancipation was being worked out. In 1859 Chernyshevskii forwarded to Herzen a communication, "Letter From a Russian Man," in which he castigated Herzen for the complaisant tone his paper had adopted towards the government, then engaged in the final draft of the degree on emancipation. Herzen printed the letter in the issue of *Kolokol* of March 1, 1860, without comment.[14] (There is no indication of the authorship but A. A. Sleptsov, a member of the secret society, *Zemlya i Volya,* credited it to Chernyshevskii. It appears in Herzen's works.)[15] Eventually, the language of *Sovremennik* became so intemperate as to draw from Herzen his famous article, "Very Dangerous," in which he issued from London a warning to the editors that their periodical was transgressing the bounds of prudence and wisdom. Moreover, it seemed to Chernyshevskii to cast some doubt on his integrity, and it was this, apparently, that moved Chernyshevskii to journey to London to interview Herzen in the summer of 1861. The encounter was cordial, for both men respected one another. Herzen's comment after the meeting was:

> An extraordinarily clever fellow and with such brains; the more striking is his opinion of himself. Why, he is convinced that the *Sovremennik* is the navel of Russia. He has consigned us poor people to oblivion. Still it seems to me that he is in a bit of a hurry to bury us—we are very much alive.[16]

14 *Ibid.,* 167–72.
15 A. Herzen, *Polnoe Sobranie Sochinenii i Pisem* (ed. by M. Lemke), T. X, 228–29.

Despite his cordiality, Herzen expressed his strong disapproval of Chernyshevskii's views (though actually more in sorrow than in anger). The two having agreed to disagree, Chernyshevskii took his departure.[17]

There are various other events involving Chernyshevskii. Quoted below is the account of a memorable meeting between Dostoyevskii and Chernyshevskii.

Dostoyevskii, having at that time returned from exile in a chastened and repentant mood, was disturbed at the course events were taking and lent his support to the forces of law and order. He tells in his *Diary of a Writer* of his approach to Chernyshevskii:

> One morning, at the door of my apartment on the knob, I found one of the most unique proclamations that had up till then appeared and it seems there were enough of them. It was entitled "To the Younger Generation." One could imagine nothing more absurd or stupid. The contents were scandalous, expressed in the most ridiculous language, such as only a criminal could conceive for some murderous purpose. I was terribly upset and depressed all day. . . .
>
> . . . Towards evening, I suddenly made up my mind to call on Chernyshevskii. Up till then I had not once visited him nor do I think he had ever been at my place.
>
> I recall it was five o'clock in the afternoon. I found Nikolai Gavrilovich quite alone, none of his servants even were at home, and he opened the door for me himself. His greeting was very cordial and he asked me in to his office.
>
> "Nikolai Gavrilovich, what does this mean?" I pulled out the proclamation. He took it from me as though he had never seen it and read it through. There were only about ten lines.
>
> "Well, what about it?" he enquired with a slight smile.
>
> "Can it be possible they are so stupid and ridiculous? Isn't there some way to put a stop to this rubbish?"
>
> He replied with deliberation, weighing his words carefully.

[16] Evgen'ev-Maksimov, *Sovremennik pri Chernyshevskom i Dobrolyubovye*, 391.
[17] *Ibid.*, 388.

"Surely you don't suppose that I have anything to do with them, or think that I could have had a hand in composing this document?"

"Of course, I did not suppose that," I replied, "and I even regard it as superfluous to assure you on that point. But in any event, they must be stopped at all cost. You carry some weight with them, and, of course, they respect your judgment."

"But I don't know any of them."

"I believe you. But it is not necessary to know them or to talk to them personally. All you have to do is express your disapproval in conversation and they will hear of it."

"Perhaps, that won't do it. And these incidents are inevitable and of no importance."

"And yet they are harmful to everyone and everything."

At that moment another guest rang the bell; I do not remember who. I left. I think it my duty to recall that I talked frankly with Chernyshevskii and it was my conviction then as it is now that he had had nothing to do with those disseminators of propaganda. It appeared to me that Nikolai Gavrilovich was not pleased with my visit. Some days later he confirmed that impression when he paid me a call himself. He stayed for an hour and I admit, I have seldom met a milder and more reasonable person, so that I could not then understand his reputation for being irascible and lacking in cordiality. It was clear to me that he wanted to make my acquaintance, and I remember this flattered me. I called on him once more and he returned my call. Later, for some reason, I moved to Moscow and lived there ten months. As a result, our short-lived acquaintance came to an end. Subsequently, he was arrested and sent into exile. I never could find out anything about his case. Even today I have no idea about it.[18]

This account of Dostoyevskii's is at variance with Chernyshevskii's own version, which is given below:

Some days after the fire which destroyed the Tolkuchii market, my servant handed me a card with the name F. M. Dostoyevskii and said that this caller wished to see me. I at once went

[18] Dostoyevskii, *Dnevnik Pisatelei za 1873 god*, 210–13.

into my reception room; there stood a man of medium height or slightly under, whose face was somewhat familiar to me from pictures I had seen of him. I went up to him and asked him to sit on the divan and sat down beside him, remarking that I was very pleased to see the author of *Poor Folk*. After some seconds of hesitation he replied to my greeting by plunging without any preliminaries into an abrupt explanation of the purpose of his visit, in brief, simple, and direct language, somewhat as follows: "I have come to you on a pressing matter with an urgent request. You are close to the persons who have burned the Tolkuchii market and have influence with them. I beg you, dissuade them from a repetition of what they have done." I had heard that Dostoyevskii's nerves were shattered almost to the point of a mental breakdown, but I had not supposed that his disorder had gone so far that he could associate me with the burning of the Tolkuchii market. Seeing that the mental disturbance of the poor invalid was of the kind that leads the doctors to forbid any argument with the unfortunate, and to enjoin that he be spoken to in a way to calm him, I answered, "All right, Fyodor Mikhailovich, I will do as you wish." He seized me by the hand, pressed it with all the force at his command, and in a voice that trembled with joyous excitement, uttered expressions of his gratitude to me for having, out of regard for him, saved St. Petersburg from being burned down, to which apparently it was doomed. Noticing after the elapse of some minutes that his burst of feeling was producing nervous tension, I asked my guest the first chance question that came into my head which was unconnected to his sickness, and at the same time interested him, as doctors direct in such cases. I asked him about the finances of the periodical he was publishing, how they covered expenses, whether there would be a chance to pay the debts with which the periodical had burdened his brother, Mikhail Mikhailovich; whether he and Mikhail might hope that the journal would support them. He began to reply on this subject, forgetting the former one. I allowed him to talk all he wanted on the affairs of the journal. He talked to me a long time; probably two hours. I hardly listened though I pretended to. When he tired of talking he remembered he had been sitting a long time with me; he took out his watch and said that he was late for reading proofs and probably was detaining me. He got up and took his leave. I accompanied him to the door and replied that he was not keeping me, that it is true I was always busy, but I was always free to put off business for an hour or two. With these words I bowed him out of the door.[19]

Although the accounts of the two participants in this incident differ in details, together they confirm the fact that in spite of the proclamation of emancipation of February 19, 1861, the atmosphere was even more tense than it had been the preceding year. There were many student disturbances in St. Petersburg during the spring of that year, which recommenced with the fall term. These disorders were accompanied by agrarian outbreaks which hampered the inauguration of the reform.

After the series of conflagrations which spread panic in the capital, Chernyshevskii was finally arrested in June of 1862. His quarters were searched, and most of his books and papers were confiscated. He languished in prison many months despite his protests of innocence and appeals for release. In the meantime, according to the account now accepted, Vsevolod Kostomarov was busy with the police in drawing the coils tighter around Chernyshevskii, and, eventually, damaging letters which allegedly passed between Chernyshevskii and others were produced which induced the police to proceed with the case.

The case passed through three stages. First, Kostomarov's evidence was presented at a meeting of the Examining Commission, which reported to the monarch. The latter referred the case to the Senate in May, 1863, and on the basis of the evidence that body decided that Chernyshevskii was a member of a criminal conspiracy; the Senate recommended a sentence of fourteen

[19] N. Chernyshevskii, *Polnoe Sobranie Sochinenii*, I, 777–78.
It will be observed that Dostoyevskii places this incident in the year 1861, while Chernyshevskii assigns it to the year 1862, the year of the incendiary fires in St. Petersburg.
It will also be observed that Dostoyevskii's version is dated 1873, while Chernyshevskii's appeared in 1888. All other things being equal, Dostoyevskii's account is more plausible. In addition, Chernyshevskii's version is far from convincing.

years at hard labor and permanent exile in Siberia. This sentence was arrived at on February 6, 1864. On April 7 the matter came before the State Council, which concurred in the opinion of the Senate, and finally the monarch himself confirmed the sentence but reduced the term of hard labor to seven years. On May 19, 1864, the ceremony of degradation was held and Chernyshevskii was stripped of his civil rights and all rank. On May 20, he set out for his long exile.[20]

Even while the case of Chernyshevskii was occupying the minds of the public, it was overtaken by events of even greater significance. At the beginning of January, 1863, the New Year was to be the occasion for calling up recruits for the Polish Army—since the Organic Act of 1832 an integral part of the Russian Army and commanded by Russian officers. By order of the Governing Committee for Poland (largely made up of Russians), the first lots were to fall on young men who had taken part in the recent disturbances. When this became known, the draftees fled the city of Warsaw and gathered in neighboring thickets. Their flight was the signal for a general rising throughout the country, directed by a secret committee in a secret location. Poland was in the grip of a general revolt that lasted well into the next year.

The revolt brought a crisis in the ranks of the revolutionary groups. There had been forming in Poland and abroad groups pledged to the cause of national independence primarily, and to the cause of reform secondarily. The Polish *émigrés* abroad had entered into contact with Herzen, who personally and in the columns of *Kolokol* gave them guarded support and encouragement. But the radical groups in Russia itself held back. Even Chernyshevskii could not afford to clash with the censors over a matter that was not vital to him and declined to take a stand in *Sovremennik* (prior to its suspension). But the truth was that the Russians had little sympathy with the Polish cause. One of them had expressed himself thus on the Polish issue:

[20] N. A. Alekseyev, *Protsess Chernyshevskogo*, Introduction.

I will not say to the Poles, "We are brothers. Give us your hand, your cause is our cause," and other fine phrases. I will tell them, on the contrary, with all frankness, the following: "I sympathize with you profoundly, as with a nation of heroes, as with a nation oppressed and especially oppressed by the people to which I belong. But nonetheless, your cause is not our cause, as the Polish movement will take place under the standard of aristocrats and priests and will not be a popular one. Up to that moment, we are united only by a common hatred for the German bastards, our masters and tyrants. . . . In any case, whatever be the lot which fate has in store for the Poles, there must be a separation of all that is Polish from Russia, and then if it is possible, a free federation; first division, later fraternal union. . . . I am sure that the younger generation of Russians will be with me and not with *Kolokol*. I cannot believe that the powerful and inspired words of Chernyshevskii have fallen on barren soil. "[21]

As a spokesman for the Polish point of view said, "We Poles would make a lord out of every peasant; you Russians would make a peasant out of every lord."[22]

The Russian government, while baffled at the revolt directed from underground, eventually found the commander who could cope with the situation—Count Muraviev. The secret committee behind the revolt was uncovered, its members taken into custody, and the rising put down with severe repressive measures.[23]

The Polish revolt created havoc in the revolutionary camp. In London, Herzen, who had long been in touch with Polish exiles and sympathized with their cause, threw his weight on their side, but with considerable heart-searching and reluctance. He felt that the Polish leaders, including the National Committee, were visionary, with no grasp of realities, and at the last minute he tried unsuccessfully to dissuade them from an armed rising.[24] However, the Polish leaders knew nothing of Herzen's

[21] F. Venturi, *Il Populismo Russo*, I, 458.
[22] N. V. Shelgunov, *Vospominaniya*, 34. Cited in Venturi, *Il Populismo*, I, 403.
[23] S. Tatishchev, *Imperator Aleksandr Vtoroi*, II, Chapters XV and XVI.

lukewarm sympathy, and in 1861 he was showered with addresses signed by hundreds of Poles in appreciation of his action in their behalf.[25]

Mikhail Bakunin, who had arrived in London on New Year's Day of 1862 after his sensational escape from Siberia, resumed his championship of the Polish cause, since it accorded well with the Pan-Slavic sympathies which he had demonstrated in the Slavic Congress thirteen years before at Prague and which he continued to demonstrate until the collapse of the revolt.[26] In general, both Herzen and Bakunin were quite at sea in gauging Russian public opinion, for most Russians rallied to the cause of their government once there were Russian casualties. The addresses submitted to the monarch were apparently spontaneous and reflected merely a natural surge of patriotic feeling at a time of crisis.[27] Herzen remarked somewhat ruefully in his autobiography that his mistake in judging Russian public opinion cost him the support of his countrymen for his *émigré* periodical, *Kolokol*.[28] It is sad to have to record that in general few Russian intellectuals were able to rise above their national prejudice in their attitudes towards the Poles.

This persistent tension in the relationship between the public and the government came to a head when an attack was made on the emperor by a revolutionary by the name of D. V. Karakozov on April 4, 1866. The event was the signal for redoubling the precautions of the police, for applying intense vigilance in scrutinizing the publications which issued from the presses, and for harrying the editors with "warnings." In general the measures of the government were successful, and the activities of secret underground societies on Russian soil became more and more difficult and hazardous, with the result that many revo-

---

[24] Labry, *Alexandre Ivanovich Herzen*, 374–75. It is to be noted that Herzen had earlier alienated the Poles by his cordial attitude towards Alexander II and had only gradually been brought around to the cause of the Poles by the criticism of Bakunin and others.

[25] Herzen, *Polnoe Sobranie*, XI, 110–26.

[26] E. H. Carr, *Mikhail Bakunin*, Chapter 21.

[27] Engelhardt, *Ocherki*, 280–87.

[28] Herzen, *My Past and Thoughts*, V, 157.

lutionaries and others escaped abroad, not only to avoid the repressive measures of the Russian government but also, in the case of the young women particularly, to obtain educational opportunities denied them at home.

By the early seventies, therefore, while Russia itself was fairly tranquil, hundreds of Russians gathered in the Swiss cities of Zurich, Geneva, and Berne, where they presented an admirable ground for agitation by the more radical revolutionary leaders. Herzen, of course, died in 1870, but his influence had long been overshadowed by that of Bakunin and others, and it was in these circles that was born the great movement "To the People," to be discussed in a later chapter.

3. Nihilism

ONE interesting by-product of the new currents, which admittedly had no immediate political results but which echoed again and again through the works of later writers, was that system of thought usually referred to as "nihilism." The term "nihilism," which came to be applied to a Russian revolutionary movement, is, of course, derived from the Latin *nihil*, and while it does not seem to have been first applied to Russian thought by him, it was certainly popularized by Ivan Turgenev in his *Fathers and Sons* in 1862. A caution must be uttered at this point that the word came to be used very loosely of all Russian revolutionists in the seventies and eighties, and even Russian writers accepted the term in this sense, since it had been sanctified by usage; e.g., Stepniak in his *Underground Russia* draws attention to this curious phenomenon:

> Here then are the two types that represent the Russian intellectual movement. The first, that of the decade 1860–70; the second, that from 1871 onwards.
> And yet fate has decreed that the former [the nihilist] who was not known and who could not be known in any other part of Europe but his own, should have no name in Europe, and

that the latter [the terrorist], having acquired a terrible reputation, should be called by the name of the other. What irony![1]

However, there are other difficulties in pinning this expression down to something definite. It is generally conceded that the most representative figure of the group was Dmitrii Pisarev (1840–68), the brilliant literary critic of *Russkoe Slovo* whose chief contribution was his denial of the principle, "art for art's sake," in favor of the theory that art must be socially useful to be justified. This principle was pushed by him to extreme lengths. He denied the merits of great artists like Raphael, great poets like Shakespeare and Pushkin, and insisted, in the language of Plato, that art was a pure imitation of original nature and therefore nature should be the object of our admiration and delight and not the secondhand reproduction of it. These ideas were not original with Pisarev, having been held by both his predecessors, Dobrolyubov and Chernyshevskii, but he formulated them in the most extreme language.

But there were other elements in nihilism. One was the denial of the validity of universal moral sanctions as well as of existing institutions. In other words, nihilism was a repudiation of most of our accepted artistic and ethical values. The most characteristic expression of this doctrine is found in Turgenev's *Fathers and Sons*, where Bazarov is a perfect reflection of it in his repudiation of all conventional values. This extravagant theory shocked contemporary Russian society and contributed to the spread in Europe of the belief that it represented a universal Russian tendency, thus helping to estrange the Western world from the intellectual developments in Russia. Its effects, of course, were not limited to the time but left a lasting impression on Russian intellectual development.

Associated with nihilism was a profound conviction that was gathering headway that Russian society could be corrected only by drastic reforms in its institutions and that it was useless to expect improvement through the slow process of moral homilies directed to the individual. As a matter of fact, the thought-

[1] *Underground Russia*, 13.

ful elements of the Russian public had been and still were sharply divided on this issue. Back in 1834 Chaadayev had denounced Russian society for its backwardness and its complete failure to find and follow any fruitful line of development, saying, "There is no natural progress, no integral development. ... We grow but do not mature, we advance but in an oblique line that leads nowhere . . . without a future in the midst of a dead calm."

Chaadayev placed his hope for a revival of spiritual life in a universal church. Although he had originally been connected with the Decembrist movement, he had abandoned his belief in the curative powers of a reform of institutions. Similarly, in the 1840's, Gogol, whose *Dead Souls* had just been published and acclaimed as a faithful picture of Russian life, disclaimed the purpose of writing a mere satire and insisted that the first volume of his great work was to be a starting point for a masterpiece that would lead to the moral regeneration of Russia and would be its inspiration in the future, appealing to the moral nature of the individual in order to direct society along the proper course.[2]

[2] Letter of Gogol to S. P. Shevyrev, Rome, February 28, 1843, in *Sobranie Sochineniia*, 340–42. "You say that it is time that the second edition of *Dead Souls* was published but that it ought to be issued with the second volume. In that case, it will be necessary to wait a long time. I am bound to repeat once more that my work was much more important and significant than might be inferred from its beginning. And if I had to labor over the first part, which surveyed hardly a tenth of what the second part is to do, almost five years, . . . how long would I have to slave over the second? It is true that I can now work with greater conviction, more zealously, with greater penetration, owing to the efforts I undertook for my education, of which no one was aware. For example, no one knew the reason I worked over my first plays, when I was writing them, taking my stand on reason (for myself) on the organization of my own brain. I saw that only this way could I accustom myself to produce a work clothed in flesh; vital, vigorous, and free from what was superfluous and extravagant; absolutely clear and perfect in loftiness of soul. After these and other exploits undertaken by me in the depth of my soul, I naturally can now advance my work more effectively and more rapidly than formerly; but one must also know that my horizon has been extended and broadened by this, so that now I must embrace what formerly I did not. And so if one can take for granted an activity that is not interrupted and never comes to a halt, it will require two years; this is the very minimum. But I do not dare even to think of it, aware as I am of my present insecurity of

Gogol's lofty moral purpose is disclosed in his book, *Selections of Correspondence with My Friends*. A copy of this book reached Byelinskii when he was abroad in the summer of 1847, and he wrote a bitter, angry letter to Gogol from Germany, denouncing him for having turned his back on reform.[3] The reply of Gogol, who was deeply wounded, reveals the fact that Gogol's purpose had been completely misunderstood or, if it was understood, regarded by Byelinskii as the deepest treason to progress.

It is obvious, therefore, that by 1847 the idea had taken root among advanced thinkers in Russia that there was no hope for progress in the slow process of individual improvement, such as had been the basis of religious instruction in Western coun-

---

life and the many preoccupations from day to day which can distract me, although I exert myself to keep clear of them and to pay as little attention as possible. . . . Do you not see that up to now everybody has taken my book for a satire and not as an account of individualities in it, which can be seen merely after reading it a number of times? Those who rail against me, for the most part, have read my book only once. See, further, how loftily and with what contempt everybody looks on my heroes. The book took a long time to write; it is necessary that people should give time and effort to understand it. It is necessary that one's opinion should be crystallized. From first impressions, I cannot guard myself. Criticism should guard against first impressions; only then will impressions take form and emerge in some way or other from the first chaos and become definite and clear. Only then can I guard against them. Believe me, I exert every effort to do my work efficiently, so that I have no life apart from it, and I have long given up all other forms of enjoyment. But in consequence of the structure of my brain I can work only after profound contemplation and play of imagination. And there is no power that can make me produce, let alone publish, anything whose immaturity and weakness I myself observe; I may die of hunger but I shall never publish a work that is not the result of considered judgment and contemplation. There is a voice which issues us orders, before which our wretched judgment is nothing. There are many things which can only be felt to the depths of one's soul in the midst of tears and prayers, but not during the distractions of daily life."

[3] The letter was dated from Salzburg on July 15, 1847. See Byelinskii, *Sochineniia*, IV, 1197–98. "The feeling of outraged self-respect can further be borne and I would have had the sense to refrain from mentioning it if that were the only issue; but it is impossible to bear the outrage you have done to the truth of human worth; it is impossible to keep silent when in the guise of religion and the defense of the *knut* you proclaim what is false and immoral as truth and virtue. . . . So you cannot see that Russia sees its salvation not in mysticism, asceticism, or pietism, but in the triumph of civilization, enlightenment, humanity. She needs no sermons."

tries, but that the correction of Russia's evils was to be found in the complete destruction of the existing system.

When we come down to the post-Crimean War period, this opinion had gained ground and had become almost, if not quite, dominant in Russian thought. For example, Dobrolyubov, in his discussion of the satire of the reign of Catherine, lays down the principle that private efforts are ineffective in bringing about improvement in society:

> The greater number of social conditions cannot be changed merely by the wishes of individuals; one must change the environment, must introduce other principles into social activity, and then he can criticize those who are incapable of availing themselves of the benefits of the new order.[4]

But if the movement for spiritual regeneration of the individual was ebbing and a new one towards institutional reform was rising, these were only eddies in the vast movement that was engulfing the whole of educated Russia. In this surge, the chief impulse came from new attitudes derived from Western Europe, originally, perhaps, from German philosophy (especially Hegel), but greatly stimulated by the new science, which was beginning to undermine many traditional beliefs. But no slight contribution was made by French socialist thought, which had begun to gain ground in the early years of the century. Its most striking characteristic was a resounding challenge to accepted beliefs and conventions—a current of thought that was to be purely negative and critical and whose work was almost wholly destructive.

In tracing this movement, which represented the most characteristic side of nihilism, it will perhaps be well to start with the publication in 1862 of Ivan Turgenev's great novel, *Fathers and Sons*, a work that almost immediately roused intense feeling, and which quickly became a storm center in the literary world. It is believed by some that the original of its principal character,

---

[4] N. A. Dobrolyubov, *Sochineniia*, I, 110.

Bazarov, was Dobrolyubov, who had recently died after having been chief literary critic of the periodical *Sovremennik,* in which capacity he had advanced his somewhat novel ideas on literary criticism.[5] The hero of the novel was distinguished by his utter defiance of ordinary standards of life, an attitude which Turgenev characterized as "nihilistic." The term immediately became popular and was soon accepted by the members of the new school of thought as a badge of honor.

The word, according to one writer, had been invented in the eighteenth century, and applied to such writers as Jean Paul Richter and Louis Sébastien Mercier, known for their critical attitudes.[6] It was apparently first used in Russia in 1821 by Nadezhdin, who applied the term to Russian writers. Turgenev was probably the first to apply the word to pessimistic philosophers like Schopenhauer and Bruno, using it in the sense of skeptic. Subsequently, others gave similar meaning to the word. Thus, a review of a work of Professor V. Berni of the University of Kazan, appearing in *Sovremennik* in 1858, stated, "Berni is trying to make sly fun of the skeptics, or, as he expresses it, the nihilists."[7]

The appearance of Turgenev's novel, which was taken as a satire on the young generation of Russian writers, called forth an immediate storm of protest, whose bitterness bore witness to the violent schism among the intellectuals of the day. Its reverberations were heard throughout the rest of the century. As the schism left permanent traces on Russian thought, we are bound to inquire about the factors that led to it. One is inevitably reminded of Peter's famous words: "It is better to

[5] There is some dispute about this. V. V. Vorovskii cites a letter of Turgenev in which the latter says: "I gave him [presumably Bazarov] a sharp and unceremonious attitude as a result of my observation of my acquaintance, Dr. D. [Dmitriev]. In this remarkable man was incarnated before my very eyes the barely developed, still in ferment, new principle which later was called nihilism." V. V. Vorovskii, "Bazarov i Sanin. Dva nigilizma," in N. I. Brodskii and I. N. Kubikov, *Russkaya Literatura. Sbornik literatur'nyke Proizvyedenii i kriticheskikh statei,* 63, 70.

[6] Franco Venturi, *Il Populismo Russo,* I, 531–32.

[7] Labry, *Alexandre Ivanovich Herzen,* 387.

pull down and rebuild than to patch up the old." But actually, most writers of the time ascribe it to a number of adventitious causes.

Let us take a look at some of the views advanced by these so-called "nihilists" during the sixties. If we turn from the extravagant opinions of Bazarov in *Fathers and Sons* to the press, we find that such aphorisms as the following passed currently: "Love is simply sexual attraction," "What is natural is moral," "Man is an animal," "The belly is the center of life," "Photography is higher than art," "The end justifies the means," and "Ten thousand heads for the good of humanity."[8]

It will be observed that in one of these maxims there finds expression the antiesthetic point of view that was to be advanced in such an extreme form some years later in the works of Pisarev. There is, of course, nothing novel in the attitude, which has often been reflected in other times and by other writers. But the idea shocked Russian literary society and prompted the satire not only of Turgenev in *Fathers and Sons*, but of Tolstoi in *The Contaminated Family*, of Dostoyevskii, of Goncharov, and even of Herzen.[9]

The intellectual currents of the 1860's were comprised of many elements, but if, for the moment, we concentrate on one particular phase and call nihilism the rejection of all conventional, moral, and artistic values, we will find various explanations of this phenomenon. Perhaps it would be well to start with contemporary accounts. Dmitrii Pisarev is generally considered the chief exponent of this particular philosophy, and his characterization of the origin of these trends is particularly valuable. In "Our University Studies," Pisarev, who later became the leading representative of the nihilist school recounts that he was a student at the University of Moscow during the period immediately following the Crimean War. Writing somewhat later of this period, he noted that in his day students at the university fell into two groups, the "old" and the "new"

[8] Engelhardt, *Ocherki*, 286.
[9] Ibid., 287–90. Engelhardt lists at least nine of these contemporary novels.

students. "Old" students were those whose chief interest was in learning and who were indifferent to the political problems of the time. The "new" students were those who eagerly read *Sovremennik* and took Dobrolyubov for their teacher. Pisarev, however, noted that "with every year, the ranks of the learned party grew thinner, partly because the scholars graduated and entered service in different departments, where they quickly merged into the general tone of the civil service; partly because some of the scholars deserted to the side of the 'new' scholars and themselves became antagonists of university learning."[10]

Pisarev points to the years 1858–59 as those that marked the transition, which he ascribes to the altered tone of society, now entirely preoccupied with social and political problems of the day, agitated by movements directed to this or that practical purpose of benefiting humanity, and little inclined to listen to the advice of the sages. If university circles were carried along on this current, it was simply because they identified themselves with the people and were following a tradition that was already established.

It would seem, therefore, that no intellectual movement to abandon all conventional and ethical values would have had much chance to succeed had not the ground been prepared for it. But it appears that the nihilists had no monopoly on this particular trait. Had not Peter himself been the first nihilist? Moreover, as Herzen remarked, "The Petersburg government has but few traditions."[11] We observe also that it is not often in Russian history that the past is appealed to in support of a claim to a right or privilege.[12] It would seem, therefore, that

10 L. A. Plotkin, *D. A. Pisarev*, 127–218. Also D. I. Pisarev, *Sochineniia*, III, IV, 57–58. Pisarev says that in the year 1858, at the time he received his appointment to write articles of literary criticism for *Rassvyet*, he himself became a "new" student.

11 Herzen, *My Past and Thoughts*, VI, 96.

12 There may be exceptions to this rule but demands put forward for reform were seldom buttressed by appeal to precedents in Russian history, but were usually couched in terms of some abstract principle or recommended by examples drawn from Western Europe. This is in striking contrast with England, where arguments for reform have usually been based on some half forgotten rule or precedent.

there was no truly conservative element in Russian public life; conservatism, such as there unquestionably was, was based largely on self-interest, relying primarily on the maintenance of the *status quo* by force, and not on any commonly accepted ideology. Issues between liberal and conservative were fought out with weapons drawn from the arsenal of Western Europe that had small relation to domestic problems. There was thus a certain measure of unreality in these battles, which were purely theoretical, and in which victory usually inclined to the side that was able to present its appeals in the most extreme form, untroubled by practical considerations. There were thus, then, no deeply rooted attachments to the past among the students, nor, in the absence of practical experience, any prudential considerations to induce caution; hence the triumph at all times in Russia of the most extreme ideas presented in the most plausible and logical form, ideas which in other countries would have been moderated in the interest of practical politics. Hence, since blind force buttressed the existing order, it was easy to convey the impression that a correspondingly greater force was what was needed to usher in a millennium.

Herzen had lent some countenance to this view. Bakunin became its chief exponent. *"Die Lust der Zerstörung ist eine schaffende Lust"* (The instinct of destruction is also a creative one).[13] Since the classes which had nothing to lose stood to profit by such destruction, it was natural that this view should appeal. But both Herzen and Bakunin, in their soberer moments, could see the danger of this confounding of good and bad in wholesale moral condemnation and destruction. Herzen deplored this complete amoralism of the nihilists. Bakunin, when he himself was the victim of such neglect of moral scruples, protested against it. As late as 1869, when a fellow revolutionist had wronged him, he raised his voice against the attempt to build a new order on so shaky a foundation. Writing to an unidentified friend from Lugano who had slandered him, he had

[13] Jules Elisard, *Jahrbücher* (ascribed to Bakunin), cited by Herzen, *My Past and Thoughts*, V, 132.

this to say: "Be sure of one thing, that one can erect nothing vital or solid on Jesuitical casuistry, that revolutionary activity must look for its prospects of success not in mean and base emotions but in lofty and humane ideals, without which no revolution can achieve success."[14]

Other explanations of this striking phenomenon have been offered. One writer advanced the idea that the triumph of extremes was due to the previous harsh regime: "We very definitely ascribe this [radical trend] to the terror of censorship with which Russian literature charges the administration of Valuev [minister of the interior]."[15]

Another common theory (at the time as well as later) was that the extremism represented a protest of the new class of *raznochintsy* against the narrow restrictions to which they had been subjected, as well as a rejection of the whole system of values under which they had grown up. Herzen thus describes the new class:

> Taking them by and large, these *enfants terribles* of ours take a perverse pride in showing themselves just as their mothers bore them—and that appearance not of the best—not just plain fat little babies, but the degenerates and unhealthy offspring of the lowest element of the St. Petersburg populace. In the place of well-developed muscles and the lusty nakedness of infancy, one can see the unhappy legacy of their forebears—polluted blood, traces of old ulcers, all kinds of sores from stocks and collars. The anteroom, the barracks, the seminary, the mean manor house of the petty squire persisted in their blood and brain without losing their distinguishing traits. So far as I know, not enough attention has been paid to this.
>
> On the other hand, the reaction from the old narrow oppressive world was bound to rouse in the younger generation distaste

---

[14] Mikhail Dragomanov, *Mikhail Bakunins Sozial-politischer Briefwechsel mit Alexander Ivanovich Herzen, und Ogarow*, 272. The editor adds this comment: "One may well say that in this letter . . . he equally contradicts everything he practiced in his life, and everything he preached by his revolutionary activity."

[15] Engelhardt, *Ocherki*, 285–86.

and fierce resentment against their uncongenial environment. On the contrary, one cannot look for moderation or justice; defiance and hatred are the order of the day; "You are hypocrites, we will be cynics; you are moral in words, our language will be foul; you are obsequious to your superiors and insolent to those beneath you, we will be insolent to everyone; you are deferential without feeling any respect, we will be rude without apology; you show respect only by external courtesy and deference, we regard ourselves as honor bound to trample on all signs of respect and to show contempt for all *points d'honneur.*"

He adds, however,

It is impossible not to realize that tsarist tutelage and the civilization of our empire has furnished a strange seedbed, in which promising sprouts have grown up into worshippers of the Muravievs and Katkov's on the one hand, and on the other into the rowdies of nihilism and desperate gangs of Bazarovs.[16]

This animus of Herzen against the nihilists was inspired by a natural aristocratic prejudice against these young upstarts. Writing as late as 1868, in an article entitled, "Once Again Bazarov," he vented his anger on the claim that these sons of priests, officers, clerks, and small landowners falsely clothed themselves in the garb of nihilism to cast him out as a man past his prime, in the name of that nihilism which he had been the first to preach when he published the article, "On Dilettantism in Science." They, on the other hand, were quite as ready to brand Herzen a revolutionary fraud, since he continued to live on a fortune invested in the backs of serfs, and to enjoy all the comforts of exploiters. "They considered Herzen an amateur of words in revolution and not of deeds."[17]

[16] Aleksandr Gertsen (Herzen), *Polnoe Sobranie Sochinenii i Pisem,* XIV, 419–21. The Muraviev mentioned was the general charged with the suppression of the Polish revolt in 1863, whose name became a synonym for cruelty and oppression. Katkov was the brilliant journalist, formerly a member of the Stankevich circle and an associate of most of the revolutionary writers, who had become at this time reactionary.

[17] These citations are taken from Labry, *Herzen,* 389; based on Gertsen, *Polnoe Sobranie Sochinenii i Pisem,* XXI, 237.

Herzen was not alone in thus explaining the rise of nihilism. A later author, writing at the beginning of the present century, found that the movement was due to the rise of an entirely new class of intellectuals, represented by the *raznochintsy*, who were, he claims, predominantly of clerical origin, though later joined by the so-called "repentant nobles."

> It was just this phenomenon in the intellectual and social life of this type of seminarist and *raznochinets* that was the first revelation of the most important phases of *bazarovshchina*. In the life and activity of Chernyshevskii, Dobrolyubov, Elisayev, and others, we find its characteristic features.[18]

On the contrary, Herzen's strictures on nihilism as a manifestation of lowerclass vulgarity are contradicted by the contribution he himself made (as he admitted above) to nihilism. Most damaging to his claim was his controversy with Michelet, the celebrated French historian. The latter had written in his book, *Legendes Democratiques du Nord*, "Everything in Russia is an illusion and a lie; they lack any sense of right and wrong; they are not men.[19] To this, Herzen replied in a letter that has become famous:

> The Russian, you say, is a liar and a thief; he is perpetually stealing, he is perpetually lying, and quite innocently—it is his nature. . . . Who is it [I ask] that the Russian deceives? Who, if not the landowner, the government official, the steward, the police officer; in fact the sworn enemies of the peasant, whom he looks on as traitors, as half-Germans? Deprived of every possible means of defense, the peasant resorts to cunning in dealing

[18] D. N. Ovsyaniko-Kulikovskii, "Istoriya Russkoi Intelligentsii," *Sobranie Sochinenii*, VIII, 62–63, 92–93.

[19] Labry, *Herzen*, 361. Michelet's remarks are somewhat expanded in Herzen, *My Past and Thoughts*, where the Frenchman is represented as saying, "They [the Russians] are without sign of humanity, of moral sensibility, of the sense of good and evil. Truth and justice for them have no meaning; if you speak these words, they are mute, they smile and know not what the words signify."

Nikolai Chernyshevskii

From Benjamin R. Tucker (*trans.*), What's To Be Done? (1886)

Ivan S. Turgenev

From A. Yarmolinsky, Turgenev (1926)

with his torturers; he deceives them and he is perfectly right in doing so.

Cunning, my dear sir, in the words of the great thinker, is the irony of brute force.

But Herzen is not content with mere defense of the peasant; he denounces the whole system of moral concepts prevalent in Europe; "The truth and justice of old Europe are falsehood and injustice to the Europe that is being born."[20] It would thus seem that Herzen had made his own contribution to nihilism by casting doubt on the validity of all moral and social standards that had prevailed up to his time. In this he was outdone by Bakunin, who in later life became the prophet of the necessity of universal destruction if the new world was to come into existence. Even Tolstoi, who certainly would have been uncomfortable in the society of the nihilists, made common cause with them in his work, *What is Art*, in which he denounced all existing esthetic values.

It is our contention, therefore, that nihilism was a Russian phenomenon, deeply rooted in Russian life, to which many writers made a contribution. There have been, it is true, eras in the history of Western Europe marked by the rise of amoralism. In nineteenth-century Russia, however, though its excesses generally came to be condemned, the tendency in Western Europe to scrutinize existing moral standards was transformed into a rejection not only of European values but of all moral concepts, a tendency much aggravated by the teaching of Marx.[21]

[20] Herzen, *My Past and Thoughts*, VI, 221–22. These convictions were somewhat foreshadowed in his article, "Dilettantism in Science," dated 1843.

[21] Marx had, of course, his own ethical values, however much these have been lost sight of, though he has been charged with "anti-cultural, nihilistic amoralism." See S. L. Frank, "Etika Nigilizma" in *Vyekhi*, 178–79.

4. Populism

THE movement of thought of the early 1860's that produced nihilism led also to the emergence of a second trend that took the place of nihilism and absorbed some of the later nihilists. It was destined to have a far greater length of life, dominating Russian thought until almost the end of the century. To this movement the name *narodnichestvo* was applied, and to its adherents, the term *narodniki*.

It is difficult to assign any exact origin to this school or to fix the date when it sprang into life. It is to be noted, of course, that during the eighteenth century, when the peasant question first emerged, there was a strong tendency to regard the condition of the Russian peasants as simply an earlier stage of the development through which the peasants of Western Europe had gone, and to assume that the Russians would pass through the same later stages and ultimately obtain emancipation and the rights of free men.

The proper method of emancipation in this scheme of thought was assumed to be simply the release of the peasants from the control of the landlord, without any special economic provision for them. This seems to have been the common view also in the early part of the nineteenth century, but about the time of the Decembrist Revolt a different attitude was becoming apparent among would-be reformers; the attitude that personal emancipation was useless unless some provision was made to enable the peasants to make a livelihood.

This view gained ground rapidly during the reign of Nicholas I, who made a number of unsuccessful attempts at emancipation. On the death of Nicholas in 1855, the new monarch, Alexander II, and the circle which surrounded him were convinced that the recent war had proved that serfdom had become a dangerous drag on Russian development; to enable the country to emerge from the almost complete collapse that attended the war, they felt that the economic structure of society would have to be radically altered. This led Alexander to set in motion the measures already described for finding some solution to the peasant problem—a series of measures that began with the famous decree of February 19, 1861.

The elaboration of a scheme for peasant emancipation was attended by spirited discussions in the press, which down to 1858 was given a considerable degree of freedom to discuss public issues. This controversy was carried on principally in the columns of *Sovremennik* and *Russkaya Besyeda* in Russia and the *Kolokol* of Herzen, published in London. The leading writer on the *Sovremennik* at this time was Chernyshevskii, and he undertook to champion the cause of the peasants against the landlords; in London, Herzen conducted a similar campaign, though in more temperate language.

As Nicholas had discovered, the peasant question was a complicated one, affected as it was by various vested interests. As time went on, the issue began to clarify itself and to turn more and more on the question of the right of the peasant to the land he had tilled. The second issue that aroused strong feelings was whether the peasant, if he received this land, should hold it as an individual rather than as a member of a commune. Down to the year 1842 few Russians had concerned themselves with this problem, and, indeed, many of them were actually ignorant of the existence of the commune.[1] However, in 1843 Baron von Haxthausen, a Prussian authority on agriculture who had been invited by Nicholas to make a tour of Russia and report on rural life, had found the institution of the commune widespread and had drawn the attention of the Russian public to its existence. This coincided with the rise of Slavophilism in Russia, a movement which glorified the old Russia before Peter's time and advocated the perpetuation of the primitive national institutions of an earlier age. Since the Slavophiles were opposed to civilization in its Western manifestation, and particularly to capitalism, the village commune seemed to them admirably adapted to the maintenance of the old institutions as a foundation for a unique national civilization.

But their opponents, the "westerners," who wished to speed up the process of assimilating Western civilization, did not agree on the question of the commune, and Herzen, who became their unchallenged mouthpiece, took over that element of Slavophile doctrine in his advocacy of internal reforms. Moreover, the historian Shchapov at this time was attracting large literary circles with his discussions of the *Raskol'niki*, dissidents who had broken away from the church in the seventeenth century. Shchapov maintained that this revolt against the church was to a great extent a protest against the policy of centralization pursued by the autocracy in the sixteenth and seventeenth centuries, which had led to the suppression of many of the indigenous organs of self-government.

The inference to be drawn from Shchapov's work was that a sound Russian economy and a healthy political organization could be secured only by the restoration of such institutions as would allow the principle of local autonomy full play.[2]

[1] For example, Turgenev, in his three-volume book, *La Russie et les Russes*, published in 1847, makes no mention of the commune.

[2] Franco Venturi, *Il Populismo Russo*, 136, claims that Shchapov really provided the ideological basis for populism in his "Zemstvo i Raskol," published in 1862. According to Venturi, M. N. Muraviev, after reading this work, exclaimed, "This is pure communism with incessant attacks on the boyars and the officials. Shchapov has depicted the *raskol* as a weapon or 'lever' for unchaining a new *pugachevshchina*."

It seemed, therefore, to political writers, that this function could be best served by the restoration of the commune in agriculture and the *artel* in urban life. This controversy coincided with the spread to Russia of the writings of many Western Europeans, including the French utopian socialists of the early part of the nineteenth century. The majority of Russian writers embraced the general theory of local organization of productive forces, and regarded the maintenance of the village commune as basic to agriculture.

When, therefore, the issue came up for discussion in the press, concerning the proper method of carrying out emancipation, the reading public had constantly presented to it the advantages of this somewhat unique solution. In the various committees and commissions named by the government, however, the division of opinion was somewhat along the line of class interests, and the landlord class, which was heavily represented in governing circles, set itself definitely against emancipation, particularly emancipation with land.

The best that the moderate element could hope for was emancipation accompanied by the purchase of land from the landlords. It would seem, therefore, that the official organs of the government and public opinion as it was expressed in the leading journals generally pulled in different directions; what is worse, neither side was disposed to listen to the arguments of the other.

The solution finally arrived at was a compromise, but the Russian mind, not being disposed to compromise, found this solution distasteful; by the time emancipation was accomplished, most of the informed public had taken up a position hostile to the government and its new reforms and were not prepared to co-operate with them.

There were thus two movements that prepared the way for populism. The first was the rise of the Slavophiles, who insisted on the restoration of earlier native institutions, not so much for economic and social advantage as from the mystical belief that they were a development of primitive Russian patriarchal society and had a moral and religious significance. The other was the influence of Shchapov, whose famous works on the *Raskol'-niki* harked back to an earlier condition of Russian society when there was a greater degree of local autonomy, which had disappeared under the centralizing trends of the sixteenth and seventeenth centuries. But it is questionable whether the Slavophile movement should have had such a significance had it not been for the study made by Baron von Haxthausen, who provided the necessary factual basis to justify the institution of the village commune.

As already pointed out, from the time of the Decembrists the plan for emancipating the peasants without land had steadily lost ground to the proposal to give the peasants the land they had been cultivating. It is true that it would have been difficult to establish the claim of the commune to ownership in the face of the government's insistence, since the time of Peter, that the land was the private property of the landholder.[3] Nevertheless, the idea of communal tenure made a great appeal at this time, partly because the ground had been prepared by the Slavophiles, but to a larger extent because of the general dislike of all the forms of economic life of Western Europe that had been assiduously spread by Herzen and those associated with him in the fifties and sixties.

The views of the educated upper classes are reflected by Herzen, who thus describes the life of the peasant in 1843:

> Poor Russian peasant! And what is saddest of all to see—the means of improving his lot are within our reach, but the greed of the landlords and the disorder among the state peasants plunges him into this situation. Alongside his wretched field are the fine fields of the landlords, with stacks of grain, ricks of hay, tilled by his own hands. What angelic self-sacrifice! If today the poor from a neighboring village come to the window, the

[3] Peter the Great put all the holdings of the serving nobility on the *votchina* basis (which made them private property and heritable) and abolished the old *pomyest'e* system, the form of conditional tenure that emerged in the early Moscovite period. V. I. Lebedev (ed.), *Reformy Petra I*, 73–74.

landlord drives them off to work . . . if they have only bread, his conscience is clear. What more do they want; they are satisfied. We wonder at the gladiators, but will they not, in time to come, wonder at us for our ruthless cruelty, the want of humanity in us? Are we any better than the colonists of Surinam, than the English in India? No, we are worse, because our peasants are better than savages; meekly and with sad resignation, they bear their cross of life; they endure it darkly with the prospect of blows, hunger, labor, and, if they are subject to *obrok*, military service and enrollment as a servant. Our Slavophiles argue about the communal idea and about a division of the fields, so among the Bedouins the right of property does not have the egotistical character that it does in Europe. But they forget, on the other hand, the absence of every consideration for the man himself; the dull unbearableness of all the persecutions; in a word, the misery of living under such conditions. Would it be any wonder if the peasant did not develop a respect for property when his strip is not his strip, when even his wife and children are not his own? What property can a slave have? He is worse than the proletariat; he is *res*, a tool for working the fields. His master may not kill him, just as under Peter in certain places you could not cut down an oak. Give him the right to be tried; only then will he be a man. [There are] twelve million people outside of the law. *Carmen horrendum.*[4]

But the chief role in popularizing this notion undoubtedly belongs to Chernyshevskii and his associates on the *Sovremennik* in the period from 1855 to 1862. Chernyshevskii, the son of a priest, was born in Samara, where he received his early education before going on to the University of St. Petersburg. He was a man of wide reading and intense intellectual activity. His early life had tended to make him sympathetic with the peasants, and his observations and studies combined to confirm him in his view that the peasant was entitled to a better deal than he was getting.

[4] V. Semevskii, *Krest'yanskii Vopros*, II, 304–305. At this time Herzen was much under the influence of the Slavophiles, with whom he broke some two years later.

In the preceding chapter we have emphasized the factors that helped to produce this complete alienation of the public from the government; we will now discuss the manner in which this hostility developed and hardened into a definite revolutionary movement in the next decade.

During the early years of the reign of Alexander II, Chernyshevskii entered the lists against his competitors, the *Economicheskii Ukazatel'* and *Russkaya Besyeda*. His views were advanced in plainest language in an article, "On Landed Property," which appeared in *Sovremennik* in 1857, in answer to an article by Vernadskii in the first-mentioned periodical. Chernyshevskii's article strongly maintained that communal tenure and cultivation of the land were preferable to a system of individual holdings, from the point of view of the population as a whole. In one passage Chernyshevskii stated his case in the following language:

> The nation possesses two elements: (1) persons especially gifted, especially happy, or especially active, who are able successfully to compete and love to take chances; (2) ordinary people who wish to live in comfort and security. For the first group there is open a vast field of private enterprise in which every opportunity is given for happiness, for special gifts, for strength or cleverness. The second must be secure in their possessions, free from the caprices of chance, so that they always have the means to work (means secure against everyone and everything in the world).
>
> This would be secured by the grant of state landed property, under the control of the commune. I am the son of my country; my country treats me like a mother; it gives me shelter; it gives me a heritage adequate for my existence; if only I take advantage of it, I can receive a share of the state property. . . .
>
> But I long for, and have the means to look for, something better than a comfortable life; I have confidence in my own powers; I have special tendencies; fine, that is my business. That means that I must renounce my security; exchanging my sure, though humble, lot for a way of life that may be more advantageous and agreeable for me, but which also may be unsuccessful. I

renounce a share in the state. I seek for myself personal private property. But if I have made a mistake, I can return to my mother and she will give back to me what I renounced in the hope of something better.[5]

Chernyshevskii follows up this general statement with what he calls a comparison of conditions in agriculture under the communal system (in Russia) with the system obtaining favor in various countries of Western Europe, including France, Prussia, and Austria. Chernyshevskii is not envisaging a system such as prevailed in the United States at that time, where the general practice was for a single family to cultivate the land and receive the whole income. Rather, he is thinking of a condition in which the land is held in large estates as, for instance, in England; the estates being divided into farms which the farmers rent from the landlord.

In describing this system, Chernyshevskii takes an estate of an arbitrary size of 5,000 *desyatins* and divides it into thirty farms, each operated by one farmer and employing twenty or more families, who thus form a greater part of the population of the estate. Under this system, the landlord receives some 25 per cent of the revenue, the thirty farmers among them 45 per cent, and the workers—twenty or more times as numerous as the farmers, with six hundred or more times as many mouths to feed as the landlord—receive only 30 per cent.

Against this system, Chernyshevskii sets the case of an equal amount of land in Russia, populated by 400 families of peasants engaged in communal agriculture, which, he grants, is somewhat less efficient than individual agriculture, producing a revenue of only twelve rubles per *desyatin* as against twenty rubles per *desyatin* in individual farming. But in this case there is no landlord, nor is there any private class of farmers to take the lion's share of the production; all of the 400 families receive equal shares, which puts them in a privileged position, if not in comparison with the landlords or the farmers, at least in comparison with the workers on the individual farms.

[5] *Polnoe Sobranie Sochenenii*, IV, 437-38.

This is the basic economic argument of Chernyshevskii. Over and over again he insists that with communal agriculture there is a more equitable distribution which more than offsets the greater efficiency of the individual farm. Applied to the whole country, therefore, this would mean that the welfare of the majority of the population would take precedence over national wealth. National wealth, hence, is not by any means to be equated with national well-being.

Of course, the figures and the arguments of Chernyshevskii do not carry much conviction today, since he ignored the main problem with which modern agriculture is concerned: namely, increasing the production per acre. Moreover, he ignored, or perhaps omitted through lack of information, the case of American agriculture, based on the one-family farm. The theoretical arguments of Chernyshevskii and his associates helped to perpetuate the somewhat unsatisfactory condition in which agriculture was left by the emancipation of 1861.

In other words, the problem of distribution preoccupied all Russians who wrote on agriculture, to the exclusion of the question of increasing production.[6] Even the figures quoted by Chernyshevskii, which are drawn from Tengoborski, showed that Russia lagged far behind the countries of Europe, in spite of the fact that the black-earth district of Russia contained some of the most fertile land in the world.[7]

In view of the fact that the emancipation of the peasants was the most important of all the reforms—and that the public's attitude towards the reforms was largely determined by its attitude towards emancipation—it would be well to review the steps by which the project reached its final form and the progress of public opinion from one of full sympathy to hostility.

It will be remembered that the Emperor Nicholas had made a series of efforts to modify the institution of serfdom, which would indicate that the issue had been a live one throughout his reign, as a result, possibly, of the Decembrist Revolt. During

---

[6] Ivanov-Razumnik, *Istoriya russkoi obshchestvemoi mysli*, II, 15.
[7] M. L. Tengoborski, *Études sur les Forces Productives de la Russie.*

this period the predominant view on the peasant question had shifted from personal emancipation without land to emancipation with land. During the forties a new element had been injected into the controversy by Baron von Haxthausen's discovery of the widespread distribution of the village commune—a discovery that was fully exploited by the Slavophiles as an argument for a return to the old patriarchal times before Peter's reign.

The government, however, was not inclined to this point of view and had already laid down a different set of principles for any solution. In the words of one writer:

> The land of the nobles was to remain the inviolate property of the landlords; the state lands, the inviolate property of a feudal government. The peasant was to be a holder, a user, an *obrok*-payer. Governmental centralization and local power was to remain in the hands of "the enlightened noble class," but the peasant delegates were to play a subservient and subordinate role—to discharge administrative functions under the direction and control of bureaucratic institutions. Lawless seizure of lands and peasants was to be stopped, violence and wrongdoing stamped out; but the old privilege of the noble class—the right to receive grants of state lands—was to be maintained and protected.[8]

Consequently, the first steps taken by the administration of Alexander II laid down the following principles in a rescript of November 20, 1857, occasioned by the petition of Kovno, Vilna, and Grodno provinces:

(1) The landlord was to retain ownership of the land; the *usadba* was to be redeemed within a specified time and become the peasant's property; the fields were to continue to be used by the peasant, in return for which he was to pay *obrok* or perform work.

(2) The peasants were to be divided into communes and placed under police supervision of the landlords.

[8] N. M. Druzhinin, *Gosudarstvennye Krest'yane*, I, 194-95.

(3) Steps were to be taken to insure the payment of all state and *zemskie* dues.

This rescript was to be followed by an *otnoshenie* of the Minister of the Interior to Nazimov, military governor of Vilna. This set a period of transition of not more than twelve years (it was not clear exactly what was to happen in this period). Still it did emphasize the points made in the rescript. Points to be settled were:

(1) Were they to insist on the peasant's right to redeem his *usadba* and to his right to use it even if he did not proceed to redeem it?

(2) Was the landlord bound at the end of the period of transition to assign the peasants their *nadyely?* Was the *obrok* to be temporary or permanent?[9]

Nevertheless, this announcement on the part of the government was received with delight in the press. Herzen, who had just begun publication of *Kolokol* in London, immediately wrote a celebrated article, "In Three Years," with its famous introduction, "Thou hast conquered, O Galilean!"[10]

Chernyshevskii also was at first enthusiastic, although he hastened to temper his enthusiasm with a caution: "As the basic principle of our desire is the matter of emancipation, we ought to accept this with a proviso that the peasants should not be left without land."[11] Chernyshevskii immediately proceeded to wage a vigorous campaign in the *Sovremennik* for his views, but within a little more than a year he had come to feel that the struggle was hopeless; with the year 1859 he ceased to concern

[9] Vishnyakov, "Khod krest'yanskoi reformy; nachalo zakonodatel'stkh rabot," *Velikaya Reforma*, IV, 144–45. The various steps in reaching the final decision on the controversial issue with regard to reform are also given in a series of chapters in Chernyshevskii, *Izbrannye Ekonomicheskii Proizvedenya*, I, 495–633, II, 5–127.

[10] Ch. Vyetrinskii, "Kolokol i krest'yanskaya Reforma," *Velikaya Reforma*, IV, 204.

[11] V. Zamayatnin, *Izbrannye Ekonomicheskii Proizvyedenya*, I, 18.

himself directly with the peasant question, contenting himself with resorting to Aesopian language.[12]

There is some indication that Chernyshevskii's views with regard to the retention of the commune had prevailed with the editing commission, for the head of that body is reported to have come out in favor of the commune in 1859:

> I am no professor and I shall not explain to you how the commune came into existence in this country. In our literature, there are abundant opinions and discussions; but the commune is present among us and, consequently, it is still necessary and we ought to preserve it. We ought to destroy nothing. When you talk of freedom, I yield to you; open the doors as wide as you like to allow every peasant to withdraw from the commune, but do not destroy the commune—let it remain.[13]

Chernyshevskii had also disclosed his irreconcilable hostility to the course of negotiations in a letter he wrote to Herzen in 1859.[14] He claimed that circumstances proved that nothing was to be obtained by Russia as long as tsarism continued to exist. The only worthwhile course to pursue was to attack it and destroy it. He used the words, "The only cure is the axe."[15] His only expressed concern with emancipation subsequent to this was in a series of communications addressed to the Emperor, "Letters Without an Address," intended for publication in *Sovremennik* but suppressed by the censor in 1862.[16]

Throughout the period from 1857 to 1861, Herzen continued to follow the program from London with close attention. His views were expressed in the *Kolokol*, the most important coming in a series of open letters to the Emperor; it was the mod-

[12] The progress of the reforms and of Chernyshevskii's polemics are discussed by A. A. Manuilov in "Reforma 19 Fevrala i obshchinnoe zemlevladenie," *Velikaya Reforma*, VI, 54–75.

[13] Manuilov, "Reforma 19 Fevrala i obshchinnoe zemlevladenie," *Velikaya Reforma*, VII, 66.

[14] Herzen, *Sochineniia*, X, 224–29.

[15] Labry, *Herzen*, 375.

[16] These letters are given in Chernyshevskii, *Izbrannye Ekonomicheskii Proizvyedenya*, II, 617–66.

erate and compromising tone of these letters that drew down on him the indignation of Chernyshevskii.[17] The *Kolokol* always appeared, it is said, mysteriously on the table in the Emperor's study, and it was made available to the editing commission. But Herzen himself seems to have been disappointed in the final settlement of 1861. In Number 21 of the *Kolokol* he gave vent to his indignation, writing, "There is no longer anything to save us from the *chinovnichestvo*." Nevertheless, on receipt of the Proclamation of Emancipation, Herzen held a celebration in his London home.

> Our celebration was gloomy. I do not know a day when one could have been more heavily and mercilessly oppressed; when our eyes were so near to tears. We, as it were, grew younger with the news of the emancipation of the peasants. All was forgotten with the hope of this new step of Russia; with beating hearts, we awaited our holiday. In the presence of Russians, Polish friends, exiles of all countries, and people like Mazzini and Louis Blanc, we tried to raise our glasses to the strains of the *Marseillaise*, and propose a toast never heard in such a gathering; to Alexander, the emancipator of the peasants.[18]

The process of his disillusionment is seen in Number 102 of *Kolokol*.

> We shall not see a free Russia. Our whole task has been to remove obstacles and clear the ground. We shall die on the threshold, not because the gendarmes stand at the entrance, but because in our veins flows the blood of our ancestors, who were flogged with the *knut* and beaten with rods; the blood of the informers of Peter and Biron; of our grandfather-hangmen, such as Arakcheyev and Magnitskii; of our fathers who convicted the Decembrists, who condemned Poland, who served in the Third Section, who piled up soldiers in the grave, who tortured peasants into the tomb; because in the veins of our leaders and our journalist bosses, such foul blood, which their ancestors se-

17 Vyetrinskii, "Kolokol," *Velikaya Reforma*, IV, 208.
18 *Ibid.*, IV, 205.

cured in the anterooms, audience chambers, and chanceries, is putrefying.[19]

There is no doubt that the periodicals mentioned, the London *Kolokol* and the *Sovremennik*, exercised enormous influence on the Russian public, as is attested by their very large number of subscribers, at least down to 1862. The question whether the controversy carried on in their columns made any material contribution to the final settlement of the problem is another matter. One authority, writing fifty years later, has this to say about the whole controversy:

> In general, did the journalism of that time contribute to the solution of the problem of communal land ownership—that is a question to which it hardly seems possible to give an exact answer; Kolyupanov blames literature for the fact that in the practical solution of the question of the commune, "not one voice decided to come out with a proposal showing the necessity of coercive measures against the commune that existed among us." It is possible that in this connection one ought to pay just due to the influence of journalism of the pre-reform era, and, of course, above all, to the Slavophiles. But the chief factor that was decisive in determining the decisions of the Editing Commission on the commune was the impossibility, obvious to any practical man of affairs, of proceeding to abolish the land structure of the country, which had taken form through historical processes. Apart from that, the *mir* was the single reliable guarantor to the state and the landlord for the prompt discharge by the peasants of the obligations laid on them. In view of this, the abolition of communal land ownership through elimination of servile dependence would have been practically impossible; thus the commune was not threatened by any danger.
>
> Samarin correctly summed up the situation when he wrote Koshelev, "I cannot understand why you are so concerned and alarmed by the question of the commune. From a practical point of view it is unimportant, for its settlement is not for a moment in the slightest doubt. It, perhaps, was the only question in which

[19] *Ibid.*, IV, 217-19.

the interests of the state and the landlords coincided with national customs. The opposition to communal land ownership in favor of private ownership came not from the landlords or the government but from scholars—or those who considered themselves scholars—in the name of so-called science. God be with you!

"It is understandable why the question of the maintenance of the commune found so ready a solution with the Editing Commission. The center of gravity lay not in this question, and the danger that really threatened the commune did not come from that side."[20]

With little doubt, the journalism of the time contributed to the disappointment of the public, and to the feeling of resentment that this particular reform, out of deference to vested interests, had been whittled down to insignificant proportions.

The cooling of public sympathy with the government in its program of reform became more and more marked after the publication of the emancipation proclamation; in spite of the moral support that rallied to the administration as a result of the revolt in Poland, the public was indifferent to reforms and came to the conclusion that more radical solutions to Russia's problems were needed. The assumption on which this conclusion was based was that the reforms were a fraud, designed solely to lull prevailing discontent.[21] The dissatisfaction continued to grow, fanned by the publications of revolutionaries abroad and at home, and culminated in the attempt of Kara-

[20] Manuilov, "Polozhenie 18 Fevrala i obshchinnoe zemlyevladenie," *Velikaya Reforma*, VI, 62.

[21] The basic reason for public dissatisfaction was simply the Russian's preference for extremes and his refusal to accept a compromise. If the idea that half a loaf is better than none may recommend itself to the Western mind, it would appear that Russian revolutionary leaders preferred to have no bread at all rather than to accept half a loaf. Moreover, the questioning of the motives of Alexander and his administration seems to us a fruitless task; every reform is doubtless designed to silence discontent, and is satisfied to achieve that end. Similarly, the charge of bad faith would only hold if the state's original intentions were of the best but were later abandoned or modified in deference to opposition. This attitude is clear from the quotation from *Nachalo* (1878), published in Chapter I.

A. I. Herzen

Nikolai A. Nekrasov

kozov on the life of the Emperor in 1866. From then on, the lines of battle were drawn more sharply. The existing indifference changed to open hostility that took a more definitely subversive character, while the government showed less and less tolerance for criticism and resorted more and more to repression. While repression was attended by some success at home, it could do little to restrain the exiles abroad. And the exodus of students to the universities of Europe exposed more and more of the young to Western influences. After the death of Herzen in 1870, these young people came more and more under the influence of Bakunin in Switzerland, and to a lesser extent, Tkachev. While the destruction of the existing order by force or propaganda might have been regarded as the immediate task, the new order envisaged by these visionaries was conceived (in the mold suggested by Chernyshevskii and his followers, as well as by Bakunin) as a federation of more or less voluntary economic co-operative institutions in agriculture and in industry, held together perhaps by some central authority but exercising a considerable degree of autonomy. It is this ideal for the future of Russia that becomes the characteristic note of populism (*narodnichestvo*), whose development we shall trace in a later chapter.

5. The Press

THE role of the press in the controversies that developed after 1855 was crucial. That media reflected not only the opinions of the various groups and classes into which society fell, but also, to some extent, the views of the government and the ruling circles—in a negative way, through the censorship which imposed restrictions on publications. It is important, therefore, to form a complete and comprehensive picture of the whole field of literature and of the organs of public opinion, and especially of the way in which they interacted, one on the other.

It was assumed on the death of Nicholas that the unhappy times were over and that the cloud which had descended on Russia in 1848 would promptly be lifted. The notorious Committee of April 2 ceased to meet.[1] The atmosphere of the capital immediately became relaxed, and everyone jumped to the conclusion that censorship was to be eased and full liberty of the press granted. Almost at once articles began to appear in the periodical press on subjects hitherto banned, such as political and even religious topics.[2] Not only did the existing periodicals

---

[1] [Petr Karlovich Shchebal'skii], *Istoricheskie Svyedenia o Tsenzure v Rossii*, 69. The date given here (1856) is apparently only approximate. Engelhardt, *Ocherki istorii russkoi tsenzury*, 202, says it was suppressed December 6, 1855.

68

treat their subjects with greater freedom, but there was also a flood of new magazines, eagerly greeted by a public eager to make up for the long fast in written news through which it had passed during the regime of Nicholas.[3]

Almost immediately, a new code of censorship regulations became a major concern of the new administration. The chief board of censors considered the matter, and there seems to have been at least a tacit agreement that there had to be a moderation of the code. Nazimov, one of its members, wrote to a fellow member, Norov:

> Without going into details on this question, I will merely say that to get out of this muddled situation into which our censorship has fallen, it is essential to return to the basic law of 1828, repealing all subsequent supplementary regulations, which actually do not help but only hamper the smooth functioning of a reasonable censorship.[4]

But even the code of 1828 had certain extremely unpopular features; e.g., that the censors were bound to search for the hidden meaning of the author. On this, as on other matters, the new monarch and his advisers had given the censors no lead. While the press was clamoring for a new and more generous code, an agonizing doubt prevailed in the chief committee on almost all issues. Should the press be allowed to discuss controversial matters with impunity? This question, of course, dealt with matters within the domain of the various ministries, and the practice that had grown up since 1828 of referring such matters to the ministry concerned proved too strong.[5] Actually, between 1855 and 1865, the number of agencies of the government concerned with censorship not only did not diminish but increased.[6]

In 1858, the decision of the government to proceed with

2 [Shchebal'skii], *Istoricheskie*, 89.
3 Engelhardt, *Ocherki*, 214–15.
4 [Shchebal'skii], *Istoricheskie*, 94.
5 *Ibid.*, 97.
6 Engelhardt, *Ocherki*, 209.

emancipation of the peasants posed the question of whether the press should be allowed to discuss this issue. Whatever may have been the attitude of the Emperor, the administration decided that discussion should be restricted to the most innocuous matters. This is well illustrated by the experience of the Slavophiles with their journal, *Russkaya Besyeda,* which they had founded in 1856. A supplement of this periodical, dealing with the peasant question, was called *Sel'skoe Blagoustroistvo.* The fate that overtook this publication, owing to the obstacles placed in its way by the government, is summarized by a recent writer:

> Having issued twelve numbers of *Sel'skoe Blagoustroistvo,* Koshelev was forced to suspend its publication. The government of Alexander II, having decided at the beginning of 1858 to publish in periodicals articles on peasant reform (in connection with which the publication of *Sel'skoe Blagoustroistvo* had been undertaken), hastened to reverse its decision. It was proposed to Koshelev that he send all the articles intended for *Sel'skoe Blagoustroistvo* to the Central Office of the Censorship. After twelve of the seventeen articles [intended] for two successive numbers of *Sel'skoe Blagoustroistvo* had been turned down and five had been mutilated, Koshelev decided to cease publication of the periodical. "They allow anyone to talk against the peasants, against emancipation, but they strictly forbid anything to be written on behalf of the peasants and emancipation. The words, 'Emancipation of the peasants from serfdom,' they delete," he complained to Cherkasskii in July, 1858.[7]

The attitude of the government toward the press is revealed in a memorandum presented by the governor-general of Moscow, Count Zakrevsky, to Prince V. A. Dolgorukov, chief of the gendarmes and head of the Third Section. This document, "A Memorandum on Various Unreliable Sects and Unreliable People," in addition to naming certain periodicals which the censors were to scrutinize continually, directed attention to certain subjects on which they were to exercise great vigilance.

[7] A. G. Dement'ev, *Ocherki po Istorii Zhurnalistiki 40–50'kh godov,* 360–61.

The periodicals picked for special attention were the following: *Russkii Vyestnik*, edited by Katkov and Leont'ev, the special censor for which was Von Krause; *Atheneum*, edited by Korsch and censored by Ketcher; and the *Moskovskie Vyedomosti*, also edited by Korsch. The memorandum noted that these periodicals had a very wide circulation among unreliable elements, and exercised great influence. The topics and the persons to which the censors were to address their attention, and the type of article to be subjected to close scrutiny, were the following:

1. The peasant question; rousing hatred of peasants for the nobles and of the nobles for the government.

2. Persons in the lower brackets of the bureaucracy on indefinite leave.

3. The *Raskol'niki*, who were being led to look for no consideration from the government and to place their hopes on a revolution.

4. The factory people; they were being seduced by foreign workers.

5. Theatrical performances; especially those plays drawn from Herzen.

6. Distribution of the works of Herzen (forbidden).[8]

There were, during these years, no actual statutes to guide the censors, apart from the outmoded law of 1828 and supplementary regulations issued since that date. Moreover, the chief board of censorship was divided between those who still favored some strict form of control and those in favor of relatively complete freedom. Periodicals, therefore, had to attempt to gauge the temper of the majority of the board, and thus seemed to be at the mercy of chance. For the first three years of the new reign, censorship functioned in this haphazard way, under a sort of tacit understanding that the press could discuss anything but was always subject to the whim of the censor. After 1858 a general reaction set in, largely due to the nod of the monarch and not supported by any legislation. It was not

[8] Lemke, *Epokha*, 7.

until 1859 that the first definite steps were taken towards obtaining a new code. This was by the standard device of the autocrat —setting up a *neglasnyi komitet* (a nonofficial committee).[9]

In this committee, the old controversy arose about whether the censors should lay down a pattern for literature to follow, instead of contenting themselves with prohibiting what has already been written. The committee was short-lived and gave up without having solved the problem. Finally, a new series of regulations drafted by Kovalevskii (one of the censors) was approved by the board and sent to the State Council for adoptition. It proposed to return to the code of 1828, but to liberalize some of its provisions; e.g., suggesting that nothing should be read into an author's words that conveyed a meaning not on the surface. The proposed regulations allowed great liberty to scholarly, didactic works and those produced by specialists, and restricted the ministries to intervention with the main board (committee). But the new plan did not meet with the approval of the State Council, which sent it back with the recommendation that a new ministry be created for censorship and that more far-reaching changes take place.[10] Pending the adoption of a new code, the code of 1828 was to be regarded as in force, and, with certain modifications, was to be followed in the period of transition; however, an appeal to the emperor was provided for.[11]

The relations between the government and the press had become a matter of some concern with the announcement of an impending program of reform. The Emperor's rescript of November, 1858, on the peasant problem, immediately called forth a series of discussions on the role of the press in the reform. One of the censors, Norov, enthusiastically welcomed the participation by the press in the discussion of reform. "A new era has dawned for Russia, and in ushering it in, literature is called upon to play an important role." An important speech calling

[9] [Shchebal'skii], *Istoricheskie*, 109–10.
[10] Lemke, *Epokha*, 22. This ministry was actually founded in 1859, with Baron Korf as minister, but was short-lived.
[11] [Shchebal'skii], *Istoricheskie*, 109–10. Also, Lemke, *Epokha*, 170.

on all the people to collaborate was passed by a censor, F. Kruze, for publication. But his opinion and that of Norov were not shared by all the censors. Vyazemskii protested that the question of reform had to be settled by the government, and he did not think that comment by writers on the subject would contribute anything to its proper solution.

The decision was finally reached that the censor should pass articles that viewed the matter of reform from "a scholarly and economic point of view." The Academy of Sciences urged that Russia turn to foreign rather than domestic sources for light on the peasant question.[12] One writer, at the end of 1858, wrote an article touching on the matter of redemption, which was passed by the censor. Then the member of the board who had officially passed it was censured. The press was flooded with articles which were held up by the Minister of Public Instruction; however, an appeal to the emperor released them, the Tsar ruling that the public was entitled to discuss the peasant situation.[13] This freedom was later extended to other political issues. But difficulties began to arise concerning the limits to which such discussions should be carried. Also involved were questions of libel, and a committee of the ministers of justice, public instruction, and the interior was formed to suggest what, if any, restrictions should be imposed.[14] Since there was still no law of censorship, the whole question was subject to rulings by administrative officials, and pressure began to increase to bring about greater vigilance against abuse of freedom of the press, to circumvent such oversight; various methods of evasion were resorted to, such as the smuggling of literary matter from abroad, secret presses, and the circulation of articles in manuscript.[15]

The severity of administrative censorship continued to increase in 1860, responsibility for the enforcement of the law being divided between regular justice and administrative

12 [Shchebal'skii], *Istoricheskie*, 100–101.
13 *Ibid.*, 106–107.
14 *Ibid.*, 113–15.
15 *Ibid.*, 119.

courts.[16] On February 7, 1860, Nikitenko wrote, "A very bad time has come for literature. The chief factor is that the Emperor has taken a stand against it."[17] An action taken against Kostomarov, the historian, for unauthorized mention of monarchs later than the time of Peter, indicates that the government had gone back on the relatively mild rule that monarchs as late as Catherine II might be discussed.[18]

In 1861 a committee of four was set up to take preliminary steps toward drafting a new code of censorship. Their recommendations did not favor the complete abolition of "preliminary" censorship, but urged that it be combined with a system under which writers and editors could be punished after publication. This committee also received recommendations from various periodicals, the tenor of which, however, is unknown.[19] Other recommendations came from the board of censors concerning the violations for which the censors should be on guard. These were based on answers to questionnaires submitted to various periodicals. It is interesting to note that almost all of the editors were in favor of complete abolition of preliminary censorship.[20]

It appears that the rules of censorship set up in 1848 had not been abolished, even though the Buturlin Committee of April 2 had been discharged. It could be argued, therefore, that these rules were still in operation. However, the work of the commission of 1861 was to terminate effectively this state of affairs.[21] On March 10, 1863, a *ukaz* (apparently initiated by Golovnin) was issued to the Senate, abolishing the old chief board of censorship (*Glavnoe Upravlenie Tsenzury*). By this decree, all government publications were released from the control of the board and remained subject only to their own

[16] *Ibid.*, 115.
[17] Engelhardt, *Ocherki*, 237.
[18] Lemke, *Epokha*, 31. Also see the discussion of the circumstances under which the Russian translation of Giles Fletcher's *Of the Russe Commonwealth* was forbidden in 1849, in S. R. Tompkins, *The Russian Mind*, 136-37.
[19] Lemke, *Epokha*, 56-58; also [Shchebal'skii], *Istoricheskie*, 123.
[20] Lemke, *Epokha*, 109.
[21] [Shchebal'skii], *Istoricheskie*, 84.

ministry. Publications on religion remained, as before, subject to the control of the Holy Synod. Matters dealing with the Tsar and the imperial family were left subject to the censorship of the Ministry of the Imperial Court. The major responsibility of censorship was now to fall on the Ministry of the Interior, although the Ministry of Public Instruction was left with general supervision.[22] In this way the power over the press passed into the hands of the thoroughly distrusted Valuev.[23] This change effectively abolished all the rules introduced between 1828 and 1862, and restored the code of the former year.

One complication now injected into the question of the censorship developed from the attempt in 1862 on the life of the Grand Duke Konstantin Nikolayevich.[24] It is noted also that the year 1862 saw the first harsh measure against the press—the suppression for a period of eight months of *Sovremennik* and *Russkoe Slovo*. A second committee on censorship, presided over by Obolenskii, came into existence in 1863, and assembled information on censorship in France, Germany, and Great Britain. The one point which the committee emphasized was that in these countries the promulgation of the law of censorship awaited the anticipated reform of the courts, especially if it was proposed to abolish preliminary censorship.[25] The report of this committee was turned over to the Minister of the Interior, who had now become the responsible minister.[26]

The regime of Valuev (1863–68) was to all intents and purposes a reign of terror. It led to a great demoralization among writers, and the official pressure was sufficient to change the tone of some of the leading papers. Perhaps the Polish Revolt of 1863 was the major factor in determining the attitude of the government. It also led to a profound split in the ranks of the writers themselves. "Two events—the Polish Revolt of 1863

[22] Lemke, *Epokha*, 129.
[23] *Ibid.*, 130. See the cartoon on p. 238 of Tompkins, *The Russian Mind*. Also see [Shchebal'skii], *Istoricheskie*, 129.
[24] Lemke, *Epokha*, 222.
[25] Engelhardt, *Ocherki*, 253.
[26] Evgen'ev-Maksimov, *Poslyednye Gody Sovremennika*, 11–13.

and the attempt of Karakozov on the life of the Emperor in 1866—brought about the reaction of 1868."[27] It is interesting to observe that the *Sovremennik* and *Russkoe Slovo* were permitted, late in 1862, to resume publication.[28] But it is probable that it was on the condition that they undertake to change their tone.[29] The result, therefore, of the events of the 1860's was a general reaction, partly due to the national feelings aroused by the Polish Revolt and partly due to administrative severity.

In intellectual circles, however, it was the heyday of the nihilists, and particularly of Pisarev, the literary contributor to *Russkoe Slovo*.[30] The attempt of Karakozov on the life of the Emperor on April 4, 1866, was the immediate occasion of the complete suppression of the *Sovremennik* and *Russkoe Slovo*.[31] It also coincided with the clash of Katkov and Valuev, in which the former was enabled to emerge victorious by an appeal to the Emperor.[32] In 1868, Nekrasov, with the final suppression of the *Sovremennik*, obtained control of *Otechestvennye Zapiski*.

In the meantime, the drafting of a new censorship law was proceeding apace. The first step was the decree of September, 1863. The final decree setting up a new administration for censorship did not come, however, until April 6, 1865. This abolished preliminary censorship and set up in its place the principle of *karatel'nyi* censorship. This decree applied only to St. Petersburg and Moscow; all other parts of the empire were still subject to preliminary censorship. It was clearly the intention that henceforth in the capitals, cases against the press for infringement of the statutory laws would be submitted to the ordinary courts and tried by them. However, the administration was not entirely excluded from control of the press,

27 Engelhardt, *Ocherki*, 249.
28 *Ibid.*, 273.
29 Evgen'ev-Maksimov, *Poslyednye*, 14.
30 Engelhardt, *Ocherki*, 285.
31 *Ibid.*, 271.
32 *Ibid.*, 281–82.

for the Minister of the Interior was given permission to issue warnings to periodicals which seemed to tread dangerously close to subversive language. The law permitted the minister to suppress the periodical on the third alleged offense. Under an aggressive minister, this procedure could involve practically a return to preliminary censorship and bureaucratic rather than judicial intervention in the affairs of the press.[33]

In anticipation of the law of April 6, 1865, the Minister of the Interior issued instructions to the censors, noting the great responsibility that lay with them still. He emphasized that the crucial question now was in permitting presses to begin publication. Permission was not to be granted save where there was adequate police personnel to supervise; that is, in the larger towns and cities. He also noted that while preliminary censorship was waived, supervision was not necessarily removed. A strict watch was to be kept on the press, to see that it was not guilty of breaking the law. In case a law was violated, it was not a matter of routine prosecution; some latitude was left to the discretion of the censor, who had to take into account a wide variety of circumstances to determine the gravity of the offense and how it should be punished.[34] The following offenses against the law were drawn to the attention of the censors as particularly heinous:

1. Publishing articles against faith.
2. Publishing articles against the monarchical principle.
3. Publishing articles against public and private morality.
4. Publishing articles against private property.
5. Publishing articles to undermine faith in government.
6. Publishing articles to incite class against class.[35]

The comment of one writer on this subject is extremely pertinent:

Now it has already become quite clear that the removal of

[33] *Karatel'nyi* censorship—the system under which the editor is held accountable before the courts for what he publishes.
[34] Lemke, *Epokha*, 390-91.
[35] *Ibid.*, 235.

preliminary censorship was not unconditional, and likewise that it was to a considerable degree fictitious. It was not unconditional because preliminary censorship was kept in existence not only for a whole category of periodicals but also for books of less than ten printed "leaves." It was fictitious because, by the rule about printing presses, lithographical establishments, and metal-lographic installments it was contemplated that every work freed from preliminary censorship could appear only after the elapse of three days from the receipt of a voucher from the censorship committee for the legal number of copies. The setting up of this three-day period gave the censorship the chance to make up its collective mind about the work to be issued. In these cases, when the censorship recognized that "By reason of the greatness of the damage to be caused from the distribution of an illegal publication, the carrying out of arrest could not be put off until the judicial sentence," the council of the chief administration and the censorship committees had the right to stop publication, on the condition, of course, that the prosecution of the accused at once be set in motion.[36]

Following the promulgation of the law a series of warnings were issued by Valuev, first against the *Sankt-Peterburgskie Vyedomosti* for printing an article criticizing a proposal to pledge part of the imperial domains for a second issue of bank notes at 5 per cent, without redeeming a prior issue. Likewise, the official organ of the Ministry of the Interior, *Syevernaya Pochta*, received a warning. Naturally, this caused a furor in the ministry, and the *Minister* felt it incumbent upon himself to explain publicly that the warning was adopted as a temporary measure, pending the organization of the courts to take over such cases. In the case of the *Vyedomosti*, the warning was allegedly rendered necessary by the danger to the government's credit.

In the first two years of the operation of the law, it is to be noted that numerous other warnings were issued, involving organs from the extreme left to the extreme right. Included

[36] Evgen'ev-Maksimov, *Poslyednye,* 91.

were the radical journals *Sovremennik* and *Russkoe Slovo;* the moderate liberals *Sankt-Peterburgskie Vyedomosti* and *Golos;* the organ of landlords, *Vyesti;* the Slavophile organs *Den'* and *Moskva;* and the ultra-patriotic *Moskovskie Vyedomosti*. *Russkoe Slovo* incurred the hostility of the government with an article by Lavrov on Comte. *Golos* was warned for disrespectful references to the Turkestan administration, Napoleon III, and the Baltic barons. *Vyesti* was warned for mentioning a (national?) assembly of *zemstva*, though this subject was discussed during the preparation of the law on the *zemstva*.[37]

Another writer draws attention to further administrative measures which hampered publication:

> Apparently the first, second, and third warning allowed by the law of April 11, 1865, had degenerated into a form of *predvaritel'naya tsenzura*, since the censors, while unable to change or erase anything, could hold up an edition or stop the publication of a paper. For example, *Russkie Vyedomosti*, having experienced official displeasure, had to submit its morning edition to the censor for approval; thereafter (i.e., after 11:00 P.M., when the edition was submitted to the censor), the paper could publish telegrams from official agents or news of a trivial nature, but could not publish major articles except those passed.[38]

The same writer also notes that authority sometimes resorted to the device of stopping the retail sale of the paper.[39]

The law of April 6, 1865, was recognized as a temporary measure, and continued to be modified. Supplementary decrees were dated October 16, 1866, December 12, 1866, June 7, 1867, June 13, 1867, and July 12, 1873. By this last decree, any matter could be withdrawn from the consideration of the press; failure to observe such prohibition rendered the paper liable to suspension for three months.

[37] Dzhanshiev, *Epokha Velikykh Reform*, 394–403.
[38] V. A. Rosenberg, *Iz Istorii Russkoi Pechati, 1863–1918*, 124.
[39] *Ibid.*

The general results of the law of 1865 (and the supplementary legislation) was summed up by one writer in the following words:

> The system of administrative prosecution, however oppressive it may be for the press, has an undoubted advantage over preliminary censorship. It would be unjust to claim that the condition of our periodical literature has not changed for the better. Time was when our literature, despite the dominance of the censorship, was more free than in the period from 1865 to 1868; but this was, in the first place, a freedom in the highest degree unstable and ephemeral; in the second, it was restricted to the sphere of general abstract questions. The abolition of preliminary censorship reduced the dependence of the press on accidental circumstances, on personal whim, and made possible the consideration of such matters as were previously forbidden to literature. Thus, for instance, Russian history only a short time ago stopped, as far as criticism was concerned, at Catherine II, or even at Peter the Great; dispassionate, scholarly research on recent events only began after the passing of the law of April 6. Analysis of government regulations—even now far from easy and not free from danger—some years ago could not be started, or even thought of. Oversight of the press exists, of course, even now, but it has lost its trivial, exasperating character; while it continues to hover over thought as formerly, it is not reflected, as formerly, in every word.[40]

The general effect of the law was to introduce a basis for relaxation. The *Vyestnik Evropy* in 1869 made an interesting comment on the period ushered in by the new program of censorship:

> At the end of the fifties and the beginning of the sixties, we had no conservative journals; all periodicals belonged to the opposition—if one assumes under this heading the desire for reform and a critical attitude towards the existing order of things. The difference between the journals consisted solely in their

[40] Engelhardt, *Ocherki*, 308.

greater or lesser degree of boldness, their greater or lesser degree of radicalism of their desired reforms. Now we have conservative journals, even ultraconservative and reactionary ones. Instead of the passive support of the censors, the government now disposes of the active support of journalism.[41]

The year 1870 marked the end of reaction in the policy towards the press, and in general terminated the program of reform (the new military law was still to come, but this was not an integral part of the internal reorganization of Russia). The above-quoted writer summarizes the trend after 1870 in the following words:

Nevertheless in 1870 was set up a sort of *modus vivendi.* The press, which had been almost wiped out and emasculated in 1868, again raised its head. There arose in 1866 the *Vyestnik Evropy* of Stasyulevich, at first a historical journal primarily. From 1870, this organ was the principal mouthpiece of liberal ideas and of the traditions of the great reforms—the *zemstva,* the courts, and municipal self-government. Its role in the seventies was similar to that of *Russkii Vyestnik.* The conservative and nationalistic organs were the *Russkii Vyestnik* and the *Moskovskie Vyedomosti* of Katkov. The organ of the St. Petersburg bureaucracy, the weather vane of views and trends of the upper bureaucracy, the organ of the center, was *Golos.* The opposition to *Narodnichestvo* was represented by the *Otechestvennye Zapiski* of Nekrasov and Shchedrin. Here the writers of the sixties found shelter and instruction, while the poets and belletrists of the forties published in *Russkii Vyestnik* and in the organ of Stasyulevich, which was enlightened, in the European sense, and correct.

Finally, radical nihilism was represented by the *Dyelo* of Blagosvyetlov. There was set up a kind of equilibrium which was maintained for ten years, despite the reaction of 1872 and a series of underground works which compromised literature and called for the repression of the censor.

The sinister influence of Dmitri Tolstoi appears in the seventies; he ascribes to the weakness of censorship the troubles vexing

41 *Ibid.,* 307.

the country. Prince Meshcherskii was also a force, although his influence was especially to be noticed in the 1880's.[42]

After 1872, it does not appear that there was any drastic change in the laws of censorship until the revolution of 1905. Lanin, writing in *The Fortnightly Review* in 1891, mentions a number of committees on the censorship from his own experience. His discussion gives a picture of the various agencies involved in censorship at this time:

> We have quite a numerous series of censures. A General Censure under the Ministry of Public Instruction (now the Ministry of the Interior); a Supreme Board of Censure; an Ecclesiastical Censure; a Censure in the Service of the Foreign Office; a Dramatic Censure in the Ministry of the Court; a Press Censure; a Censure of the Secret Police; a new Pedagogical Censure; a Censure of Law Books. If we reckon up all the officials occupied in censuring, we find that they are more numerous than the books that are published each year.[43]

Lanin's other comments published in the same series of articles drew attention to the rather complete control of the government over the entire process of publishing, from type foundry to bookstore. General comments imply an all-seeing and ever pressing vigilance on the part of the authorities over all publication. But, he admits, there was some legal basis for this. The judicial reform of 1864, for example, provided machinery for dealing with infractions of the censorship law in the capitals.

It is to be noted that religious publications and those of a scholarly character were generally immune from the regular censorship, as were books of more than twenty printed sheets. That left most pamphlets and novels printed in periodicals still under the law of preliminary censorship.[44]

The development of Russian literature after 1855, particularly periodical literature, was nothing less than phenomenal.

[42] *Ibid.*, 311.
[43] Vol. XL, 801. "Lanin" was a pseudonym adopted by Dr. E. J. Dillon, long the St. Petersburg correspondent of the London *Daily Telegraph*.
[44] Engelhardt, *Ocherki*, 258.

The periodicals that furnish the most striking examples of this intense intellectual activity are *Sovremennik* and *Otechest-vennye Zapiski*, but they are closely followed by *Biblioteka dlya Chteniya, Russkii Vyestnik, Russkaya Besyeda,* and *Russ-koe Slovo*. At the beginning of Alexander II's reign, there was an intense rivalry between the first two mentioned. Neither, perhaps, had assumed the characteristics for which they were later noted, but both were generally regarded as independent and aggressive.

Sovremennik had been founded by Pushkin in 1836, and after his death passed into the hands of a publisher named Pletnev. In 1846 it was purchased by Panayev, who seems to have leased it to Nekrasov with the understanding that he would be entitled to publish articles of his own whenever he wished. Panayev seems to have died about 1860, but Nekrasov continued to lease the periodical from his family until it was finally suppressed in 1866.

Nekrasov had been famous as a poet, but it would seem that his real claim to distinction was as an editor, in which capacity he showed an astonishing gift for recognizing ability in young writers and in recruiting and holding them. In 1846, for instance, he succeeded in attracting the services of Byelinskii, who had been a contributor to the *Otechestvennye Zapiski*. The same year Nikitenko, who was on the chief board of censors, joined the periodical as editor.[45] A list of contributors to the periodical in 1847 is almost a roster of the great names in Russian literature at this time.[46]

Byelinskii, V. G.	Maikov, A. N.
Gamazov, M. A.	Nebol'son, G. P.
Granovskii, T. N.	Nestroyev
Guber, E. I.	Nekrasov, N. A.
Goncharov, I. A.	Nikitenko, A. V.
Dal'-Luganskii, V. I.	Nadyezhdin, N. I.

[45] Evgen'ev-Maksimov, *Sovremennik v 40–e–50–e gg.,* 31–35.
[46] *Ibid.,* 64.

Dostoyevskii, F. M.   Odoyevskii, Knyaz, V. F.
Zasyadko, D. A.   Panayev, I. I.
Herzen, A. I.   Pletnev, P. A.
Kavelin, K. D.   Perevoshchikov, D. M.
Komarov, A. S.   Redkin, P. G.
Korsh, E. F.   Sologub, Graf, V. A.
Kroneberg, A. I.   Strugovshikov, A. N.
Ketcher, N. K.   Turgenev, I. S.
Mel'gunov, N. A.

It will be observed that this list contains the names of many who later differed violently. After the Crimean War their number was increased by the addition of Leo Tolstoi, who returned to St. Petersburg in the spring of that year. He had already attracted attention with his *Tales of Sevastopol*, and Nekrasov, with a view to heading off *Sovremennik's* rival, *Biblioteka dlya Chteniya*, whose editor was bidding for the young writer's services, offered him a tempting contract. Under its terms, Tolstoi—together with Turgenev, Ostrovskii, and Grigorovich—in return for giving Nekrasov's periodical an exclusive claim on his productions, was to receive a share of the dividends in addition to his pay.

It is apparent that every effort was made to hold writers by attractive terms and other means of encouragement. One of these means was the granting of generous advances to gifted writers in order to retain their services.[47]

All accounts agree that during the late fifties the contributors to the *Sovremennik* were more or less a happy family, but then differences began to develop. It is obvious to anyone that the contributors represented various stations in life, and persons of the noble class did not feel too comfortable in their relations with *raznochintsy*, many of whom were recruited from the church. Perhaps this rift is best illustrated by Turgenev, who in 1855 published his *Rudin*, whose hero is generally con-

[47] Evgen'ev-Maksimov, *Sovremennik pri Chernyshevskom i Dobrolyubovye*, 71, 119–20.

ceded to have been Bakunin. But as time went on, a note of enmity developed between Turgenev and Dobrolyubov, and the publication in 1861 of *Fathers and Sons* marked a definite break of Turgenev with his former colleagues, since this novel was little more than a caricature of the character of Dobrolyubov.[48] By this time, Tolstoi had already severed his connections and had acquired other interests. Dostoyevskii had been sent to Siberia, whence he did not return until 1861. In general, therefore, the contributors who bore distinguished names had dropped out, and the remaining staff was recruited from the clergy, bureaucracy, and other members of the *raznochintsy*. Of the remaining writers, by far the most brilliant were Chernyshevskii and Dobrolyubov. The latter, who joined the staff at the solicitation of Chernyshevskii, very quickly took over the literary editorship, while Chernyshevskii (who became practically the editor at this time) devoted himself to political and economic questions.

As we have seen, Chernyshevskii went along with the government to some extent until 1859, when he broke with it and took up a position of uncompromising hostility. This was not directly revealed in his periodical, since he printed no articles on emancipation between 1859 and 1861 and barely mentioned it at the time of emancipation. He did, however, resort to indirect methods (such as Aesopian language) to show his intense dislike of the plan.

By 1861 the *Sovremennik* was drifting into rough water. Its subscriptions had declined. In 1861, Dobrolyubov died, and in 1862, as a result of the growing unrest of which he was suspected to be the center, Chernyshevskii was arrested and the periodical suspended. The period of repression (from 1862 to 1868) was not interrupted by the press law of 1865, which, as we have seen, introduced a modified form of the system prevailing in Western Europe.

[48] *Ibid.*, 544. Evgen'ev-Maksimov states on the authority of Chernyshevskii that "actually he [Turgenev] was trying to get back at Dobrolyubov when he wrote his novel."

The periodical press in Russia went through a striking development in the post-reform years, either spontaneously or in reaction to administrative measures. Some account must be taken of the ebb and flow of interest in these journals in order to follow the development of Russian thought.

It must always be borne in mind that literary activity was shared in the Russian Empire by the two capitals—Moscow and St. Petersburg—about equally. It was natural that in the ancient capital, Slavophile sentiment should be the most powerful force, and we are not surprised, therefore, to learn that the Slavophiles had two organs there recognized semiofficially as theirs—the *Parus* of Sergei Aksakov and the *Russkaya Besyeda* of Koshelev. The westerners were also represented by *Moskovskie Vyedomosti*. A group of contributors to the latter, becoming dissatisfied, left that periodical and founded their own paper, *Atenei* (*Atheneum*), which soon, however, died of inanity. A further addition to the Moscow press was *Moskovskoe Obozryenie*, a critical journal which carefully preserved the anonymity of all its contributors.

The capital, St. Petersburg, had three important publications: *Sovremennik*, radical in tone, which as we have seen above occupied first place; *Otechestvennye Zapiski*, mildly liberal; *Biblioteka dlya Chteniya*, *Ekonomicheskii Ukazatel'*, the latter a free-trade organ advocating free competition and personal property in land; *Iskra*, a somewhat satirical journal founded and supported by poets and humorists, known for its clever cartoons; and *Russkii Vyestnik* (of Katkov).[49]

It is interesting to observe that during the sixties there was almost unanimity (with the possible exception of *Sovremennik*) on the question of reform. The organs of the Slavophiles, *Parus* and *Russkaya Besyeda;* the moderate right publications, *Moskovskii Vyedomosti* and *Russkii Vyestnik; Sankt-Peterburgskie Vyedomosti*, edited by Valentin Korf, representing the center; the *Golos*, edited by Krayevskii; *Vyestnik Evropy*, the moderate left organ of the *narodniks*, edited by Stasyulevich;

[49] Engelhardt, *Ocherki*, 239.

Otechestvennye Zapiski; and *Dyelo,* the radical journal edited by Blagosvyetlov—all united in support of the program of reform, however much they later came to differ.[50]

The fortunes of the press and the public reaction to it are reflected in the subscription lists. For example, the pioneer *émigré* paper, Herzen's *Kolokol,* founded in 1857, had by 1860 increased its circulation to 2,500; later, as a consequence of the Polish revolt, it dropped to 500.[51] *Sovremennik* had a subscription list from 1847 to 1854 of between 3,000 and 4,000. After the accession of Alexander and the relaxation of censorship, it rose rapidly; by 1859 it had reached 6,000, and by 1861, 7,000. Although the increased circulation improved the financial position of the publication, competition for contributors and the practice of making generous advances to hold them made a serious drain on the till.[52] Subscription figures for other magazines during the early sixties are equally instructive. While in the prereform period 4,000 to 5,000 was the maximum, *Moskovskie Vyedomosti* in 1863 had 12,000 subscribers; *Sankt-Peterburgskie Vyedomosti* had 8,000; *Den'* (one of the Slavophile organs) had 8,000; *Iskra* (the magazine of humor), 7,000; *Otechestvennye Zapiski* had 4,000; *Russkie Vyesti,* 5,700; *Sovremennik,* 7,000; and *Russkoe Slovo,* 4,000. In the years after 1855, all kinds of new publications blossomed, to flourish for a time and then shrivel under the winds of adversity. One writer gives the number of periodicals published in 1863 as 301.[53] The post-emancipation period brought heavy casualties; *Den',* *Moskva,* *Russkaya Besyeda,* *Moskvykh*—all Slavophile organs—fell by the way.[54]

There were other factors, however, besides government re-

[50] *Ibid.,* 20. Someone characterized the *Golos* by a shibboleth, "It is impossible on the one hand not to recognize and on the other hand to recognize."

[51] *Ibid.,* 240.

[52] Evgen'ev-Maksimov, *Poslyednie,* 112–16. Chernyshevskii said that his yearly income was approximately 10,000 rubles.

[53] Engelhardt, *Ocherki,* 18–19. Lemke (who probably arrives at his figures in a different way) gives the number as 195. See *Epokha Tsenzur'nykh Reform,* 269.

[54] *Ibid.,* 305.

pression that determined the trend periodical literature took. One was the rise of the modern newspaper in the early sixties, which to some extent hurt the periodicals. Another event that had wide repercussions in the field of current literature was the Polish Revolt of 1863. Addresses of public bodies, including the nobility of the province of St. Petersburg and the city council of the capital, gave the lead to a nationalistic movement, and Katkov, who had up till then stood mostly with the liberals, began to beat the drums of nationalism. The famous diplomatic controversy that developed between Alexander II and Russia's later adversaries in the Crimean War, represented by Palmerston and Napoleon III, enabled him to appear as the champion of Russian patriotism. Katkov's organ, *Russkii Vyestnik*, became immensely popular; the London *Times* called it the foremost journal in Russia. His *Moskovskie Vyedomosti* also caught the wind of popularity and prospered mightily, though its fulminations began to embarrass the government. Eventually, in 1866, it drew its first warning from Valuev; the attempt on the life of Alexander that came the next day perhaps saved Katkov. It so enhanced his popularity that the students of the University of St. Petersburg paraded in front of his press building and called on him to continue the good work. He was eventually saved by Dmitri Tolstoi, the minister of public instruction, perhaps at a signal from the Emperor.[55]

One difficulty of the times was that there seem to have been no respectable organs to reflect moderate or conservative opinion. *Vyestnik Evropy* (Stasyulevich) in 1869 bewailed this fact, for which no remedy, at least from private initiative, appeared in sight.[56] However, the government had endeavored to correct this situation in 1862 by founding *Syevernaya Pochta*, the editorship of which was entrusted to N. F. Pavlov, a close friend of Valuev. This periodical was to give the public an education in conservatism; one of its first numbers contained an article by B. N. Chicherin, "Myery i granitsy" (Measures and Bounds),

[55] *Ibid.*, 278.
[56] *Ibid.*, 308.

88

in which the writer emphasized the limits to individual freedom and the need for moderation.[57] From this time on, the press passed through difficult times, as has already been seen in connection with the suspension of *Sovremennik* and *Russkoe Slovo* and the arrest and trial of Chernyshevskii. With the new law of 1865, the government was in a position to put an end to the hitherto prevailing uncertainty, and, through both the courts and the administration, exert strong pressure on editors. *Sovremennik* and *Russkoe Slovo* disappeared in 1866 after the attempt of Karakozov. Pisarev's arrest and imprisonment (1864–66) deprived the nihilists of one of their spokesmen. Blagosvyetlov's *Dyelo* only partly filled the gap. It appears that more and more the press was being forced to adopt a colorless rather than a conservative tone, as, for example, did *Golos*, the mouthpiece of the higher bureaucracy in St. Petersburg, which expanded its list of subscribers from 4,947 in 1865 to 22,632 in 1877.[58] The important periodicals that remained after the suppression of *Sovremennik* and *Russkoe Slovo* were *Dyelo*, *Otechestvennye Zapiski*, *Vyestnik Evropy*, *Literatur'naya Biblioteka*, *Biblioteka dlya Chteniya*, *Zhenskii Vyestnik*, and *Vsemirnyi Trud*.[59]

The development of the press in Russia in the seventies was marked by a general moderation of tone. This seems to have been due to a sort of *modus vivendi*, as Engelhardt in one passage seems to suggest, or to the inherent weakness of the Russian press, accustomed as it was to constant surveillance.[60] One gets the feeling that from 1870 on the press suffered from a progressive decline so far as its public appeal was concerned. There were no names in the latter part of the century to compare with Chernyshevskii, Dobrolyubov, and Pisarev, and the gen-

[57] Lemke, *Epokha*, 92.

[58] Engelhardt, *Ocherki*, 384.

[59] *Ibid.*, 273. Nekrasov took over *Otechestvennye Zapiski;* this same year, Pisarev broke with Blagosvyetlov and his *Dyelo*.

[60] *Ibid.*, 311. Engelhardt ascribes it in a later passage (p. 316) to *opeka* (tutelage), implying that the government had by this time managed to attain the purpose it had so long striven for of bringing the press under rigid control.

eral air was one of inanity. That fact inevitably raises the question, "Was this due to censorship?" To this, one writer has the significant answer that if, by some miracle, the Russian press were suddenly released from censorship, it would still continue to show the same characteristics as before. As proof, he offers the fact that despite the greater degree of freedom the press gained under Alexander II, as compared with the regime of Nicholas I, it remained substantially what it had been in the previous reign.[61] This suggests what any careful student of Russia has probably long suspected, namely, that it is idle to blame the censors for the condition of the Russian press; that the arbitrariness of the one and the submissiveness of the other are merely complementary; that if, by some chance, the censors and the editors could change places, they would continue to act in their new capacity just as did the earlier occupants of the role.

A second characteristic of the press reflects one of the weaknesses of Russian life—the tendency in intellectual circles towards specialization.[62] This results in an educated Russian's being abreast of the times in some respects, but in others being capable of entertaining the most irrational ideas. In this connection, Pisarev said:

> The head of every representative of this society consists of a number of rooms that do not communicate with one another, each of which contains a distinct philosophy. In one chamber, for instance, one finds Darwin's theory of evolution, or Moleschott's materialism, or Comte's positivism. In a second chamber, Hegel's metaphysics. In a third, the belief in lucky and unlucky numbers, in graphology and spiritual revelations, in ghosts and miracle-pictures of saints or their relics.[63]

This somewhat disorganized mental equipment may have ludi-

[61] Nagradow, *Moderne russische Zensur und Presse*, 110–11.
[62] *Ibid.*, 54–58.
[63] This citation from Pisarev, the author has not been able to identify. It probably comes from the article, "Our University Studies," published in 1863 in Vol. III of his works.

crous consequences when the individual is called on to pass judgment. He may commit the same folly as the *Zemskii Nachal'nik* who boasted of his liberalism in having reduced the customary number of blows inflicted on a culprit (apparently some hundreds) to the comparatively low total of ninety.

Out of this complete lack of a uniformly critical faculty came another characteristic weakness—condescending contempt for the

> poor nations of Western Europe, who groan and, if not actually [at least figuratively], are crushed by the yoke of capitalism; and for the proletariat, who are oppressed by militarism and religious intolerance. Only in Russia is all quiet and tranquil, so that one cannot hear of such terrible things; everything in the Tsar's empire is happy and contented. The Russian peasant is no proletarian, for he has land which he himself tills. The Russian Army is the strongest in the world . . . for it has no Jewish muskets.[64]

This nourishing of the idea that the Russians are the happiest and the most advanced people was charged even to scientific and learned periodicals. The truth is that even in the Tsarist times, there was, to all intents and purposes, an "iron curtain" which effectively prevented Russians from forming a true estimate of their own country and of the rest of the world.

Nagradow discusses at some length another characteristic of the Russian people—their lack of objectivity. He notes that the periodicals of Western Europe go to great lengths in discussing a problem, to get all the facts; otherwise, they would be shown up by their political opponents, and thus humiliated and discredited. On the other hand, the Russian press never hesi-

[64] "Many learned Russians engaged in economic or technological studies look with disdain on German industry, which, they have read in 'foreign' works, turns out 'cheap and inferior products.' These Philistines fancy that German goods have this feature in comparison with the corresponding Russian goods, while actually, as everyone knows, the latter are both costly and inferior—the products of the *Kustarny* industries alone excepted." Nagradow, *Moderne russische Zensur und Presse*, 60. For passage quoted in text, see page 58.

tates to have recourse to the most questionable methods—any methods other than objective presentation of facts, including sneering at the naïveté of anyone who doubts their statements or does not accept their argument, and casting suspicion on their opponents and their sources of information.

> In other words, all controversy is conducted on a frankly partisan basis, so that the reader's doubts are swept away and he is left with the idea that there is only one side to the argument. This lends, in a discussion of all Russian questions, a certainty that is completely lacking in the discussion of great issues in the press of Western Europe.[65]

After the death of Katkov (in 1886) and of Ivan Aksakov and Saltykov-Shchedrin, and after *Otechestvennye Zapiski* was suspended, the conservative nationalist press had disappeared, as did the legal *narodnik* press. *Russkoe Obozryenie*, which came into existence at the end of the eighties, languished and died of public indifference. *Russkii Vyestnik*, after Katkov's death edited by F. N. Berg, was moved to Moscow, where it became dull in addition to being conservative. In the same way, the radical magazines also lost their savor.[66]

The periodicals that now dominated the scene were *Vyestnik Evropy*, *Russkaya Mysl'*, and *Russkoe Bogatstvo*, none of which made any appeal to the younger generation, however distinguished their editors and contributors were. Among newspapers, *Russkie Vyedomosti* acquired a reputation for incorruptibility that was unique.[67] On April 21, 1898, it was suspended for having published an appeal by Leo Tolstoi for "collecting contributions for the aid of the Dukhobors." Actually, the offense of Tolstoi was not only in having published the appeal but in having failed to comply with the order of the governor-general that the money be turned over to him; the paper was in no way involved, but as the Dukhobors (shortly

[65] *Ibid.*, 146.
[66] Engelhardt, *Ocherki*, 21.
[67] Rosenberg, *Iz Istorii*, 206.

to emigrate to Canada) were then in a state of more or less open revolt against the government, the Grand Duke Sergei Aleksandrovich ruled that it was a crime for the paper to publish an appeal on their behalf. Plehve in 1900 suspended the paper for having discussed the possibility of a constitution.[68]

Russkie Vyedomosti was again under fire in 1905 and 1913.[69] in 1914 it was singled out for special distinction by the Free Economic Society, receiving a gold medal for its inestimable services to culture and the political consciousness.[70] It lived on in the years of World War I as *Svoboda Rossii*, under the law of April, 1917, which allowed free discussion in the press (under the Provisional Government). After the death in 1918 of Count Mirbach, the German ambassador, all bourgeois papers were suppressed, and finally, in 1922, all publications were put under "preliminary censorship."

Other features of the Russian press in the late nineteenth and early twentieth centuries call for some comment. While the government had never officially ventured to acquire complete control over the press, it had made some use of the press for its own purposes, so that the idea became widespread that every Russian organ reflected official opinion. Despite the fact that Gorchakov had protested that most magazines expressed their own views and that the government was not called on to confirm or deny stories told or opinions expressed, the administration was forced to exercise a close censorship over utterances of the press, especially on foreign affairs, just as if their opinions were official.[71]

Moreover, there were in Russia a large number of organs openly subsidized by the state, including publications in German, French, English, Turkish, Bulgarian, Serbian, Czech, Ukrainian, and other languages, used for presenting the government's case to a wide group of readers. These, of course, supplemented government publications used to carry the same message

[68] *Ibid.*, 125.
[69] *Ibid.*, 133 and 253.
[70] Rosenberg, *Iz Istorii*, 259.
[71] [Shchebal'skii], *Istoricheskie*, 90–91.

abroad to foreign readers.[72] An example of the latter is *Bulletin Russe,* issued by the Ministry of Finance to inform foreign readers about Russia's financial position, and to reassure holders of Russian bonds in regard to their security.

One other point to be noted is that Russian journalists long continued to practice the use of Aesopian language, and this made journalese a peculiarly esoteric jargon. Lev Tikhomirov, the famous member of the executive committee of *Narodnaya Volya,* recounts that having lived abroad for eight years and having become accustomed to the frank and precise language of the Western European press, he found himself in despair when he returned to Russia and had to read Russian publications. He is quoted as having said that in deciphering "this Russian cuneiform script, Beelzebub himself would break a leg."[73]

But Russian thought was not reflected solely in the "legal" press. There is also to be considered the "illegal" press, made up of two distinct categories: the underground publications, printed in secret presses hidden away from the prying eyes of the Third Section, and the many *émigré* publications which, through all the latter part of the nineteenth century and the early years of the twentieth, continued to be printed abroad and smuggled across the frontiers. A roster of these would begin with Herzen's *Kolokol,* founded in 1857 in London and published continuously till 1867, and (if we include only the period down to the revolution of 1905) would include *Iskra,* the organ of the Social Democrats, and *Vpered,* which Lenin founded when he had broken with the *Iskra* staff. A list of these publications was compiled by E. E. Kluge and published at Zurich in 1947 in *Die Russische Revolutionäre Presse in der Zweiten Hälfte der Neunzehnten Jahrhunderts, 1855–1905.* It is quite probable that Kluge's list is not complete, for these fugitive and somewhat ephemeral publications, like their edi-

[72] Nagradow, *Zensur und Presse,* 21.
[73] *Ibid.,* 65, 84–85. A good example of Aesopian language is given in Chapter VI, where Lavrov is quoted as identifying justice with the pursuit of human interest, although his meaning is just the opposite.

tors, frequently led a precarious life. If discovered, the periodicals were confiscated and destroyed; to possess them was criminal. But no account of Russian thought can fail to take them into account as mouthpieces of contemporary views on great issues.

The greatest of all these was, of course, *Kolokol,* which was read by the emperor and put at the disposal of the Editing Commission of Emancipation. It unquestionably influenced in some degree the emancipation program. Other publications, such as *Rasprava* of Nechayev, the *Vpered* of Peter Lavrov, and *Nabat* of Tkachev, had a considerable vogue for a time. But the publication of such periodicals was beset with difficulties—financial and otherwise—and few had a prolonged existence. Revolutionary fashions were constantly changing, and a popular organ such as Herzen's *Kolokol* might, by misjudging public opinion in Russia, suffer a disastrous decline in subscriptions and in popularity, as, indeed, *Kolokol* did as a result of the Polish Revolt. Yet these publications continued to be a powerful factor in Russia down to the revolution.

During the revolution of 1905, a condition little short of anarchy prevailed when control over the press was lost by the administration. In keeping with the almost universal unrest, numerous publications sprang into life to meet the demand for information on the politics of the day. Some of these were party organs, such as *Vyestnik Russkoi Revolyutsii* and *Revolyutsionnaya Rossiya,* published by the Social Revolutionaries; *Ryech,* the organ of the Constitutional Democrats (this may be said to have replaced Struve's *Osvobozhdenie,* as Struve and his followers merged with it); *Vpered,* founded by Lenin after his break with the Mensheviks, and *Izvyestiya,* the organ of the Soviet of Workers and Peasants' Deputies. One deserving special mention is *Byloe,* a periodical devoted to the history of the revolutionary movement in Russia.

The dissolution of the Second Duma and the election of the Third inaugurated a new era, in which the regulations that had been ignored during the disturbed period from 1905 to

1907 were enforced by the administration. The radical and opposition periodicals, therefore, had to moderate their tone, under threat of complete suppression. Those which refused to adopt a more moderate attitude transferred abroad, if they possessed sufficient resources, or, more often, ceased publication.

The press in Russia during the nineteenth century cannot be judged by standards that apply to Western Europe. Although the censorship had some significance, it was not the determining factor in making the Russian press what it was. It should be noted, first of all, that journalism in Russia never pretended to be anything but partisan, and the Russian journalist was not bound to observe the ordinary standards of veracity and fair play. He could not, therefore, be judged by any criterion save whether his views ran parallel to those of the administration or counter to them. To avoid being caught in this trap, he usually resorted to Aesopian language, which sometimes baffled the reader as well as the government. Journalism thus became a battle of wits between the censor and the author, with the latter endeavoring to outwit the former by giving expression to views that ran counter to those of the administration without seeming to. The contest between the two, therefore, was never in the field of facts, but always that of opinion, and not subject to any test other than that of conformity. It would seem that it was not a battle in which victory could go to the side which was most reasonable, but one in which the supreme arbiter was force. Most Russian writers, however much they might inveigh against the repression of the censorship, believed deep down in their hearts that governments were entitled to forbid expression of hostile views. Freedom of the press usually meant freedom for me but not for my opponent. It is readily understandable why in 1917 the Bolsheviks exploited to the full the freedom of the press allowed by the Provisional Government, yet immediately abolished it once they had gained power.

6. *Going to the People*

THE attempt of Karakozov on the life of the Emperor on April 4, 1866, was followed by the rescript of May 13, which may be called a turning point in the relations of the government with the people. Alarmed by the spread of dangerous ideas, the administration decided on severe repressive measures and made use of its coercive powers in the fight. On the other hand, the public, especially the moderate element, was confirmed in the attitude long advocated by the more radical element that no understanding was possible with the forces of autocracy.

The last years of the sixties saw this cleavage become more marked. There were still those who held to the view that the Tsar and the administration were sincere, and that they were making genuine efforts at reforms to improve the lot of the people; a small minority of the journalists openly rallied to the support of the government in its struggle with the forces of disorder. Their most notable representative was Katkov, just reconciled with Aksakov and now an avowed champion of the old Russia and her national greatness. But neither the patriotic conservatives nor the timid liberals had the ear of the public. The great majority of the intellectual class—now beginning to be called the "intelligentsia"—had become openly hostile to the government and the existing order, a phenomenon destined to have such momentous consequences that some consideration of its significance is in order at this time.[1]

As we have seen in Chapter II, immediately after the Crimean War openly subversive sentiments began to get a footing in the institutions of higher learning, the students abandoning their academic pursuits in favor of the more enticing but less solid occupation of drawing up idealistic blueprints for the future of Russia. There being no conscious historical tradition in Russia and no practical experience of politics, few young people had any grasp of the difference between the ideal and the practical. Hence, when they had selected a new principle on which society ought to be organized and its social relations regulated, to proceed to act on it seemed to them the simplest thing in the world. Dobrolyubov propounded the new principle of realism in literature and Chernyshevskii began to advocate the distribution of land among the peasants, convinced that the wider the distribution, the greater would be the national well-being. Emancipation with land was to be the magic wand that would transform the rural countryside into model villages of contented peasants, its advocates completely ignoring the backwardness of peasant agriculture, which under any circumstances constituted a constant menace to such prosperity and even to the lives of the peasants. Holding this view, the students could not imagine why the government might hesitate to go all out for the property rights of the peasants; such hesitation could only be ascribed to malign influences ready to sacrifice the interests of the peasants to the greed of the landowners. The refusal of the government to take counsel of the extremists in the matter of peasant reform was thus accepted as a challenge to open war, rather than as a bid to compromise.

It cannot be said that this attitude towards reform was anything new in Russia. Catherine's passion for enlightened reforms had cooled after the Pugachev revolt. Even Alexander I had not found things propitious after the Napoleonic wars, and

[1] Ivanov-Razumnik, *Istoriya*, II, 104.

had abandoned his early hopes in favor of his Holy Alliance and the Bible Society. The truth was that reforms of all kinds were hindered by the traditional belief that compromise means weakness, and should be a signal for stepping up rather than abating demands. An example of this is provided by an incident that occurred shortly after the famous split in the ranks of the Social Democratic party at the Second Congress—held in London in the summer of 1903—when Plekhanov, at the League of Russian Socialist Democrats Abroad, endeavored to persuade Lenin to withdraw his opposition and compromise. "There are moments," Plekhanov said, "when even the autocracy is compelled to make a compromise." "Then it is said to be wavering," retorted Liza Knuniantz.[2] This conviction that compromise is a sign of weakness and calls for redoubled opposition apparently doomed any possible collaboration between government and intellectuals and precipitated the final break that led to open acts of violence against the administration. This tendency to go to extremes took several different directions, of which only a few can be mentioned.

The break between government and people can be traced back to the period immediately following the Crimean War. From a statement by Pisarev, we are tempted to believe that it was among the student body that the discontent first made itself manifest. But it would seem that the university disorders of 1861 had a relatively simple cause, namely, the "gown versus town" privileges which the students enjoyed and which led to clashes with the police as early as 1857. During the "honeymoon" of the reforming movement, good humor and tolerance were shown by the Tsar, while at Kiev, the kindly Pirogov took the side of the students, whose adolescent outbursts of high spirits were assessed at their true value.[3] On the other hand,

[2] N. K. Krupskaya, *Memories of Lenin*, I, 110.

[3] An account of these outbursts is to be found in A. N. Georgievskii, *Kratkii Ocherk pravitel'stvennykh myer i prednachertainii protiv studenchiskikh bezporyadkov*. It consists of a secret report prepared by Georgievskii, a clerk in the Ministry of Public Instruction in 1891, later smuggled abroad and published by Struve in *Osvobozhdenie* at Stuttgart. Why these harmless

Ivanov-Razumnik blames the decree of emancipation of 1861 for the hardening of the attitude of the public towards the government, as well as the resentment at the government's failure to heed the counsel of the powerful intellectual figures and of *Sovremennik*, exercised in the peasants' behalf. One is inclined to question, however, the effect of such adventitious circumstances and to fall back on the words of W. E. H. Lecky:

> The doctrine that the opinions of a given period are mainly determined by the intellectual condition of society, and that every great change of opinion is the consequence of general causes, simply implies that there exists a strong bias which acts upon all large masses of men, and eventually triumphs over every obstacle. The inequalities of civilization, the distorting influences arising out of special circumstances, the force of conservatism, and the efforts of individual genius produce innumerable diversities; but a careful examination shows that these are but eddies of an advancing stream, that the various systems are being all gradually modified in a given direction and that a certain class of tendencies appears with more and more prominence in all departments of intellect. Individuals may resist the stream; and this power supplies a firm and legitimate standing-point to the theologian; but these efforts are too rare and feeble to have much influence upon the general course.[4]

Actually the swing of the intelligentsia, which became markedly hostile to the government and the existing order, had its roots in the very character of the groups and in the nature of the intellectual life of Russia. An analogy is often drawn between the intelligentsia and the great crusading orders of the Middle Ages—both fired by a sense of devotion to a mission that made them see controversial issues not as something to be reduced to formal logic, but as challenges to their militant ardor. It was

---

demonstrations were ultimately transformed into subversive activities is not at first clear. From Pisarev's account of student life at this time, one is tempted to believe they were merely a manifestation of the general spirit that was showing itself everywhere. See *Byloe*, November, 1906, 309–12.

[4] *History of the Rise and Influence of Rationalism in Europe*, I, Intro., 14.

easier to rouse the younger generation by such an appeal than to school it in the more severe discipline of ordered thought and formal education. The younger student body thus became, to no small degree, the nucleus of the new intelligentsia, whose origin has been the cause of so much speculation. It is safe to say that the revolutionary leaders properly estimated the value of recruiting from this group those who would become the leaders of the coming generation.

The "intelligentsia" is not, according to the Russian meaning, to be confused with the "intellectuals." The intellectuals of Western Europe are persons engaged in intellectual activity and in spiritual creativity, especially in the capacity of scientists, writers, artists, high school teachers, pedagogues, and the like. The Russian intelligentsia displayed a completely opposite character; persons might belong to it who had nothing to do with intellectual work and were not even very "intellectual." Many Russian scholars and writers, on the other hand, could scarcely be considered members of the intelligentsia, in the unique Russian meaning of the word. For the Russian intelligentsia, as a social phenomenon, reminded one of a monastic order or a sect. It had its own special and intolerant code of ethics, a philosophy obligatory on its members, its own customs and habits, and represented a type of individual that could be recognized from an external appearance that set him apart from the members of other groups. So the Russian intelligentsia was neither a distinct professional nor economic group, but rather an ideological association which arose out of the most diverse social elements—the clergy, the lower ranks of the civil service, the *myeshchane*, and, after the abolition of serfdom, the peasants. It had, accordingly, formed a social stratum which stood above classes and orders, one that embraced all ranks of life—the so-called *raznochintsy*—bound together exclusively by ideas, especially social ones.[5]

[5] N. A. Berdyaev, *Sinn und Schicksal des russischen Kommunismus*, 25.
The origin of the term "intelligentsia" is somewhat in doubt. It seems to have been first applied in the sixties, perhaps beginning with Turgenev. The intelligentsia were a group of fanatical, devoted, and intolerant people, fed constantly from below by the rising youth. It was, perhaps, failure to

In this confused period, a number of diverse currents of thought were in conflict, one of which would ultimately emerge victorious in the next decade. Of the originators and propagators of the various philosophies, only a few can be mentioned.

The first of these is Petr Nikitich Tkachev, a member of the lesser landed nobility from Velikiye Luki, who became identified with the revolutionary movement as early as 1861 during the student disturbances at the University of St. Petersburg, his participation in which led to his first imprisonment. Tkachev was in and out of prison throughout the sixties, and finally succeeded in escaping to Switzerland in 1874. Tkachev's ideas, though they had much in common with those of Bakunin and others, were initially inspired by Jacobinism, and he later found a kindred soul in Blanqui. But his most noticeable contribution to revolutionary thought was his belief that revolution could be brought about only through the violent seizure of power by a minority, without waiting for a long period of propaganda to prepare the minds of the people. Tkachev had also read and assimilated much of the teachings of Machiavelli, and it seems to be largely through him that there entered the Russian revolutionary movement a cynical reliance on force and guile to attain revolutionary aims.

Tkachev introduced an element of urgency into the discussion of revolutionary methods. In his controversy with Lavrov, he insisted that the trend developing in post-reform Russia was turning it into a capitalist country; a new class of peasant farmers was forming, which would buttress the capitalist system: "But however slowly these classes take shape and gather strength, the situation of the people will inevitably get worse, and the chances of success of a violent revolt will become more problematical."[6] Tkachev's preference for out and out conspiracy, led by an elite group, for seizure of power led him not

recognize this that led to the crisis noted by Zhelyabov at the end of the seventies, when he remarked that the "revolution was living off its capital." There is no doubt that there is no western counterpart of the intelligentsia.

[6] Tkachev, *Sochineniia*, III, 70.

only to quarrel with Lavrov, who advocated a long period of preparation for revolt,[7] but also brought him into collision with Bakunin and his advocacy of a federation of autonomous groups. Tkachev condemned such a program, which, he felt, would only lead to failure.

> Every idea of creating a movement for the foundation of a federation of autonomous groups was a utopia; could not have provided an effective weapon for struggle; would have been incapable of any prompt or decisive action; would have opened the doors to internal dissension and argument, to vacillation and compromise. Further, such a federative conception had its roots in the mentality and morality of the bourgeoisie, based as it was on individualism and egotism. Revolutionaries, even in their organization, had to show that they put what was collective above what was individual.[8]

Tkachev was associated with Bakunin in Switzerland in the early 1870's, but the two men finally parted company. Bakunin founded his own newspaper, *Narodnoye Dyelo*. Eventually, Tkachev launched his journal *Nabat* (*The Alarm Bell*), which appeared between 1875 and 1881.[9]

An even more important personality in the revolutionary movement at this time was Sergei Gennadevich Nechayev, a member of the working class born in the industrial region of Ivanovo-Voznesensk, famous for its production of textiles, and sometimes called the Russian Manchester.[10] Forced into a life of labor at an early age, he managed to educate himself and, in 1865, at the age of seventeen, he went to Moscow, where he came into contact with various revolutionary groups—including that of Ralli, the disciple of Buonarroti, and that of Tkachev, with whom he collaborated. Nechayev soon gained a reputation for extreme fanaticism, and acquired great prestige among

[7] *Ibid.*, III, 54.
[8] *Sochineniia*, III, 228. Cited by Venturi, *Il Populismo Russo*, II, 68.
[9] E. E. Kluge, *Die Russische Revolutionäre Presse in der Zweiten Hälfte des Neunzehnten Jahrhunderts, 1855–1905*, 199–201.
[10] Venturi, *Il Populismo Russo*, I, 587–632.

the Russian revolutionaries. He made trips back and forth across the frontier, as well as over the length and breadth of Russia. In Switzerland, he made contacts with Herzen and Ogarev, as well as Bakunin. After Herzen's death in 1870, Nechayev conceived the idea of reviving *Kolokol,* which had been discontinued in 1868. However, he lacked Herzen's literary skill and wide circle of literary friends, and the revived periodical ceased publication shortly.

As has been said, he established relations with Bakunin, and with his collaboration composed the *Catechism of the Revolutionist,* one of the famous documents of revolutionary history. The first seven paragraphs give a key to the ideas of Nechayev, and to a lesser degree those of Bakunin.

1. The revolutionist is a doomed man. He has no personal interests, no affairs, sentiments, attachments, property, not even a name of his own. Everything in him is absorbed by one exclusive interest, one thought, one passion—the revolution.

2. In the very depth of his being, not merely in word but in deed, he has broken every connection with the social order and with the whole educated world, with all the laws, appearances, and generally accepted conventions and moralities of that world which he considers his ruthless foe. Should he continue to live in it, it will be solely for the purpose of destroying it more surely.

3. The revolutionist despises every sort of doctrinairism and has renounced the peaceful scientific pursuits, leaving them to future generations. He knows only one science, the science of destruction. For this and only for this purpose he makes a study of mechanics, physics, chemistry, and possibly medicine. For this purpose he studies day and night the living science of human beings, their characters, situations, and all the conditions of the present social system in its various strata. The object is but one— the quickest possible destruction of that ignoble system.

4. He despises public opinion. He despises and hates the present-day code of morals with all its motivations and manifestations. To him whatever aids the triumph of the revolution is ethical; all that which hinders it is unethical and criminal.

5. The revolutionist is a doomed man. He is merciless toward

the state and toward the entire system of privileged educated classes; he in turn expects no mercy from them. Between him and them there is a continuous and irreconcilable war to the bitter end—whether it be waged openly or secretly. He must be ready to die at any moment. He must train himself to stand torture.

6. Rigorous toward himself, he must also be severe toward others. All tender, softening sentiments of kinship, friendship, love, gratitude, and even honor itself must be snuffed out in him by the one cold passion of the revolutionary cause. For him there is only one satisfaction, consolation, and delight—the success of the revolution. Day and night he must have one thought, one aim—inexorable destruction. Striving coldly and unfalteringly towards this aim, he must be ready to perish himself and to destroy with his own hands everything that hinders its realization.

7. The nature of a real revolutionist precludes every bit of sentimentality, romanticism, of infatuation and exaltation. It precludes even personal hatred and revenge. Revolutionary passion having become a normal phenomenon, it must be combined with cold calculation. At all times and places the revolutionist must be, not that towards which he is impelled by personal impulses, but that which the general interests of the revolution dictate.[11]

From Switzerland, Nechayev claimed that a peasant revolution was imminent in Russia, and that he had an organization ready to exploit it. His *Principles of the Revolution*, written also in collaboration with Bakunin, advocated the use of terror by the revolutionaries. With some encouragement, he organized a society called the *Narodnaya Rasprava*, which published a periodical of the same name, only one number of which appeared, in 1869. Eventually, the revolutionaries began to doubt the imminence of a revolution and the strength of Nechayev's organization.

During his sojourn in Russia in 1869, he had brought about

[11] Nechayev, *Catechism of the Revolutionist*, from Max Nomad, *Apostles of Revolution*, 228–33.

the assassination of Ivanov, a young member of his organization whom he suspected of treachery. The discovery of Ivanov's body put the police hot on the trail of *Narodnaya Rasprava*.

Nechayev planned to launch a peasant revolution on the tenth anniversary of the emancipation. He had, however, already overstrained the credulity of the Russians in exile, and Bakunin had broken with him. Nechayev became involved in various outbreaks in Western Europe, and was finally betrayed to the Swiss police in 1872 and turned over to the Tsarist government. He was first sentenced to ten years, and finally to life in exile in Siberia, where he died in 1882. The fate of Nechayev, as we will see, had considerable influence on the progress of the growing revolutionary movement in Russia.

A third powerful element in the revolutionary movement at that time was that associated with the name of Nikolai Chaikovskii and which appeared in the Medical-Surgical Academy of St. Petersburg. While the group was called the *Chaikovtsy*, actually the man who gave the name to the organization dropped out of the revolutionary picture, and the leadership was taken over by M. A. Natanson, who actually exercised it for a much longer period.[12] The *Chaikovtsy* was made up primarily of students from the above academy and other educational institutions, and included many revolutionary leaders who later became famous.

This movement was just taking form at the time of the Nechayev trial, and on the evidence at hand it appears that it changed the emphasis from revolutionary violence to propaganda. We have the following statement on the subject:

> At the time of the Kushelevskaya commune, during the summer months of 1871, the trial of the followers of Nechayev dragged out. The trial was public; accounts of it were printed every day in the newspapers. "And it is easily understood," says N. V. Chaikovskii, "that every detail of this trial became for us a salutary lesson for our own future career. . . . All that was

[12] Venturi, *Il Populismo*, I, 584–86.

openly expounded in the courtroom in regard to this affair (that of Nechayev) at a time when our own convictions were taking form was experienced as something absolutely negative, which we ought not to repeat in our own career." Such a severe verdict on *nechayevshchina* and the Jesuitical system of its organization—in spite of the attractiveness of the thought of a struggle for the ideal of truth and justice—is found in all the memoirs of the time, without any exception, which treat in any way the Nechayev trial.[13]

The most interesting evidence, however, was that of Madame Breshkovskaya:

> The "to the people" movement made its real beginning after the Nechayev trial. This was the first case which was officially and widely reported in the papers. In this way the public was informed of the entire history of the conspiracy, of the political opinions of the chief participants, and of the opinions of scores of liberal-minded lawyers. This publicity was very effective propaganda, and the revolutionary movement from the outset gained useful information as to what kinds of activity a secret society had to avoid and what it might hope to accomplish. The trial demonstrated the necessity for mutual trust and the strict observance of all rules and agreements.[14]

The *Chaikovtsy*, during the early stages, spread considerable propaganda among the workers in the industrial sections. Sophia Perovskaya, Sinegub, and Peter Kropotkin were among those who prosecuted this branch of the revolutionary work.[15] Eventually, however, their hopes of revolution began to be placed more and more on the peasant, and by 1873 it was in this direction that their eyes were turned.

It is to be observed that the *Chaikovtsy* placed the first emphasis on self-education and that they circulated among themselves the important literature which provided the mental diet

[13] D. M. Odinets, "V Kruzhkie Chaikovtsev," from *Nikolai Vasil'evich Chaikovskii* (ed. by A. A. Titov), 41–49.
[14] E. K. Breshkovskaya, *Hidden Springs of the Russian Revolution*, 334.
[15] Ludwik Kulczycki, *Geschichte der Russischen Revolution*, II, 79.

of the revolutionaries of this period. D. M. Odinets, on the authority of Shishko, gives a list of the writers whose books were circulated in the group. They include Chernyshevskii, Dobrolyubov, Pisarev, Nekrasov, Kostomarov, Shchapov, Sergeyevich, Mordovtsev, Khlyebnikov, Buckle, Berne, Lassalle, Shpielgagen, Emma and Lucinda Schweitzer, John Stuart Mill, Darwin, Draper, and Spencer. Specific works mentioned include: "Historical Letters," Lavrov; "The Condition of the Working Class," Flerovskii; *Kapital*, Marx; *History of Ten Years*, Louis Blanc; "The Comedy of Universal History," Chere; "The Proletariat in France" and "On Associations," Scheller-Mikhailov; "The Renegades," Sokolov; and "Makers of Gold," Tschoke.[16] These were obtained through the operation of secret presses, or by clubbing together to buy books.[17]

The number of members of the *Chaikovtsy* has been a matter of some speculation. Venturi, on evidence given in 1928 by three veteran revolutionaries, N. A. Karushin, M. F. Frolenko, and A. Kornilova-Morozova, estimates the number at thirty active members and fifteen collaborators. This, however, is only the group in St. Petersburg. To this must be added nineteen members in Moscow, eleven in Odessa, eight in Kiev, and units of unknown size in Kharkov, Orel, Kazan, and Tula.[18]

This group had some connections abroad, and in 1872 opened negotiations with Peter Lavrov in Zurich to collaborate in the publication of his new periodical, *Vpered*. Thus the movement in Russia was linked to that in Switzerland.[19] There were special factors operating in the case of Russian *émigrés* in Zurich. In the first place, the universities of Russia had not yet opened their doors to women, and the girls of well-to-do families who wished to obtain an education were likely to emigrate. Many went to Switzerland.

"What is all this knowledge," the young girls asked them-

16 Odinets, "Chaikovtsev," *Chaikovskii*, 61.
17 Kulczycki, *Geschichte*, II, 72.
18 Venturi, *Il Populismo*, II, 785.
19 Kulczycki, *Geschichte*, II, 82.

selves, "but a means of acquiring a more advantageous position among the privileged classes to which we already belong? Who except ourselves will derive any advantage from it; and if no one does, what is the difference between us and the swarm of blood-suckers who live by the sweat and tears of our poor fellow-countrymen?"

And the young girls deserted medicine, and began to frequent the sittings of the "Internationale" and to study political economy and the works of Marx, Bakunin, Proudhon, and of all the founders of European socialism. In a short time the city of Zurich from being a place of study was transformed into an immense permanent club. Its fame spread throughout all Russia and attracted to it hundreds and hundreds of persons, men and women.[20]

This emigration had taken some considerable proportions by 1872. It is possible that these young people would have finished their studies and gone back to Russia to enter service there, had not the Russian government at that time issued a *ukaz* withdrawing all passports and demanding their return.[21] But the students had fallen under the influence of Lavrov and Bakunin, the latter of whom had already sounded the note that was to be the watchword of the new movement. This appeal of May, 1869, was worked out in collaboration with Nechayev and read as follows:

Go to the people; there lies your road, your life, your science. . . . Educated youth ought to become, not the object of charity, the dictator, the guide of the people, but merely the midwife of the people's liberation, the concentrator of the energies and the force of the people. To acquire the ability and the right to serve their cause, you must blend with, identify yourselves with, the people. Do not devote yourselves to science, in the name of which they seek to shackle you by depriving you of all your strength. That science should perish, together with the world of which it is the expression. A new and quickening

20 Stepniak, *Underground Russia*, 21.
21 *Ibid.*, 21.

science will unquestionably arise later, after the victory of the people, from the liberated life of the people themselves.[22]

This appeal found its counterpart in one issued in Moscow in 1873 by one of the followers of Dolgushin, Bervyi-Flerovskii. His appeal really echoes the sentiments of Bakunin: "Go to the people and tell them all the truth, even to the last word; tell them that man should live according to the law of nature. According to this law all men are equal. All are born naked, all are born alike, tiny and weak.[23]

The two currents of humanity were thus fused in that extraordinary movement which took place in the summer of 1873—known as the "mad summer"—the almost complete exodus of the intellectual leaders of the revolutionary movement to the country. The movement had not only the support of Bakunin and Dolgushin, but also that of Lavrov, who took a most sanguine view of the probable effects, and seems to have believed that this campaign of propaganda would call a whole army of peasants into life.[24] The enthusiasm among these people was extreme, and has been well described by Stepniak:

Nothing similar had been seen before, nor since. It was a revelation, rather than a propaganda. At first the book, or the individual, could be traced out, that had impelled such or such a person to join the movement; but after some time this became impossible. It was a powerful cry which arose no one knew where, and summoned the ardent to the great work of the redemption of the country and of humanity. And the ardent, hearing this cry, arose, overflowing with sorrow and indignation for their past life, and abandoning home, wealth, honours, family, threw themselves into the movement with a joy, an enthusiasm, a faith, such as are experienced only once in a life, and when lost are never found again.

I will not speak of the many, many, young men and young women of the most aristocratic families, who laboured for fifteen

22 Venturi, *Il Populismo*, I, 599–600.
23 *Ibid.*, II, 809.
24 Ivanov-Razumnik, *Istoriya*, II, 107–108.

hours a day in the factories, in the workshops, in the fields. Youth is always generous and ready for sacrifice. The characteristic fact was that the contagion spread, even to the people in years, who had already a future clearly marked out and a position gained by the sweat of their brows; judges, doctors, officers, officials; and these were not among the least ardent.[25]

This exodus was directed for the most part into the traditional country of peasant risings, into the lower and middle Volga, the Ukraine, the valleys of the Dnieper and the Don, where it was assumed that the response to the movement would be more enthusiastic.[26]

Most of the persons who participated in this movement prepared themselves for some trade or calling that would find an outlet in peasant communities, and, in addition to their training, provided themselves with simple tools and equipment. These crafts, however, were only a front behind which they proposed to carry on their secret propaganda. A vivid account of this is given in a book by one of the most famous participants in this movement, Madame Breshkovskaya, called *Hidden Springs of the Russian Revolution*.

The persons participating in the movement, however, were doomed to disappointment. Few of them were acquainted with peasant life, and even when they were their acquaintance was only a casual one, such as would be set up between a member of the gentry and his peasants. Strange craftsmen coming into the community were looked upon with distrust, and the peasants preferred to give their work to someone they knew. In few cases did these *narodniki* succeed in winning the confidence of the peasants. The police quickly became alarmed at the rate at which this movement was developing and within a short time had taken steps to counter it. Since the peasants were suspicious or even openly hostile, the young enthusiasts could not count on support from the rural population, and in some cases were even denounced by the peasants. The landowners and others

[25] *Underground Russia*, 25.
[26] Venturi, *Il Populismo*, II, 823.

were quickly alerted, and action taken by the administration resulted in some 770 persons being locked up, of which 612 were young men and 158 young women. Of the 770 persons arrested, a few were cleared, approximately 450 were given their liberty provisionally, and about 250 were held in prison. Contrary to what one might have expected, the landowners were more favorably disposed than the peasants to the strangers in their midst, and many cases were reported in which the gentry extended protection to the revolutionaries.[27]

The "to the people" movement did not, of course, come to an end with these setbacks, but continued in one form or another until 1878. By that time, however, it was recognized by the participants to have been a complete failure, with the result that those who managed to evade the police began to drift into the cities, there to discuss among themselves the causes of their failure and the course the future revolutionary movement should take. This heart-searching was further emphasized by the warning of Tkachev, issued in 1876, that the Russian peasants were not ready for a revolution and could not be prepared within the foreseeable future, but that the proper means of initiating the revolution was by violent seizure of power at the center of government.

The group participating in the "to the people" movement had no common program and seldom agreed on basic principles. Two particular groups stand out, the so-called Troglodyts and a group that preferred to agitate among the workers in the cities. In the summer of 1876, however, steps were taken to form a party, the *Zemlya i Volya*, whose banner was raised on the square of Our Lady of Kazan in St. Petersburg on December 6 of that year. This party came ultimately to stand for all of the revolutionary elements in Russia and began to publish

[27] Venturi, *Il Populismo*, II, 824-25. This information is contained in a report to the Tsar by Count Pahlen in 1874, which subsequently found its way into the hands of the revolutionary leaders and was published in Geneva. The report emphasized the role of Bakunin and Lavrov in promoting this movement, although this opinion is heavily discounted by some of the revolutionary writers.

Going to the People

a periodical under the same name as that of the group. The first number appeared in October, 1878; a supplement called "Listok Zemli i Voli," published at intervals between the regular issues, continued until the breakup of the party.[28]

The party stood, of course, for the division of the land among the peasants as well as the granting of full freedom. The latent differences in the party, however, eventually produced serious schisms. One of these, perhaps was due to the so-called Chigirin incident, in which a young revolutionary, Stepanovich, forged a decree of the Tsar granting the peasants land and urging them to take possession of it. This led to a serious local revolt which had to be put down by force.[29]

A sudden change of tactics by the government brought the revolutionary movement out in the open and made it the subject of public discussion. In March, 1875, the committee of ministers, after some deliberation, decided that:

> One of the chief causes of the now well-attested, shameful indifference of reliable social groups to the propagation of the subversive principles now being proclaimed is the general ignorance that has hitherto prevailed, not only among the general public but also among the upper ranks of the administration. . . . The committee is profoundly convinced that . . . the memorandum of one of the most active agitators cannot appeal to respectable members of society, or even to unbalanced or uneducated persons. This states that for the attainment of their end, streams, torrents, rivers of blood must flow. . . . The committee believes public opinion ought to be roused against this teaching . . . that the most natural and direct way to obtain . . . wide and favorable publicity is through the courts, by which the sinister nature of the teachings . . . will be revealed.[30]

Thus, it was decided that as many as possible of the political

[28] Kulczycki, *Geschichte*, II, 254.
[29] E. K. Breshkovskaya, *Hidden Springs of the Russian Revolution*, 172–73. Whatever the results of the Chigirin incident, it marked the injection of Machiavellian principles into the revolutionary movement, which could not but embarrass the more scrupulous and high-minded revolutionaries.
[30] Tatishchev, *Imperator Aleksandr Vtoroi*, II, 549–50.

113

prisoners undergoing detention would be brought to trial. They were to be tried in batches. In the first trial, held from January 18 to 25, 1877, fifty of those who had staged the demonstration before the church of Our Lady of Kazan were charged. Other trials followed later in the year, and on January 23 of the year following was held the most famous trial of all, that of 193 persons.

But the government's program misfired. The administration and the police were somewhat halfhearted and inclined to sympathize with the accused. Moreover, the new court rules allowed the prisoners privileges of which they took advantage—the right to refuse to attend court and the right to challenge the competence of the court. The statements the prisoners made in their own defense were resounding challenges to the whole existing order. Most of the prisoners were acquitted and the others received relatively mild sentences. In general, the effect on public opinion was exactly the opposite of what was anticipated by the government.[31]

The last phase of the "to the people" movement came in 1877, when there was a considerable exodus to Saratov, where the so-called Commune of Saratov was founded. Similar developments took place at Samara. The commune at Saratov was raided in this year, and most of its members made their way back to St. Petersburg after being released.[32]

Gradually, the growing disillusionment and the resulting controversies over the future course of the revolution led to a split in the *Zemlya i Volya* which became too serious to be patched up. The growing realization that propaganda alone would achieve nothing prompted the more extreme elements to agitate for thoroughgoing political reforms and to take steps to force the government to make concessions.

---

[31] Accounts of these trials (especially the last) are to be found in Stepniak, *Underground Russia*, 29-31; and in E. K. Breshkovskaya, *Hidden Springs of the Russian Revolution*, 148-69. It is to be noted that Madame Breshkovskaya was herself one of the accused and was one of the few who were found guilty and given a somewhat severe sentence.
[32] Venturi, *Il Populismo*, II, 941.

The attack on General Trepov, the governor-general of St. Petersburg by Vera Zasulich on January 24, 1878, and her subsequent acquittal on March 31 of that year, were greeted in the capital with almost delirious joy. In the development of revolutionary thought, however, it indicated that the most extreme faction was getting the upper hand in the *Zemlya i Volya*, and that a campaign of terror was about to begin.[33]

Excesses followed in quick succession, and many arrests occurred during the spring and summer of 1878. Eventually, a conference of *Zemlya i Volya* was called in Voronezh, to agree, if possible, on united action. Some days before the Voronezh conference, a group of fourteen extremists gathered at a place called Lipetsk. They called for a program of action and terror, and proposed the formation of a central executive committee to direct terrorist activities. The meeting then adjourned to Voronezh, where the other members of *Zemlya i Volya* participated. The result of this was a final split, and two separate factions emerged—*Narodnaya Volya*, the terrorist group, and *Chernyi Peredyel*. Plekhanov, one of the main figures in the parent body, adhered to the *Chernyi Peredyel* faction.[34]

The chief theorist of the "to the people" movement was Lavrov, a man of noble origin (province of Pskov) whose early training was for the army, but whose intellectual tastes inclined him towards philosophy and literature. He was an associate of Chernyshevskii at the beginning of the sixties and was drawn into the revolutionary movement, which led to his arrest in 1866 after the attempt of Karakozov and to his deportation to Siberia, whence he escaped abroad in 1870, reaching Paris and eventually Zurich. While in exile in Siberia, he wrote, under the pseudonym of Mirtov, his famous *Istoricheskie Pis'ma*, a series of philosophical essays which embody his beliefs. In 1873 he founded *Vpered*, which he continued to edit at Zurich and London till 1876, when it was discontinued.

[33] Kulczycki, *Geschichte*, II, 232. Also see correspondence in *Nachalo*, April, 1878, found in [V. I. Yakovlev], *Revolutsionnaya Zhurnalistika Semidesyatykh Godov*, 57–59.
[34] Kulczycki, *Geschichte*, II, 281–89.

Lavrov's contribution to Russian thought was a considerable one, and to some extent he broke new ground as advances in science and scientific thought made it necessary to do so. His point of departure is that speculation in the realm of human affairs must not try to adopt the methods of science, or try to assimilate thought in the social field to thought in the scientific field. To quote his own words:

> It is possible (and even probable) that in the universe in general, consciousness has only secondary importance; but for man, it has a value so unique that he will always classify his own acts and those of his fellows as conscious or unconscious, and will see them, in each case, in a different light. . . . The part consciously chosen in social life, a conscious struggle in the ranks of a certain political party to achieve a fixed historical transformation, that has and will always have for man quite a different meaning from that of an automatic activity which will manifest itself under analogous conditions. So one must, when one is concerned with grouping historical events, give the first place to conscious influences. . . .[35]

In another passage, Lavrov develops his views even more fully:

> However overwhelming be the evidence of objective knowledge which proves to man that all the acts and thoughts of his choice are only the necessary consequences of a series of prior events, external and internal, physical and psychical, the subjective consciousness of the arbitrary nature of his acts and his thought remain an illusion necessary for all times, right up to the general determinism which regulates the external world, as it does the spirit of man. . . . That allows us to place alongside the domain of theoretical knowledge the domain of moral conscience, and in this last domain to take as the point of departure the primitive, subjective fact of free choice existing for us . . . this is what gives a solid base for practical philosophy, and it is

[35] Lavrov, *Lettres Historiques*, 25-26. This is the French translation of *Istoricheskie Pis'ma*. The Russian original was not available.

this that has allowed me in these letters to speak to the reader of the moral duty of the individual; of the moral necessity of a struggle of individuals against social forms that are growing old; of the moral ideal and of the historical progress that comes from it.[36]

Having thus provided this somewhat unstable foundation for man's moral and social life, Lavrov proceeds to indicate how moral laws can be applied to everyday life. In a curious passage in a chapter on "The Extent of Progress of Humanity," he inserts this statement:

> The development of the individual cannot proceed unless he can bring about in himself the need to apply critical thought to all that he sees; he must, moreover, be convinced of the immutability of the laws regulating phenomena, and he is bound finally to understand that justice is, in the last result, identical with the pursuit of human interest.

To this passage the author has appended a footnote dated 1889, which would indicate that it was not published in the original. This note clearly states what is apparently couched in the original in Aesopian language, and seems to prove the exact opposite of what is stated in the text. This footnote, in part, reads as follows:

> To prevent any possible misunderstanding it is necessary to explain these last words—something I have not been able to do in a book published in Russia.
> In present-day society, which is based on universal competition, to identify justice with personal interest appears absurd. Those who, in our time, profit from the blessings of civilization, can only do so by enriching themselves and continuing to augment their riches. But the capitalist process of accumulating

[36] *Lettres*, 155. The view that Lavrov considered freedom an illusion is challenged by V. V. Zen'kovsky in his *History of Russian Philosophy* (tr. by George L. Kline), I, 354. The French translation to which the writer had access makes use of the word "illusion" and hardly leaves any doubt of Lavrov's meaning.

riches consists, by its very nature, in deceiving the worker, in making dishonest speculations on the stock exchange, in selling, as one form of merchandise, his intellectual faculties or his political or social influence. I doubt whether the most confirmed sophist would dare to call these proceedings just.

He then goes on to show that the ordinary criteria by which we test actions, e.g., twinges of conscience, the approbation or the disapprobation of the public, are futile; conscience can be stifled or become hardened; public approval can be secured easily with the display of wealth which has been amassed, and even those who grudge us our success not only hasten to give their modicum of admiration but also seek to emulate us. Lavrov continues:

One must agree that in the present state of society, not only is personal interest not identical with justice, but it is actually diametrically opposed. To have the greatest amount of enjoyment the individual must stifle in himself the very notion of justice; he must apply all his critical faculties to the exploitation of everything and everyone around him in order to be able to enjoy the greatest possible success at their expense; he must remember that if he gives way, even for an instant, to considerations of justice, or even to a feeling of sincere benevolence, he will soon become, in his turn, an object of exploitation at the hands of those who surround him. The owner must oppress the worker on pain of being robbed by him. The head of the family must watch with a suspicious eye his wife and children; otherwise, he will be deceived by them. The government is forced to have a police force everywhere; otherwise, its power will pass into the hands of its adversaries. . . . War is everywhere, and you must have your arms ready every minute and against every man.

Then the two things are one; either the identification of justice with personal interest is nonsense, or else the present social regime is a pathological one. . . . a society based on war of all against all is a society that has no legality; no police will be able to maintain a society which is dissolving and which demands a radical reform. . . . Should we try to cure the symptoms of this malady or should we search for the roots and take measures against them? And if the source of the evil resides in the very foundations of the present social regime, does not the radical transformation of all the economic, political, and social relations between man require a new formula to express the very principle of these relations? Should we not, after transforming the abnormal situation to a normal one, take as the basis no longer the struggle of all against all, no longer universal competition, but the solidarity most intimate and extensive between individuals . . . ? And what is social solidarity if not the consciousness of the fact that individual interest coincides with the interests of the community.[37]

In the chapter entitled "The Cost of Progress," Lavrov develops a hypothesis then becoming increasingly popular in Russian society; namely, the debt of the privileged classes to the mass of the people. He notes that while progress is due to a minority of exceptionally gifted persons, it is really purchased with the blood of countless generations of obscure persons who have perished in the struggle for existence, who have done the world's hard work and have secured for the minority the leisure and the security to devote their energies to intellectual activity. In this way the ideas of truth and justice which originate in the small privileged minority are really paid for with the blood and sweat of the great majority.[38]

Perhaps the most startling of all the ideas of Lavrov are contained in a letter entitled "Le Contrat et la Loi." The author considers first of all the theory of the social contract, which he dismisses rather casually, and then proceeds to discuss the place of the contract in ordinary human relations. He challenges the principles on which the contract is based, claiming that in its very essence the idea of the contract is fundamentally wrong. His arguments are contained in the following paragraphs:

[37] *Ibid.*, 44–46.
[38] *Ibid.*, 67–81. This application of this moral obligation on the part of the privileged to the lower classes is developed in Chapter V.

Society is made up of the stronger and the weaker persons, of exploiters and exploited; the latter suffer from the sins of the former and distrust them. But circumstances may arise when, in spite of their strength, the former cannot attain their ends without the co-operation of the latter. So they buy this co-operation by guaranteeing, to some extent, the weak against their own power. This contract between the powerful and the weak is made at a time when the strong happen to be weaker and the weak happen to be stronger. It thus brings into the social regime a greater degree of justice than it had formerly.

Little by little, the advantage of such a contract becomes evident; it becomes impossible not to perceive the direct improvement which it brings to social life. People begin to idealize the contract. It is strengthened by magic rites which threaten violators with inevitable penalties. Crowds of invisible spirits are invoked who become its witnesses and, so to speak, its participants. . . . The contract acquires a character of subjective sanctity. The ideal of the honest man is generalized in the images of poets, in the conceptions of thinkers. It enters into the habits of society. The violator of a contract sees his condemnation everywhere—in the smile of his acquaintances, in the cold salutation of a friend, in the hint of the scandal-monger. From the fantastic world of myths and the subjective world of convictions, honesty passes into the real world by becoming the most sacred of social ties.[39]

Lavrov claims that, contrary to popular belief, the "conventions of social life do not form a counterweight to prevent dishonest actions, since the fate of those who break contracts is far from uncomfortable." However, the advantages of the contract to the strong are such that the contract is placed under the protection of the law and is secured by all the resources of the state.[40]

He goes even further and seeks to justify the repudiation of any contract that has ceased to be advantageous. His arguments against the carrying out of a contract that has become

[39] *Ibid.,* 197.
[40] *Ibid.*

irksome is based on his belief that when its performance ceases to be the result of good feeling towards the other party, the carrying out of the contract becomes a purely mercenary action designed solely to enable a person to avoid the reproaches of others and himself. He argues further that the man who demands the fulfillment of a contract that is unprofitable to the other party is a criminal if the other party has signified his unwillingness to carry it out. Moreover, he states that the person who discharges such a contract is himself committing a criminal act.[41]

It is difficult for the outsider to grasp the enormity of this sweeping indictment of contracts, which seem so large a part of our daily life. Lavrov assumes that contracts are never made by two persons of their own free will, but in every case dictated by the person who is in a position to do so. This, of course, runs contrary to the experience of the Western world, where contracts are normally entered into for the very reason that it is human nature for a person to seek to avoid fulfilling an agreement that has ceased to be profitable. But, as today I am forced by the law to carry out my undertaking, despite its disadvantages, I may tomorrow be the gainer from a contract which another may wish to repudiate. In other words, we assume that in carrying out contracts there is an order of reciprocity which Lavrov completely ignores. This, of course, seems to be one of the fundamental differences between Russian thought and that of the West. The revolutionary writers are constantly making an appeal to the rights of the poor, as opposed to their would-be exploiters, but there seems to be no understanding of the principle of reciprocity in human relations. It would be interesting to trace just how far this principle has been openly applied in the field of international affairs. However, the Russian government must take account of the principle of reciprocity which underlies most international law. There is one instance where an agreement arrived at in an international congress in 1856, to which Russia was a party, was repudiated

[41] *Ibid.*, 194.

as soon as the most powerful of her opponents became involved in a major war. This was in 1870, when the Franco-Prussian war broke out. The Russian government announced that it was preparing to ignore the neutrality of the Black Sea. The best that the European countries could do was to secure the written consent of the powers that signed the Treaty of Paris, in order to give the violation the appearance of legality.[42]

Lavrov's program, as revealed in his periodical *Vpered* (started in London in 1874), called for a reorganization of society along what the Russians call socialist-federative lines; i.e., he conceived that future society would be made up of groups of rural communes and craft *artels*, held together somewhat loosely by a central government. He held that a liberal constitution was unfavorable to the interest of the masses, but that it held out one temporary advantage; namely, that it would promote the ideal of liberty of thought and expression. He laid greatest emphasis on organizing the peasants and accustoming them to political activity in their village assemblies. But Lavrov parted company with Bakunin in believing that a revolution must wait on the political maturity of the peasants and could not be carried out by popular risings directed by an elite minority. In this he was challenged by Chaikovskii, who asserted that without a revolutionary psychology, it was not possible to promote the welfare of the people. He saw little purpose in trying to lift the level of the masses through science, if society remained bourgeois.[43]

[42] Besides being part and parcel of the capitalist world, the contract was basic in medieval Europe, for feudalism was essentially contractual. Indeed, some see in these relations the germ of the later constitutional monarchy and the basis of the social contract.

[43] *Obshchestvennoe dvizhenie pri Aleksandre II*, 158–59.

7. Narodnaya Volya

THE attempt of Vera Zasulich on the life of General Trepov on January 24, 1878, came one day before the final decision of the Senate in the trial of the 193 political prisoners. The result (as disclosed in the government publication *Pravitel'stvennyi Vyestnik*) was that the mild sentences given the accused were in many cases increased to the legal limit, while the effects of this strictness were extended to the new revolutionary actions which followed. The trial of Vera Zasulich was concluded on March 31, and resulted, as we have seen, in her acquittal amidst scenes of delirious excitement.[1] For fear that her acquittal might be reversed or that she might be rearrested, she was spirited away by her confederates and sent abroad.

This incident led the government to modify its method of dealing with the revolutionaries; one of the changes was to allow the provincial administration to exile to eastern Siberia persons implicated in activities to subvert the political and social order. Here they could be kept under close surveillance.

Further incidents, however, such as the murder of Baron Geikin, captain of gendarmes, on the streets of Kiev on May 24; the demonstration at Odessa against a sentence passed on Koval-

[1] Tatishchev, *Imperator Aleksandr Vtoroi*, II, 552.

evskii; and the murder of General-Adjutant Mozentsov, the head of the Third Section and the chief of the gendarmes, on August 4 (allegedly in revenge for the severe penalties against the 193), induced the Emperor to summon a meeting of the Council of Ministers at the Winter Palace on August 8, 1878 (the day of Mozentsov's funeral).[2] As a result of this meeting, the right of arresting suspects, which since the law of May 19, 1871, had been limited to the person conducting the investigation, was extended to the officers of the corps of gendarmes and, in their absence, to police chiefs and county *izpravniks*. This step could be taken even against persons participating in street demonstrations. Such persons could further be, by administrative procedure, transported to Siberia and settled in special colonies. Moreover, it was decided to withdraw cases involving attacks on officials from the jurisdiction of the regular courts and to entrust them to special administrative courts.

On August 20 the Emperor followed this up with a special appeal to the youth attending educational institutions, urging them to concentrate on their studies and refrain from dangerous and subversive acts. In the meantime, fresh trouble had broken out in St. Petersburg among the students of the medical-military academy, and it was about this time that the revolutionary organization *Narodnaya Volya* emerged.[3] Despite the new repressive measures, fresh excesses occurred, including the murders of Prince Kropotkin, governor of Kharkov, police agent Reinstein in Moscow, and the chief of gendarmes, Drenthal—all in the spring of 1879. These attacks culminated in the attack of Solov'ev on the Emperor in the grounds of the Winter Palace. This last measure convinced Alexander of the inadequacy of the measures hitherto adopted and led him to take the exceptional measure of naming three governor-generals with special powers, General-Adjutant Gurko of St. Petersburg, General-Adjutant Totleben of Odessa, and General-Adjutant Loris-Melikov of Kharkov, all of whom had distinguished themselves

[2] *Ibid.*, II, 553.
[3] *Ibid.*, II, 554–55, 557.

in the recent fighting in the Balkans. A special commission deliberated from May 10 to May 17 and made a series of recommendations to the Tsar, calling for a limitation on the power of the justices of the peace, for repressive measures against the press, for stricter oversight of the persons employed by the *zemstva*, for elimination by the cities of revolutionary agents, and for various measures intended to prevent the spread of subversive ideas among the peasants and other groups.[4]

The elementary and secondary schools came in for some consideration, and Count D. A. Tolstoy, the minister of public instruction, urged that greater care should be taken in the selection of teachers. The proposals of the special commission were approved by the Council of Ministers, whose only addition was that the elementary and secondary schools should endeavor to discourage students of humble station in life from entering the institutions of higher learning, and thus, so far as possible, help to stem the general tendency to pass from one status of life to a higher one, a movement that was apt to provoke social unrest.

In the meantime, the famous meeting of the revolutionaries had, as we have seen, taken place at Voronezh on June 21, and at that meeting the extreme group seceded from the *Zemlya i Volya* and founded the *Narodnaya Volya*, while the moderates continued their program of propaganda under the name of *Chernyi Peredyel*. The former now represented those who were convinced that efforts to promote an economic revolution, which had formed the basis of the "to the people" movement, were useless unless political liberty was first attained; hence, they addressed themselves directly to the task of wringing from the government by force and threats concessions which would allow the people of Russia to participate in the work of the government.

It might be added that this program made a wide appeal, outside of the ranks of the revolutionaries themselves, to a large body of the public, on which *Narodnaya Volya* could count

4 *Ibid.*, II, 558–60.

for at least a benevolent neutrality in the coming struggle with the state. Like the *Zemlya i Volya*, the *Narodnaya Volya* now formed its own executive committee, which continued from time to time to address pronouncements to the people. Some of the members of this extreme group prepared themselves for their task by engaging in scientific studies to enable them to make and to handle the deadly explosives (dynamite and nitro-glycerine) which were then coming into use. Almost immediately after mastering this art, they began a series of attempts to kill the Emperor. One of these occurred on November 19, 1879, when one of the sections of the imperial train was blown up near Moscow. This phase of their activities culminated in the blowing up of a part of the Winter Palace in February, 1880, on which occasion the Emperor was saved from death only by a chance delay of the imperial family in entering the dining room.

As a result of this fresh outbreak of violence, the monarch appointed a special commission under the chairmanship of Valuev, minister of the interior. The commission took the high-sounding name of the Supreme Regulating Commission for the Maintenance of the Governmental System and Social Tranquillity. Its chief instrument was Count Loris-Melikov, who was given military authority over St. Petersburg and the surrounding territory, as well as supreme control over all governors, governor-generals, garrison commanders, and all departments of the government.[5] Loris-Melikov, therefore, assumed the responsibility of restoring order and public confidence, and continued his efforts until August 6 of that year, when the commission was disbanded. His plan, outlined in a report to the Emperor in early April, was first to tighten the country's counterrevolutionary measures by bringing about greater harmony and collaboration between the various departments of the government. His second aim was to establish effective measures for detecting and punishing those guilty of subversive activities; thirdly, he hoped to find some way to induce the people of

[5] *Ibid.*, II, 577, citing a *ukaz* to the Senate on February 12, 1880.

Russia to abandon their attitude of indifference or neutrality toward the revolutionaries and to rally to the government.[6]

Loris-Melikov worked on these measures during the spring of 1880, the twenty-fifth anniversary of the accession of Alexander II. The report of April was approved by the Emperor, and its provisions put into effect. Loris-Melikov informed the monarch, however, that some means had to be found to lessen the discontent and thus deprive the revolutionists of a fertile ground for propaganda. He urged the grant of some form of a constitution which would provide a deliberative body of popular representatives, to have at least consultative powers. This idea found some favor with the government, and apparently led to the drafting of a tentative constitution which was signed by Alexander in March of 1881, on the very day, it is said, of his assassination.

In the meantime, despite the desertion of one of the chief conspirators, Goldenberg, from the revolutionary party and his betrayal of party secrets and party ramifications, the government had little success in rounding up the subversive elements. Most of the revolutionists were living under assumed names and with false passports. Eventually, on August 6, 1880, perhaps as a result of a lull in the acts of violence, the monarch decided to discontinue the activities of the Supreme Regulating Commission, believing that its aims were achieved. The powers that it had taken over from various government agencies were restored to them. The further conduct of the campaign against the revolutionaries was made the task of the minister of the interior, and Count Loris-Melikov was named to this position. At the same time, the Third Section of the Imperial Chancery was abolished and its police powers transferred to the Minister of the Interior, who had charge of the regular police force.

Loris-Melikov began his service as minister with wide-sweeping recommendations to the Emperor with regard to the collaboration of the various agencies of the government, including the Senate, whose members were drawn into a commission

[6] *Ibid.*, II, 590–91.

which was to canvass the situation in the areas most affected by the revolutionary disturbances and make recommendations to the government. He pressed at this time the scheme for representative government, which he had espoused in the latter part of 1880, and some progress was made. Further reforms also were considered. However, his work was brought to nought by the underground activities of the revolutionaries, which had assumed a serious and all-embracing character. Toward the end of December, the chief leader of the *Narodnaya Volya*, Alexander Mikhailov, was taken into custody, but in accordance with revolutionary practice, his assistant, Zhelyabov, took up the work, with the assistance of Sofia Perovskaya. A number of alternative schemes were devised to kill the Emperor, one of which involved mining a street in the capital which the Emperor's carriage frequently took in passing to and from the Winter Palace. The conspirators opened a cheese shop here and drove a tunnel from the basement under the street, where the explosives were lodged and connected with the house by a fuse. This scheme, however, was frustrated by the arrest of Zhelyabov on February 27, and the discovery of the tunnel.

In the meantime, Sofia Perovskaya had completed her arrangements for having the Emperor intercepted on a journey from the church in the Winter Palace to a special review at the Mikhailovskii Palace on March 1. The Emperor did not follow his customary route, but proceeded along the Katherine Canal. Sofia Perovskaya guessed correctly that he would return the same way on his trip back to the palace, and posted her fellow-conspirators to intercept him. The first bomb, thrown by Rysakov, killed and wounded some of the imperial escort and bystanders. The Emperor stopped his carriage and stepped out to question Rysakov, now held by his guards, but a second conspirator, Grinevitskii, was posted there in anticipation of such a situation. The bomb he hurled landed at the Emperor's feet, where it exploded with great force. The Emperor was thrown against the railing of the canal, his body almost torn apart. He was picked up by the few persons who survived the explosion, placed on a sled, and conveyed back to the Winter Palace, where he died at 3:35 in the afternoon on March 1 (13), 1881.

Following this event, the executive committee, in the person of Lev Tikhomirov, penned an "Open Letter to the Tsar," addressed to the young heir who now assumed the throne as Alexander III. Tikhomirov explained the motives of the act of his organization and called on the new Emperor to proceed with far-reaching reforms that would complete the work his father had left unfinished, and in particular demanded a constitutional government. Thus the *Narodnaya Volya* appeared to have achieved its main purpose.

Let us turn now to the basic theories underlying the *narodnik* movement. As Peter Lavrov was the ideologist of the "Going to the People," Nikolai Mikhailovskii was the spokesman of the *Narodnaya Volya*. His greatest contribution was a series of articles which appeared in the *Otechestvennye Zapiski* in 1869 and were published under the title "Chto Takoe Progress," in Volume IV of the second edition of his works.[7] These articles are an attack on the position of Herbert Spencer, who maintained that progress in society consists in proceeding from the simple to the complex, and who emphasized the principle of the division of labor, by which he claimed society is able to make progress by restricting the individual's efforts and initiative to one specialty in which he is an expert. Mikhailovskii challenged this, and maintained that the division of labor which had come in with modern industry, while it facilitated the increased production of all the necessities of modern life, nevertheless stultified the individual by dooming him to an existence in which he would repeat the same operation every hour of the working day, and every day without variation. According to Mikhailovskii, that was not progress at all. He, therefore, denounced the principle of the division of labor and insisted on the co-operation of individuals, in which everyone would engage in all the operations necessary for production of a given

[7] Ovsyaniko-Kulikovskii, *Istoriya Russkoi Intelligentsii*, VIII, 152–53.

commodity; in that way all the faculties of the individual would be developed. This form of communal labor, of course, had its best application in the operation of agriculture. Mikhailovskii did not face the question of how it could be applied in modern industry, with its assembly-line methods. This philosophy became one of the major planks in the platform of the *narodniki*.[8]

Mikhailovskii followed Lavrov in insisting that while determinism is basic for the natural sciences, where human affairs are concerned the moral life must have some other foundation. This foundation he finds in the subjective method. Indeed, most of his attack on Spencer is based on the view that Spencer has tried to apply the basic method to sociology, to which it is not applicable; therefore, his whole argument falls to the ground. Mikhailovskii quotes Comte, who says:

> It is necessary to make every endeavor to insure that the scientific conviction that social phenomena are subject to unchangeable natural laws does not develop into a persistent inclination towards fatalism or optimism, which are equally immoral and dangerous; and so only those who can successfully engage in the study of sociology whose ethical level is sufficiently developed.

Developing this point, Mikhailovskii insists that political matters depend on ethical values:

> Moral appraisal is the result of subjective processes of thought, while positivism claims as its greatest merit that it uses the objective method in sociology. Further, if the objective method fully corresponds to sociological research, why is a high ethical standard required?

He maintains further that a consideration of human affairs demands first of all the knowledge of a desirable objective toward which efforts should be directed. "Where there is no

[8] This discussion is found in Volume IV, pages 1–187, in the second edition of Mikhailovskii, *Sochineniya Mikhailovskago*.

teleology, there cannot be moral laws, and consequently neither denial nor approval."[9]

He, therefore, provides an excellent foundation for the revolutionary thinker: that having furnished himself with a definite objective, the revolutionary is able to proceed towards his goal with a single mind. In an interesting passage, he expounds his view on the difference between the spirit in which scientific phenomena and human life should be treated.

Here are two books; one deals with the phenomena of nature. It is written calmly, dispassionately; it links fact with fact, and without any hindrance arrives at a generalization. That is not the case in the book which deals with man. You see that man is overwhelmed by the perceptions which are aroused in him by the process of the exchange of ideas; in every line you can almost feel the beating pulse of the hand that writes; the man loves, hates, smiles and weeps; you can make out the traces of anger and tears on the soulless paper. The exposition is confused, uneven, alongside of purely scientific thought; there is biting, polemical trickery, a challenge to the foe, the smile of triumph and of disdain; there again unchallengeable observation, unchallengeable conclusion, and again, dejection of subjective outbursts. But the mass of acquired knowledge grows and grows. Truth is just like water poured drop by drop on a stone, only the stone is too hard and the water contains some alien mixture. There is no doubt that in the science of nature, truth has succeeded in extruding *odium theologicum,* and also has succeeded in eliminating the corresponding element in the science of society. Statisticians and psychologists, sociologists and economists, political theorists and historians contribute their share to the social science of the future, but all things are jumbled together in confusion until the demands and needs of the people are touched with a shower of the dispassionate, cold, and blinding light of the science of nature.[10]

It is impossible to exaggerate the importance of this develop-

[9] Mikhailovskii, "Chto Takoe Progress," *Sochineniya Mikhailovskago,* IV, 87.
[10] *Ibid.,* IV, 79–80.

ment in Russian thought and Mikhailovskii's contribution to it. It apparently became commonplace in *narodnik* philosophical circles to accept the view that the methods of objective observation and the careful formulation of a hypothesis based on observation have no place in the treatment of human affairs, and that man lives his moral and mental life in a world of his own, dominated by a conception of the goal towards which he thinks society should be moving. Mikhailovskii does not explain exactly how any agreement on the exact nature of this goal is to be reached, or how a goal can be set up that would appeal to all. In other words, he does not face the problem of the attainment of general moral concepts, and in that respect he breaks completely with the tradition established by Socrates that moral concepts, to be binding, must be generally agreed on, and this agreement can only be attained by reason.

8. *The Reaction*

THE assassination of the Emperor on March 1 removed from the scene a monarch who, whatever his weaknesses, had inaugurated and carried through a vast program of reform, and at the time of his death was contemplating a further reform—the grant of a constitution. His death was a culmination of a long reign of terror for which *Narodnaya Volya* was responsible, the aim of which was to force the government to carry out a more extensive program of reform. Immediately following the assassination, the executive committee of that organization issued a series of proclamations addressed to the new Emperor, in which they reminded him that his father had met death for failure to comply with their demands and warned young Alexander not to follow in his footsteps. The demand was for complete political freedom. Another proclamation called on the people to be calm, and explained the motive for the crime and the aims of the organization. These first proclamations were followed on March 10 by a letter to the new monarch defending the act as a punishment for his father's having blocked needed reforms. The letter pointed out that there were now only two alternatives: a continued program of terror, or a peaceful grant of the needed reforms, which would enable the revolutionaries to cease their acts of violence and co-operate with the government.[1]

The specific demands on which the revolutionaries concentrated were complete amnesty for all participants in the acts of terror; the summoning of a representative body of the whole Russian people, to be chosen in free elections without any restrictions and with complete equality of all classes; complete freedom of the press; and freedom of speech and of assembly. It is noteworthy that nothing was said about giving land to the peasants, which problem was apparently to be dealt with by the representatives of the people.[2]

On the side of the government there was confusion and uncertainty. The directing figure in the contemplated reforms having been removed, the administration hesitated. Certain members of the imperial family and of the entourage surrounding the new monarch declared themselves in opposition to them. The chief factor was probably the rise of a new group of advisers. The most significant of these was Konstantine P. Pobyedonostsev, a former professor of law at the University of Moscow and a former tutor of the young Emperor. Pobyedonostsev was known for his opposition to practically all the reforming trends. His opinions on current affairs were published in Moscow under the title *Moskovskii Sbornik* in 1897, and a glance through the table of contents will reveal the modern windmills against which our Don Quixote proposed to tilt. Chapters include "The Modern Democracy," an attack on democracy; "The Great Lie of Our Time," a denunciation of parliamentary government, and "Trial by Jury," an attack on the jury system.

This extraordinary man who cast a shadow over public life in the late nineteenth century apparently had his spiritual and intellectual roots in an entirely different soil from that which had produced Western culture. It is not, therefore, surprising

[1] This letter is given in *Byloe*, March, 1906, 36–39. Copies of it were widely circulated, so its contents were known to the Russian public.
[2] Kulczycki, *Geschichte*, II, 376.

that after a period of temporizing under the plea that the matter was to be turned over to a special committee headed by Loris-Melikov, the new Emperor was finally induced to take the matter into his own hands and to announce that there would be no abandonment of the principle of autocracy.

A second figure hardly less influential was Vyacheslav Plehve, a man of Polish origin whose views coincided with those of Pobyedonostsev and who was made minister of the interior with a view to crushing the revolutionary movement. Plehve's appointment was a signal that there would be no letting up in the policy of repression.

Before discussing the changes that shortly took place, it might be worthwhile to note how this period appeared to persons living in Russia at this time. Madame Breshkovskaya thus speaks of this period in retrospect:

> The barbarous reaction in the eighties made revolutionary work in Russia almost impossible. All the dishonest elements in the country were called to help the administration repress all thought and protest. After the spirited educational work of the sixties and the revolutionary activities of the seventies, it seemed as if Russia had become petrified. Analytical work continued, however, to prepare the way for new phases of the struggle. In these days of world-wide cataclysm these early efforts may seem insignificant, but they were necessary as the preliminary cracking of the fetters which bound the Russian mentality and were the beginnings of a movement which spread all over Russia and gave mighty impetus to the steady and ever widening current of mental progress and civic consciousness.[3]

Besides these persons actively engaged in administration, there were others no less influential, notably the journalist Katkov, who had been active in the sixties and had now become the leader of a strong nationalist group publishing two periodicals, *Moskovskie Vyedomosti* and *Russkii Vyestnik*. Katkov not only supported the government in domestic affairs,

[3] E. K. Breshkovskaya, *Hidden Springs of the Russian Revolution*, 331-32.

but he was extremely influential in the field of foreign affairs, where he began to promote the idea of a Franco-Russian alliance.[4] A third important figure apparently was the publisher Suvorin. In a sense, these persons constituted themselves the spokesmen for the reaction which set in with the reign of Alexander III.

But they were hardly entitled by their intellectual gifts to influence the public, and the government was more inclined to rely on repressive measures, which were redoubled in extent and intensity. For the first time the police began to make extensive use of *agents provocateurs*, and during the years that followed, members of the revolutionary organizations were induced to put themselves at the government's service and betray the secrets of their group.[5] Such informers were G. D. Goldenberg, the assassin of Kropotkin (the governor of Kharkov in 1879), Sergei Degayev, and Lev Tikhomirov, the head of the executive committee of *Narodnaya Volya*. It was the employment of these agents, more than anything else, that demoralized the movement. The government even went so far as to offer rewards openly to anyone who would betray the murderer of Colonel Sodakin, the head of the secret police, to which the *Narodnaya Volya* replied with a threat of death to any would-be traitor.[6]

It must not be supposed that the harsh measures of the government dampened the ardor of the revolutionaries. According to Kulczycki, the *Narodnaya Volya* still comprised 500 persons, while not less than 10,000 were to some extent collaborators.[7] The party continued to publish its own organ on a secret press at the capital, under the editorship of Tikhomirov and Morozov, while abroad in Geneva there appeared the *Vyes-*

[4] K. P. Pobyedonostsev, *K. P. Pobyedonostsev i ego Korrespondenty*, I, 712. Letter of Katkov to Pobyedonostsev, July, 1887; see also *Dnevnik Lamsdorfa*, January 29, 1887.

[5] Kulczycki, *Geschichte*, II, 525.

[6] "Sovremennoe Obozryenie," *Vyestnik Narodnoi Voli*, No. 4 (1885), 235–36.

[7] *Geschichte*, II, 355–56.

tnik Narodnoi Voli, which Lavrov published during the last years with the assistance of Tikhomirov.[8]

During the years 1881–83, while the revolutionary party was debating whether to continue its program of terror, to suspend it, or to substitute a series of planned outbreaks in places remote from the capital, the administration itself suffered from divided counsel. The Emperor was young and inexperienced, and even his two trusted advisers, Pobyedonostsev and Ignatiev, disagreed on tactics if not on principles. There was a powerful element among the aristocracy that was in favor of the grant of a constitution. Perhaps the most influential member was the Grand Duke Constantine Nikolayevich, but there was in addition a group consisting of Count Vorontsov-Dashhov, Peter Shuvalov, and Loris-Melikov, which during this period, either with or without the permission of the monarch, opened negotiations with representatives of the *Narodnaya Volya,* Nikoladze, and Borozdin. The negotiations were drawn out for some time since these men had no authority and had to consult with Mikhailovskii in Russia and Tikhomirov and Lavrov in Geneva. Negotiations turned on the emancipation of Chernyshevskii, the granting of reforms, and also the question of a constitution, although there was no unanimity in the organization on this point. Eventually, however, the new minister of the interior, Dmitri Tolstoi (who replaced Ignatiev in 1882), through the treason of Sudekin and Degayev, was enabled to ferret out many of the secrets of the revolutionary organization and to lay his hands on many members. This victory

[8] There seems to be some confusion concerning the length of time the *Narodnaya Volya* was published. Gessen relates, apparently under the date of 1883, that as a student at the University of Odessa he made the journey to Kharkov to bring back a bundle of the ninth issue of *Narodnaya Volya.* However, Kluge seems to imply that *Narodnaya Volya* ceased publication in 1881, though he states that twelve numbers were published. *Vyestnik Narodnoi Voli* appeared from some unknown date until 1886, when, with the issue of the fifth publication, Lavrov and Tikhomirov announced its discontinuance. It may be that Gessen confused the two periodicals, but the matter still remains somewhat uncertain. See Gessen, *V Dvukh Vyekakh: Zhiznennyi Otchet,* 50–52, and Kluge, *Die Russische Revolutionäre Presse,* 199–299.

stiffened the resistance of the administration to the demand for reforms, and after 1883 nothing more was heard of them.

These and other negotiations furnish some evidence that there was, immediately after the assassination of Alexander II, a chance for the introduction of a constitutional government, which seems to have been thwarted by the reactionary men who surrounded Alexander III.[9] However, it must not be supposed that the movement for reform was entirely paralyzed. The revolutionary journals published abroad, especially the *Vyestnik Narodnoi Voli*, appearing at Geneva during these years, contain eloquent testimony that the movement was far from dead, though with many of its leading members in prison and in exile, it tended to break up into groups. There was to some extent a suspension of revolutionary activity pending the coronation of Alexander III, which took place in 1883, but the years that followed showed great activity. Each number of *Vyestnik Narodnoi Voli* had a section called the "Chronicle of the Russian Revolution," which offer ample evidence that the revolutionary movement was widespread. One somber item published in Number 4 (1885) gives a list of the revolutionaries who left Moscow for Siberia on May 14. None of these figures is well known, but the very fact that dozens of persons were involved in this movement attests its magnitude. Many of the converts were university students in medicine or law. A considerable number were technicians, and the sons of priests quite frequently appeared in the lists:

> May 14, 1884, a new party of administrative exiles left Moscow for Siberia. Among them were the noble, Arkadii Tyrkov' (to Krasnoyarsk); the priest's son, Fedorov; the noble, Vasilii Rastopin (to Tobolsk for two years); the gymnasium student, Negvolod; the workman, Kostyurin; the son of a photographer of Kazan, Krelin; the workman, Bitkin; the son of a priest, Georgievskii; the student of medicine, Orlov; the gymnasium student, Litvinov; the workman, Golovetskii; the candidate for mathematical studies, Byelovezhskii; candidates for law, Mos-

9 Kulczycki, *Geschichte*, II, 439–62.

olov, Melenchuk, Kipiani, Chryedayev; the student of the Junker school, Mel'nikov; the captain of artillery, Shepelov; the technologist, Gorbachevskii; the civil servant, Tkachenko; the officer of Uhlans, Protasov; the engineer-technologist, Fridenson; the technician, Yemil'yanov; the workman, Pirozhenko; the students Bychkov, Gorinovich, Nyemirovskii, Fundaminskii, Sophia Bordskaya (to Tomsk for two years), Dichiskulo, and Lyutki; and the Princess Shervalidze.[10]

The Polish revolutionary movement also began to take form, and although there was some collaboration, there was no actual fusion with the Russian revolutionary organization.[11]

One of the last acts of terror was the attempted assassination of Lieutenant Colonel Katanskii of the gendarmes, at Kiev on October 8, 1885, by Mariya Kalyuzhnaya.[12] It was reported at the same time that during the period covered by the aforequoted issue, some two hundred persons had been arrested.[13]

During these years the outside world for the first time became aware of the struggle going on in Russia and was curious about its causes and about the fate of the unfortunates who suffered in the revolt. There were a number of persons admitted by the government to Russia whose avowed purpose was to pry into the secrets of Russian justice and inform the outside world of the nature of this contest. In the year 1881, an American, J. W. Buel, went to Russia and attempted to put himself in contact with the revolutionary elements as well as with representatives of the administration, to get, if possible, both points of view. He also accompanied convoys of convicts dispatched to Siberia, and has given a lively account of his experiences.[14]

The most famous account, however, is that by George Kennan. Kennan had been with the expedition organized by Western Union, which left America in 1866 for Siberia to begin

[10] "Khronika Russkoi Revolutisii," *Vyestnik Narodnoi Voli*, No. 4 (1885), *Sovremennoe Obozryenie*, 232.
[11] Anatole Leroy-Beaulieu, *L'Empire des Tsars*, II, 568.
[12] "Khronika," *Vyestnik*, 229–30.
[13] *Ibid.*, 221.
[14] *Russian Nihilism and Exile Life in Siberia.*

the construction of that part of the great telegraph line that was to link the United States with the Russian empire and with Europe.[15] Kennan apparently had heard a good deal about the political prisoners during his sojourn in Siberia, and having entered the field of journalism, he suggested to *Century* Magazine that it back him in an effort to secure all the information possible on the revolutionary movement and the lot of the political prisoners exiled to Siberia. He made his journey in the years 1883–85, and has left us a very valuable narrative of his trip.[16]

A third account is that of Harry DeWindt, an Englishman who apparently visited Russia under the aegis of the Russian government and also traveled through Siberia, frequently meeting the convoys of prisoners.[17] The accounts of these three are all vivid and as reliable as eyewitness accounts can be expected to be. There, is, however, definite disagreement concerning the suffering of the prisoners and the barbarity of the treatment they received. Both Kennan and Buel used strong language in describing the conditions under which they traveled, and particularly the accommodations provided for them at the various stages of their journey. However, DeWindt, who made the journey somewhat later than the others, is far more lenient towards the Russian authorities. This disparity may possibly be due to reforms instituted by the government, and thus his statements can hardly convict the others of untruthfulness. However, he does point out one thing which emphasizes the fact that the works of the other men must be read with caution: that their understanding of the revolutionary movement was obtained secondhand from the lips of the revolutionaries themselves. Neither Kennan nor Buel had made any study of the movement, and they relied on the statements of the prisoners with whom they came in contact and were certainly given a one-sided account.[18]

[15] S. R. Tompkins, *Alaska*, 181–82.
[16] *Siberia and the Exile System.*
[17] Harry DeWindt, *Siberia As It Is.*

The Reaction

The last conspiracy to which the *Narodnaya Volya* gave rise came in 1886 and 1887. It appears to have been organized in the institutions of higher learning in St. Petersburg. The conspirators are known to have included the following: Alexander Ulyanov,[19] Peter Shevyrev, Andreyushkin, Generalov, Ospanov, and Volokhov. During December of 1886, they decided on a renewal of terroristic activity, directed against the Emperor himself. Their general plan was simply the program of the executive committee of the old *Narodnaya Volya*. They calculated that on the anniversary of the death of Alexander II, the Emperor would visit the Fortress of Peter and Paul and pass through the capital. This occasion was to be seized to carry out his assassination. In preparation for this event, the conspirators rehearsed on successive days on the Nevskii Prospect. The police had already intercepted a letter from Andreyushkin to a friend in Kharkov, hinting at the proposed attempt; when, therefore, on the morning of March 1, the same persons for a second time were observed behaving in a somewhat suspicious manner and carrying some objects under their coats, they were at once arrested and subjected to examination. The result was that the whole plot and its ramifications were uncovered and fifteen persons were finally brought to trial. Ulyanov made

[18] Kennan reports that he met a Dr. Weimar who had been arrested in 1882 and, in spite of the absence of any evidence that he was a member of *Narodnaya Volya*, was sentenced to hard labor in Siberia. DeWindt points out, however, that in spite of this claim, references to the sources disclose that Dr. Weimar helped plan the escape of Peter Kropotkin from prison in St. Petersburg in 1880, and that actually Kropotkin escaped on Dr. Weimar's horse. It is obvious that Kennan rather naïvely believed that the revolutionaries whom he interrogated were the innocent victims of a conspiracy on the part of the government to get rid of all the liberal elements in Russia. Actually, the young men and women whom he talked with had been participants in a war against the government, and some of them had taken part in violent crimes. They regarded this as a legitimate war and themselves as soldiers who had succumbed to superior forces. The assumption, therefore, of a role of guilelessness hardly accords with the facts, and Kennan certainly showed himself somewhat naïve in his approach. It is questionable, of course, whether any foreigner who has not made a profound study of the revolutionary movement could interpret it, or could give a sound appraisal of any persons engaged in it or of the evidence associated with it.

[19] Alexander Ulyanov was Lenin's older brother.

a defiant speech to the court, setting forth the reasons for his attempt and denouncing the government.

All fifteen were condemned to death, but the court recommended them to the clemency of the Emperor, and the majority of them were not pardoned but had their sentences commuted. In the case of four, however, the Emperor confirmed the sentence of death. The four were Ulyanov, Generalov, Andreyushkin, and Shevyrev. The sentence was duly carried out on March 8 in the Fortress of Peter and Paul.[20]

Among accomplices who were not direct participants in the attempt were some Poles, including Joseph Pilsudski, who helped to found the Polish state at the conclusion of World War I. Landau, in his *Pilsudski and Poland* (page 18), says that Joseph's brother Bronislaw was also sentenced to a term on the island of Sakhalin.

The famine of 1891–92 practically ended the activities of the already demoralized revolutionary party, the *Narodnaya Volya*.[21] But it is not easy amid the claims advanced by writers, most of them doctrinaire, to arrive at any exact conclusion. It would perhaps be tempting to believe that the *narodniki* were forced to accept the unpalatable truth that the equitable distribution of land which they had concentrated on would be of slight use unless some way were found to expand its productivity. It might be well to pause for an instant to pass rapidly in review the various factors involved in this major catastrophe.

It must be borne in mind that the administration of Alexander II had conceived the program of emancipation of the peasants during the heyday of the views of the Manchester school; and throughout his reign, so far as we can judge from the policies followed, these views continued strongly to influence, if not actually dominate, government policies on economic issues. The general public, however, was probably not strongly influenced by the ideas of economic liberalism, since

[20] Kulczycki, *Geschichte*, II, 508.
[21] General Alexandre Spiridovich, *Histoire du Terrorisme Russe, 1886–1917*, 35.

these were alien to the spirit of Russian life. They had no hold on the intelligentsia at all, since the latter had generally accepted the views of Herzen that the *bourgeoisie* of Western Europe were hopelessly corrupt and decadent, and had come to place their hopes on the peasants and the rural commune. The peasants themselves accepted the blessings of emancipation without enthusiasm. They were glad to be free from the exactions of the landlord and his representatives, but apparently they could not understand why a reform so far-reaching as emancipation did not secure without cost to them the land which they had hitherto cultivated. They had little understanding of the financial provisions of the decree, but they were told by their leaders that they were being overcharged for the land and were being further penalized by the loss of the so-called "cutoffs," as well as by a reduction in the land they cultivated. There was little understanding of the government's apparent hope that the relaxation on the bonds of serfdom would allow the peasants to exercise their own initiative and enterprise to raise their standard of living. Life continued much as it had before. The peasants plowed and harvested in the traditional way, with little thought of improving their methods, and the burdens imposed on them as a result of the compulsory redemption payments, which might have easily been borne had some thought been given to the improvement of their methods, seemed to them, and actually were, intolerable under the existing conditions. The sole exception to the general stagnation in agriculture was the private estates of the landlords.

It seems, therefore, that the government and the peasants were pulling at cross purposes, and when in the 1870's the Slavophiles, in the person of Konstantine Aksakov, and the followers of Frederick List, in the person of the journalist Katkov, joined forces in an attempt to reverse the government's policy of *laissez faire*, they found wide support and were able to popularize the ideas of national self-sufficiency and regimented economy, both of which were more in keeping with traditional Russian views.[22] There was thus a hopeless disagreement on fundamental economic issues, which eventually landed the country in confusion at the end of the century.

There can be little doubt that exceptional meteorological conditions precipitated the famine.[23] But there can be just as little question that the situation was much aggravated by other factors that might be considered subject to human control. But we are here concerned with its impact on public opinion and the manner in which this impact was reflected in the press and governing circles. Witte, in his *Memoirs,* does not mention the famine, though he himself was dispatched to the Volga by the Emperor to report on the visitation of cholera which followed in the famine's wake. The famine would not have made a ripple on Russian life had it not been for the public appeal addressed to the outside world by Count Leo Tolstoi, an appeal that embarrassed the administration and somewhat belatedly forced it to take cognizance of the disaster. Thereafter the bureaucratic wheels ground slowly, too slowly to prevent distressing loss of life.

It would be interesting to record that the famine shocked the country into heroic measures to save as many lives as pos-

[22] This resulted in the adoption of a very prohibitive tariff by the Russian government in 1891.

[23] I found in the archives in Leningrad in 1937 a full report by an unnamed government official on the famine and on the climatic conditions that preceded it. According to this account, the previous year, 1890, had been dry, and the spring of 1891 was cold and some of the wheat had been frozen and had to be reseeded. The growing season was almost rainless, and in many places there were no crops at all, or a very sparse and short growth which scarcely returned the seed. Such a calamity was not unknown in marginal areas like the Volga country, but the situation was much aggravated by the pressure brought to bear by the government to secure payment of redemption dues, which led the peasants to draw on their reserves, if any.

It is perhaps noteworthy that the Russian government had, as a part of a national undertaking, established a large number of weather stations, whence reports were collected and passed on to an international weather bureau. Yet, in spite of this, there was no effort made to render these reports available to any of the authorities, let alone to the peasants or the landowners, to whom they might have been of some practical benefit. The notes I made on this occasion were, on some trivial pretext, retained by the Soviet authorities, so that the report cannot be quoted. However, I have retained in my mind the major points made in the report.

sible and into taking steps to prevent a recurrence. But apart from the efforts of the state and some private philanthropy at home and abroad, the Russian intelligentsia showed little interest in the death of a few thousand peasants. Plekhanov, the leader of the Marxist group, "Emancipation of Labor," maintained that it was not a socialist's duty to engage in measures of relief, but rather to help destroy the system which made such a calamity possible. Korolenko, who saw the situation at first hand, used it to denounce the remissness on the part of both the central administration and the local authorities, whom he accused of combining to minimize the twin disasters of famine and cholera.[24]

Truth to tell, the sufferings of the peasants were the happy hunting ground of theorists on both sides—the *narodniki*, who wished to perpetuate the commune and were inclined to blame the introduction of capitalistic practices into rural life, and the Marxists, who were less interested in the suffering than in proving to the discomfiture of their enemies that the commune was breaking down, and that the disaster was a necessary concomitant of the class struggle; that things would not be better till they became bad enough to bring on the revolution.

It is no part of our task to analyze agricultural conditions in Russia in the nineties, since this subject has been dealt with copiously by various Russian economists.[25] To the outside observer, one fact stands out above all others—that the production of Russian agriculture was notoriously low, actually lower than the yield per acre in the Balkans.[26] This, combined with the rapid growth of the rural population, could not but produce a precarious situation.[27]

Most writers have emphasized the policy of the government, the change in agriculture in the direction of capitalism, the

[24] Vladimir Korolenko, *Golodnyi God*, 60, 68, 93.
[25] For a list of these works see the section on "Peasant Agriculture" in the bibliography for this chapter.
[26] Geoffrey Drage, *Russian Affairs*, 315.
[27] Georgii Pavlovskii, *Agricultural Russia on the Eve of the Revolution*, 81ff.

tariff, the redemption payments—all of them aggravating factors. But the stark reality of low productivity, combined with the high birth rate of the rural population, could not fail to lead to disaster. The signs of progressive deterioration in the physique of peasant recruits called up for the army alarmed the minister of war, Kuropatkin, and led him to issue a solemn warning that "41 per cent of the population of European Russia produce less than enough wheat to keep themselves from starvation for a year."[28] Aggravating this factor was the excessive export of grain found necessary to compensate for the falling prices on the Liverpool market.[29] Few of the intellectual revolutionaries contemplated any other solution of the problem of agriculture than redistribution of land. The increased use of fertilizer, the adoption of new strains of livestock or of new crops, the application of mechanical power, the thousand and one means by which the American farmer has added so phenomenally to his production, are rarely mentioned. Chernyshevskii, in an interesting passage, speculates somewhat casually on this subject, but without attaching any importance to it:

> The peasants of the Urals, if they perpetuate their present system of land holding to the time when very powerful machines are introduced for grain raising, will undoubtedly be glad that they have kept their system, which allows the use of such machinery as requires farming on a large scale of thousands of acres.

All discussions of agriculture thus turned on the question of land distribution with almost no attention to its improvement, except on the landlords' estates, where there is evidence that there was a steady improvement under the direction of managers often brought in from Germany. It was from this source that the bulk of the exports was drawn, and any redistribution of the landlords' estates could not but tragically cut down the

---

[28] A. A. Kuropatkin, *Zadachi Russkoi Armii*, III, 31.

[29] Apparently caused by the lowered costs of ocean transport of grain from American wheat fields.

Nikolai A. Dobrolyubov

Courtesy Russian Embassy

Leo Tolstoi

From G. K. Chesterton, Leo Tolstoi

production of cereals and other farm products. Peasant agriculture was notoriously static and inefficient.

One other somber fact ignored by most of the writers of the period was that the demands of the armed services placed on the budget an all but intolerable strain. It was idle, therefore, to talk of reducing the peasants' burdens by shifting them to other shoulders; the middle class could not bear them, and the upper classes, whether through their own fault or not, were often in bad financial straits and could not make up for the loss. The abortive effort of Tsar Nicholas II to call a halt in armaments through the peace conference at the Hague is one evidence of the vicious circle in which Russia had placed itself by playing the role of a great power in Europe without the actual resources to be one.

9. The Beginnings of Marxism in Russia

ON the break up of the party *Zemlya i Volya*, the members of *Chernyi Peredyel* (Black Partition) dissociated themselves completely from the terrorist movement and restricted themselves largely to propaganda. This was not confined to the peasant question, for there were two organizations called into existence for agitation among the industrial workers: the South Russian Union of Workers at Odessa (organized in 1875) and the Northern Union of Russian Workers (organized at St. Petersburg in 1879).[1] These groups launched the first industrial strikes in Russia.

The most prominent figure in the *Chernyi Peredyel* was George Plekhanov. In the aftermath of the fierce struggle that developed between the terrorists and the government, the Black Partition was not spared. Its press was discovered and seized, and the members of the group only saved themselves by flight. Plekhanov, Axelrod, Ignatov, Vera Zasulich, and Deutsch made their way to Switzerland, where they established themselves in Zurich. Here they organized the *Osvobozhdenie Truda* in 1883, and began the publication of a Library of Russian Socialism, the first number of which was *Sotsializm i Po-*

[1] Ye. Yaroslavskii, *Istoriya VKP (B)*, I, 26–28.

liticheskaya Bor'ba. Plekhanov spent his exile in a study of Marx.

The works of Marx had been known in Russia since 1870, when the Russian translation of *Das Kapital* appeared. The general theory was therefore known to all the revolutionaries, who referred to Marx on many occasions in their works. However, no very serious effort had been made to use Marx as a basis for their revolutionary teachings, and in their practical revolutionary work the Russians had treated the industrial workers of the city as indistinguishable from the peasant population, with which they undoubtedly identified them. Some of the old members of the *Narodnaya Volya* had carried on agitation among them, but this was the exception rather than the rule. It was Plekhanov who first saw the possibilities of the teachings of Marx as material for a new approach to revolution. The works of Marx undoubtedly opened his eyes to the enormous potentialities of the industrial workers.

This was his principal contribution. He took issue with his former associates in *Narodnaya Volya* on fundamental questions of policy.[2] He claimed that their hopes of attaining socialism through the peasants were vain; that the country was not yet ready for socialism and had to first pass through the stage of capitalism; and that the chief hope of establishing socialism was the new industrial proletariat. He did, however, throw the *narodniki* a bouquet by referring in terms of warm approval to their work for political freedom and a constitution, work which corrected the defect of earlier socialism and anarchism emphasizing the economic struggle to the entire neglect of the political.[3] This work was followed one year later by a second, *Nashi Raznoglasiya (Our Differences)*, which took a much sharper tone. While much of his previous work had been pointed at Lavrov, it was now Lev Tikhomirov, the secretary of the so-called executive committee of *Narodnaya Volya*, to

[2] The writer is under obligation to the Columbia University library and Samuel H. Baron for permission to use the latter's dissertation submitted for his Ph.D. degree in 1952, "Plekhanov and the 'Emancipation of Labor' Group, 1883–1895."

[3] G. V. Plekhanov, *Sotsializm i Politicheskaya Bor'ba*, 72–74.

149

whom it was directed. Plekhanov surveyed both the industrial and the agricultural life of Russia and made the bald statement that it was useless for the revolutionists to argue about the merits or demerits of the peasant commune or to urge measures to save it; Russia had entered on the stage of capitalism; the peasant commune was doomed; obviously socialism had to come after the firm establishment of capitalism in both industry and agriculture.

On one point of tactics, Plekhanov advanced the idea that although the proletariat were the hope of the future, they could not of themselves overthrow absolutism, but had to collaborate with the *bourgeoisie* for this purpose. But he emphasized that they must not allow the *bourgeoisie* to take command and, by setting up a constitution that favored them, make their domination secure. The proletariat had to use the revolution to establish freedom and equality for all. On the question of land, since Plekhanov did not believe in the possibility of maintaining the commune and as a socialist could scarcely favor an agriculture based on individual proprietorship, he contented himself with a rather equivocal platform of nationalization, without specifying what this involved.

One other revolutionary idea which Plekhanov attacked was that of Tkachev, who had advocated the violent seizure of power by an elite group which would set up a provisional government and inaugurate socialist reforms in the name of the people. This program of conspiracy which Tkachev sponsored had some attraction for the revolutionary mind, particularly after the collapse of the "To the People" movement, when the socialists lost faith in the ability of the peasants to understand or sympathize with the views of the intelligentsia.[3] While Plekhanov thought that the peasants could not at that time grasp the importance of the revolutionary struggle, he believed that when the time came, if extensive propaganda was spread among them, they would be in favor of the "nationalization of the land." This equivocal catch word, which was destined to play a role in the revolution of 1917, was thus launched on its way, to be used to draw the peasants along on the course which the Social Democrats wished to take.[4]

At this time the group headed by Plekhanov had not entirely broken with the old *Narodnaya Volya*, and negotiations took place between them for a joining of forces, but Plekhanov emphasized the necessity of his *narodnik* friends' giving up their exaggerated hopes concerning the peasants and accepting the Marxist view that the future of the revolution depended on the proletariat. It is to be noted that after the defection of Tikhomirov the terrorist movement became more and more discredited, and the *narodniki*, under Mikhailovskii (who remained in Russia as editor of *Bogotstvo* and did not emigrate), tended to become a liberal constitutional movement.[5] Since this, to some extent, agreed with the general spirit of the times in favor of constitutionalism, Plekhanov urged that the proletariat join forces with the liberal elements to secure the overthrow of tsarism.[6]

In his second work, *Nashi Raznoglasiya*, Plekhanov went into more fundamental questions, discussing the economic development of Russia in industry and agriculture. As we have seen, he emphasized that Russia had already embarked on a capitalistic course, and had an opportunity to follow the example of the countries of Western Europe in the development

[4] *Ibid.*, 80–82. The program of nationalization in 1917 tacitly allowed the peasants to seize the landlords' land and divide it among themselves, but still left the state free to reassert its control of the land at some future time. This future time, of course, was 1929, when the program of collectivization got under way.

[5] See David Footman, *Red Prelude*, 255, "Revolutionary Who's Who." Tikhomirov was head of the executive committee of *Narodnaya Volya* and signed on its behalf the famous letter to the new monarch, Alexander III, in March, 1881. He was coeditor of *Narodnaya Volya*, the St. Petersburg organ of the party. Escaping abroad in 1882, he became coeditor of *Vyestnik Narodnoi Voli*, the organ published by the émigré revolutionaries. After recanting in 1888, he was granted amnesty by the government, and returned to become a defender of the regime he had spent so many years attempting to destroy.

[6] Plekhanov, *Sotsializm*, 79. "We ought to follow the excellent example of the German Communists, who, in the words of the Manifest, 'have marched side by side with the *bourgeoisie*, as far as it has shown itself revolutionary in the struggle against absolute monarchy.'"

of large-scale industry and the growth of an industrial proletariat. This work, in addition to reiterating what he had said
the previous year on the question of the peasants, quoted statistics somewhat liberally to demonstrate that the emancipation
of 1861 had worked out badly, the peasants having been overwhelmed with obligations comprising their redemption dues
and taxes, which in many cases were more than the total income
from the land. These statistics were, of course, only samples,
and Plekhanov did not make clear whether the income derived
by the peasants included the products of the farm which they
themselves consumed. Even here, his main purpose was to
prove that the village commune was dissolving and the land
was passing into the hands of individuals who were exploiting
their neighbors. This reinforced his earlier contention that Russia was becoming capitalistic. He again reiterated his appeal
for collaboration with the liberals, in which regard he found
himself in accord with *Narodnaya Volya*:

> In the calendar of *Narodnaya Volya*, I read that "in regard to
> the liberals, they ought, without dissembling their own radical-
> ism, to point out that in the present setting of the tasks of the
> [various] parties, our interests and theirs make it expedient to
> work together against the government."[7]

Plekhanov, at the time of the famine of 1891, in common
with the other revolutionary leaders, urged his followers not to
co-operate with the government in any way in helping to relieve
the famine.[8]

During the late eighties and early nineties the revolution
made little progress in Russia. The members of the Emancipation of Labor group continued to eke out a precarious livelihood
in Switzerland, publishing polemical articles which were smug-

---

[7] Plekhanov, *Nashi Raznoglasiya*, 80.
[8] "O zadachakh Sotsialov v bor'be s golodom," in Plekhanov's works, III,
410–11, as cited by Baron in his "Plekhanov and the Emancipation of Labor
Group, 1883–1895." See also Bertram David Wolfe's *Three Who Made a
Revolution*, 90.

gled into Russia, but which seemed to make comparatively little impression. After the famine of 1891–92, however, the tempo of events seemed to quicken. Russia was going through a marked industrial expansion. Factories were springing up, and peasants were flocking to the towns to find work. It seemed to Plekhanov that for the first time the efforts of the long years in exile were to bring fruit. From 1893 on, we hear of Marxist groups in St. Petersburg that were extremely active. Plekhanov himself continued to write, and in 1895 he published, under the pseudonym of "N. Bel'tov," a study of history, *K voprosu o razvitii monisticheskogo vzglyada na istoriyu*. This was a frank attack on Mikhailovskii and the so-called subjective sociology. On the other hand, Plekhanov urged the acceptance of an interpretation of history based on a materialist philosophy.

There now appeared on the scene in Russia a new figure, Vladimir Ilyich Ulyanov, a young man from Simbirsk. Ulyanov was a brother of the Alexander Ulyanov executed in 1887 for his part in the attempt on the life of Alexander III.[9] Like Alexander, Vladimir had from his earliest days at the University of Kazan associated with intellectual revolutionaries and had become acquainted with the teachings of Marx. For his revolutionary activities he was expelled from the university in 1887. In 1891 he was permitted to complete his study of law at St. Petersburg, where he took the examinations and received a certificate; he then returned to Samara, where his mother had settled. His practice of law at Samara was short, for he moved to St. Petersburg (as we are told by Madame Krupskaya) in the autumn of 1893, where he threw himself at once into revolutionary activities and became a member of a very active circle of Marxists.

We have an interesting characterization of Lenin at this period from the pen of a former member of a (later) socialist revolutionary party, Victor Chernov. Chernov met Lenin in a revolutionary gathering at this time and described the meeting in these words:

[9] See Chapter VIII for details of this plot.

Someone secretly pointed out another. "Just watch that young man with a bald spot; he is an interesting person, a power among the Marxists of St. Petersburg; his brother was hanged in connection with the business of the *Narodnaya Volya*." It was Vladimir Ulyanov (Lenin). His lisping voice rang with confidence and a feeling of superiority. With great heat, V. P. Vorontsov challenged him. "Your assumptions are without foundation, your statements unproven. Show us what gives you the right to make such claims; show us your analysis of figures, and your facts. I have a right to the assertions [I make]; I have worked them out; my books speak for me. Now, on the other hand, Nikolai-On has given his own analysis (at that time, his *Ocherki* had just appeared). But where is your analysis? Where are your works? There are none." The tone of this argument made no impression on us and did not discredit him in our eyes, for we were well aware that every novel movement cannot at once produce fundamental works.

Ulyanov countered skillfully, shrewdly; remaining perfectly cool and with a light touch of good humor. Their encounter, however, quickly degenerated into a confused wrangle; it had to be interrupted, as it more and more took on a personal character and lost the interest of the gathering.[10]

It is instructive to pause for a moment to contemplate this group of revolutionaries that probably had been won over by the work of the Emancipation of Labor. Some of these persons afterwards became famous: Ulyanov (Lenin), Peter Struve, Potresov, Krzhizhanovsky. They were a heterogeneous lot, recruited from all ranks of society but bound together by a fanatical spirit of devotion to what they considered a cause. Madame Krupskaya, in her *Memories of Lenin*, introduces us to this circle, which was engaged in all kinds of revolutionary activities, including teaching in Sunday schools, writing articles, haranguing groups of workers, and spreading propaganda leaflets. But one looks in vain for any sort of explanation of the hidden springs of action that powered this movement. In this we have, of course, the whole problem of the revolutionary in-

[10] Victor Chernov, *Pered Burei*, 74.

telligentsia, and one is constrained to ask himself how it was that a group of highly intelligent, well-educated young people had been recruited and inspired with this fanatical devotion, through what heart-searchings they had gone, what personal and other tragedies had stirred their minds, what the clue was to their disillusionment with life in general and the old regime in particular. We are left to guess.

Trotskii recalls that when he first met Lenin in London, the latter had already divided the world into two hostile camps—"we," the revolutionaries, and "they," the rest.[11] It is this "we-they" psychology that marked the professional revolutionary, of whom Lenin is the outstanding example. No revolutionary writer has given us any satisfactory explanation of the steps by which they arrived at this stage. Madame Kaidanova, in her *Ocherki po istorii narodnogo obrazovaniya*, bewails the fact that at the very time when she was beginning her life's work of teaching, so many of the young people not only refused to take part in the constructive work of society but were engaged in a far-reaching conspiracy to destroy the existing order. One must assume that there had been no break in the revolutionary tradition of the Russian youth from the time of the great reforms.

It would seem that at that period, as Pisarev pointed out, the young people attending the universities had definitely split into two groups; the "old" students and the "new" students. The old students devoted themselves to their studies, were careful of their attendance at classes, and were concerned about the attainment of a certificate. They looked forward on the completion of their studies to entering "service," starting at the foot of the long ladder of the table of ranks. The successive rungs of the ladder would mark the steps of their progress. The life to which they looked forward would be secure, and perhaps somewhat monotonous, but they might at least regard their achievement with some satisfaction if it contributed to the welfare of the country. The new students, on the other

[11] Leon Trotskii, *Lenin*, 8.

hand, scoffed at such prospects. They had absorbed the revolutionary teachings of French socialism, of the *narodniki* (and later of the Marxists), and were too impatient for results to await the long, slow progress of reform; they believed that more thoroughgoing and enduring results could be attained by social or political revolution. These young men were recruited for the most part in the universities. Some of them, indeed, were in receipt of government stipends reserved for needy students, but they had little thought of repaying them in service. They had become members of what has been likened to a militant religious order, a band of blood brothers sworn to destroy the existing order and build a better world. Such was the Russian intelligentsia of this period.

It is astonishing for us to imagine persons of substantial families and gentle breeding sitting in solemn conference and talking with all the glib confidence of youth of the destiny of the human race, and of the most violent contribution they are prepared to make to it. Social intercourse was restricted to their circle: their joy, sorrow, love, hatred, quarrels, reconciliations, all shared with one another, were their own signs of normal human relations. One is struck by their cold-blooded indifference to the welfare of the millions who were to be pawns in a game they were playing with the political forces of the existing regime. To the stranger who reads their memoirs, this complete detachment from, and lack of concern with, the human element, except in a purely theoretical way, is shocking. One does not have to presume that Madame Krupskaya, who played the role of devoted wife and daughter, was a Lady Macbeth; yet she was typical of the revolutionary women, who seemed to be completely free from any human weakness or even ordinary human feeling. Such emotional attitudes as they had were reserved for their own circle, and apparently everything outside of that circle belonged to a purely impersonal world where feeling had no place. This detachment of the intelligentsia from the world of human reality is in striking contrast to their claim to be realists. They would seem to be, rather, theorists who lived, if not in an ivory tower, at least in a realm remote from ordinary human affairs. Their singlemindedness, fanaticism, and complete preoccupation with the distant future appalls us and leaves us groping for an explanation.

It must be noted that the new revolutionary workers of the nineties, however bitterly they attacked their predecessors of the two previous decades for their wrongheadedness, were nevertheless under very deep obligation to them. The whole technique of conspiracy which they were forced to learn had been imparted to them by the older generation, to whom they paid somewhat grudging tribute. It would seem, therefore, that the art of conspiracy which first became manifest in the sixties was never lost, but persisted either above ground or under ground through the troubled eighties.[12] It contained the older tradition of the Decembrists and of secret societies in Europe at the beginning of the century. Perhaps it is an art that is never lost, but it had a peculiar attraction for the Russians, and it is this addiction to underground conspiracy, to cloak and dagger methods and programs of terror, that made the Russia of the late nineteenth century stand out from the general tone of European life. Some are prone to look for the roots of this in the violent peasant upheavals of an earlier age; some would blame it on the oppression of the tsarist regime. Whatever the explanation, it is one of the most astonishing phenomena of modern times, and it has prolonged itself into the twentieth century, where it threatens the whole world with national and international chaos. The professed objective is a better world, but apparently this goal can be reached only over the bodies of victims of countless hecatombs.

Ulyanov, or Lenin, as he later became known, began writing in 1893, his first article being "Novye Khozyaistvennye Dvizheniya v Krest'yanskoy Zhizni," which was a review of a book by Postnikov on *Peasant Agriculture in South Russia*, published

[12] In this respect the Social Democrats were under obligation to the old *Narodnaya Volya* party, from which they learned the technique of conspiracy. See N. K. Krupskaya, *Memories of Lenin*, I, 11.

in Moscow in 1891. Further articles followed, but his first important publication was "Chto Takoe'Druz'ya Naroda' " (Who Are the Friends of the People). This was a series of articles attacking Mikhailovskii and the *narodniki* and denouncing the latter for its claim to be a revolutionary party representing the peasants. Lenin pointed out that Russia had already entered on the capitalist stage, that the peasant commune was doomed, that peasant agriculture itself was becoming capitalistic, and that the real hope of the Russian revolution lay in the industrial proletariat.

Lenin went abroad in 1895, and on his return fell into the clutches of the police and was sentenced to prison, where he remained until 1897, during which period he began his great work, *The Development of Capitalism in Russia.* He was again arrested in 1898 and sentenced to exile in Siberia. Here he was joined by Madame Krupskaya and her mother, and his marriage to the former took place in his remote exile. Lenin remained in exile until 1901, and thus was absent from European Russia when the first congress of the Social Democratic party was held at Minsk in 1898. This historic event has some interest as a landmark, but actually the persons who participated in it were not of the first rank, and since they were all arrested by the police immediately, the work of the party devolved on those members who were émigrés in Europe. The revolutionary work, however, went on during these years, and Lenin and all the others continued to write.

On his release in 1901, Lenin went abroad and joined the members of the former Emancipation of Labor group at Munich, where almost immediately they began to print the organ of the party, *Iskra. Iskra* was printed at Munich, Leipzig, and finally London, from 1900 to 1905. During his period of residence abroad, Lenin was a member of the editorial board until 1903, collaborating with Plekhanov, Martov, Potresov, and Dan. However, fundamental differences were developing on matters of policy. Lenin's point of view was developed in an article, "What Is To Be Done?" In this article he stressed the importance of the task before the Social Democrats of forming a strong, disciplined group of conspirators, bound together by a common purpose and allowing freedom of discussion only to the point where a decision is reached, after which the minority must bow to the majority. Another point on which he differed from Plekhanov was in his attitude toward non-Marxist groups. While Plekhanov had, in the works mentioned, emphasized the necessity of collaborating with the *bourgeoisie* to bring about the overthrow of tsarism, Lenin claimed that there must be no collaboration between the two, that Marxists must go their own way and allow the *bourgeoisie* to go theirs. The latter might contribute to the overthrow of capitalism, after which the Marxists would step in and exploit the situation in their own interest, without any regard to the interest of the *bourgeoisie*. In contrast with Plekhanov, who took a dim view of the peasants, Lenin was convinced of the possibility of exploiting the revolutionary capacity of the peasant masses, believing that under the leadership of the proletariat, they would be sufficient to overthrow the existing regime.

This difference of opinion became more and more marked, and at the congress of 1903 in London the split became too deep to be patched up. While Plekhanov endeavored to reconcile both points of view and to work with Lenin to promote the interests of the party, the latter felt that all attempts at compromise were obscuring the real issue; namely, that the Marxists must go their own way without any abatement of their program, and must maintain the same implacable hostility to the *bourgeoisie* that they showed towards the autocracy and the old political order.

The question was of the correct tactics to pursue to bring about the destruction of the existing system.[13] It is quite clear

[13] On the question of tactics, the Social Democratic party was actually divided three ways. Plekhanov and his supporters urged that the Marxists make common cause with the *bourgeoisie* (the liberals) in the overthrow of tsarism. Lenin held to the view that, whatever the liberals did, the proletariat should stand shoulder to shoulder with the peasantry to seize power and prevent the liberals from entrenching themselves. Trotskii differed from both,

that Lenin could not be brought to collaborate with his colleague, whom he felt was betraying the cause of socialism by the slightest degree of collaboration with bourgeois elements. At the congress, by the withdrawal of the Bundists, Lenin was able to secure a vote in favor of his policy; in spite of this, Plekhanov continued to work for party harmony, and the new editorial board of the *Iskra* was enlarged by taking in members so inclined. This enraged Lenin and he resigned from the board. He gathered around him his own faction, the members of which were known as Bolsheviki, and shortly started his own organ, *Vpered*. Efforts to heal the breach were made again and again but congresses of the Social Democratic party were completely dominated by either the Bolsheviki or the minority faction, the Mensheviki. Outside the party they maintained the illusion of unity, but actually they had become, by 1905, two distinct parties.

---

insisting that the Russian people alone could never achieve a revolution, but would have to call on the proletariat of other European countries to help bring it about. These competing views are brought out by Donald W. Treadgold in *Lenin and His Rivals: The Struggle for Russia's Future, 1898–1906*, especially 156–60.

10. Social Revolutionary Party

THE old *Narodnaya Volya* had ceased to exist as a party, but it had left imbedded in Russian consciousness *narodnik* ideas which had caught the imagination of the Russian intellectuals. The period from 1885 to 1900 was scarcely favorable to the progress of revolutionary ideas. The police had shut down the underground activity and had pretty thoroughly scattered and demoralized the conspirators, even those who escaped the official dragnet. But other factors worked for stabilization and consolidation of the existing order. For one thing, Russia entered on a period of prosperity, immensely stimulated by the policies pursued by Witte in his capacity as minister of finance. There was enormous expansion of industry, largely financed by foreign capital either arranged by government loans floated in Paris or coming from private sources encouraged by favorable conditions to invest in Russia. There was thus, in the major industrial centers, every appearance of well-being and comfort. It is true that the country districts did not fare as well. Two major famines—that of 1891–92 and that of 1897–98—revealed the low production of agriculture and the overpopulation of the countryside. But the larger landowners, who practiced a more efficient exploitation of their ancestral acres, managed to maintain a fairly constant surplus of foodstuffs for export. And, in any event, famine was a constantly recurring phenomenon of rural life, and local or widespread shortage of food was not considered important in the cities.

This was also a period of disillusionment. The fond hopes of the sixties and the seventies for a revolution that would usher in a new and better order had been belied. The rush of world developments in invention and industrial expansion, the opening up of the East as a market for the goods of the West, and the enormous strides of Germany and the United States could not but awaken echoes in Russia and beckon that country along the same path. After all, there was something inevitable about the progress of civilization, and Russia seemed about to follow the capitalistic path of her western neighbors, however little it might agree with the native spirit. Russia seemed, therefore, to halt between two courses, and in her vacillation presented a picture of indecision, of doubt, of inaction, and frequently of complete futility. That mood is reflected by the writers of the time, who had lost the visions of Herzen, of Chernyshevskii, of Perovskaya, and of Zhelyabov, and were inclined to stagnate in desuetude. The general tone of polite society was one of futility, of preoccupation with the immediate present and creature comforts. If modern civilization could secure the latter, all were prepared to come to terms with capitalism. The prevailing spirit of the time, as described by the writers, was that of "political myeshchanstvo"; i.e., the spread of a spirit of meanness and covetousness, of acceptance of all that is base and selfish and material, with nothing to inspire or to elevate.

It was into this atmosphere that the famine of 1891–92 broke, with its challenge and its shock to all the vocal groups of the public. Forces long dormant gathered up all the elements of discontent in a new revolutionary movement. Some of these have been described: the renewed activity of Plekhanov and his Zurich circle; the formation of new revolutionary groups who were drawn into the circle of Marxist ideas. It also kindled into life once more the slumbering ideals of the *narodniks*.

Georgi V. Plekhanov
A bust by I. Ginzburg
Courtesy Russian Embassy

Nikolai Lenin

Courtesy Russian Embassy

Social Revolutionary Party

According to one historian, the first steps to revive the revolutionary party were taken in 1893 on the initiative of a man named Rappaport, who founded *Soyuz russkikh sotsialistov-revolyutsionerov* (the Union of Russian Social Revolutionaries) —a conspiratorial organization.[1] However, it appears that further, more definitive, steps toward the formation of a party professing the old *narodnik* teachings were first taken in 1897, when a meeting was held in Voronezh in August of representatives from Voronezh, Kiev, Poltava, St. Petersburg, and Kharkov. This group adopted the name "Socialist Revolutionary party," and appointed a committee to draw up a program.[2] The second conference was held at Poltava in November, 1897, at which the proposed program was submitted and approved. This program called for intensive propaganda among peasants, intellectuals, workers, and students at the universities. A passing mention was made of the possibility of reviving terrorism, but only as a means of defense. It appears that the matter dragged on for a year and a half, when a third conference was called at Kiev. At this conference the use of propaganda was emphasized as a necessary means to secure political liberty. On the question of terrorism there were conflicting points of view. However, the fatal shooting of Bogolyepov, minister of public instruction, indicated that among at least some of the rank and file of this movement there was a definite preference for violent measures. A great demonstration at St. Petersburg before the cathedral of Our Lady of Kazan, on March 4, 1900, indicated some broad support for the movement. The result was that a new start was made in 1900 by the committee appointed at Voronezh; in 1901 a manifesto was drawn up, indicating that the primary objective of the movement was the destruction of the autocracy and inviting workers, peasants, students, and others to join. An appeal was even made to the *bourgeoisie*.

This movement was not exactly welcome to the Social Democratic party formed three years earlier, which felt that

[1] Kulczycki, *Geschichte*, III, 448.
[2] Spiridovich, *Histoire du terrorisme russe, 1886–1917*, 91–107.

163

the new organization was a challenge to it, and *Iskra* made a bid for its members to join the Social Democrats.[3] In the meantime, there had come into existence the Union of Social Revolutionaries of the North and also the Workers' Party for Political Emancipation of Russia. These groups early in 1901 entered into contact with the southern groups and agreed to publish the *Vyestnik Russkoi Revolyutsii (The Messenger of the Russian Revolution)*. Finally these various interested groups agreed on union, which was signalized by a meeting between a number of émigrés and the representatives of the Russian groups, who went abroad for this purpose. *The Messenger of the Russian Revolution* became the theoretical organ of the new party, and *Revolutionary Russia (Revolyutsionnaya Rossiya)*—published abroad—became the popular organ for the party. In its manifesto the party reserved to itself the right to resort to terror when it saw fit. It appears that there came into existence at this time a so-called "Fighting Organization" of the Social Revolutionary party. The party, in collaboration with the Social Agrarian League, embarked on a program of extensive propaganda.[4]

The first fruits of the program of terror begun by the party was the assassination of Plehve, minister of the interior, in July, 1904, in St. Petersburg.[5] The assassination, apparently carried out by the "Fighting Organization," turned the head of its members, and they now insisted that they be given a free hand by the party, with the right to draw up their own statutes and control their own organization. This "Fighting Organization" seems, at the time, to have consisted of three members: Azeff, Savinkov, and Schweitzer. Without consulting the central committee of the party, they proceeded to arrange for further assassinations.[6]

[3] *Iskra*, June, 1901.
[4] Spiridovich, *Histoire*, 144–46.
[5] *Ibid.*, 183ff, 186ff.
[6] The notorious career of Azeff and his astounding success as leader of the "Fighting Organization" while in the pay of the police, is given in Boris Nicolaevsky's *Azeff the Spy*. His final unmasking is described in a later chapter.

In the meantime, Russia had become involved in a combination of domestic and foreign complications that became more and more bewildering with each year of the new century. In addition to the famine, the agrarian unrest, and the industrial crisis which came at the turn of the century, Russia had embarked on a perilous program of expansion in the Far East, which brought serious consequences. The aggressiveness of the western powers, including Russia, at the expense of China, led to the Boxer Revolt of 1900, as a result of which the Foreign Legations Quarter in Peking was subjected to siege. This led to the dispatch of an international army to Peking and the occupation of much of Manchuria by Russian forces, with a view to protecting Russia's stake in Manchuria, the Chinese Eastern Railway. Japan had long been resentful of Russia's policy of aggrandizement in northern China, and now, having secured herself by a treaty with Great Britain, proceeded to check Russia's advances. The Russian government, or rather the Russian tsar (Nicholas had already taken matters out of the hands of his responsible ministers), persisted in believing that Japan would never defy Russia and refused any policy of compromise, with the result that the Japanese attacked the Russian fleet in the Far East on the night of February 4, 1904, and declared war the next day. The war with Japan was a bitter humiliation for Russia, since there was an almost unbroken succession of defeats, and she was compelled to make peace on terms not much short of unconditional surrender. But the worst blow that Russia received was internal. At home the peace terms produced a crisis of the first magnitude.

During the year 1904 discontent became more widespread and intensified, and in this ferment of public opinion both revolutionary parties found themselves supported by various organizations which claimed the name "liberal." Such were *Osvobozhdenie* (The Union of Liberation), created by Peter Struve in Germany, and the Union of Zemstva. These groups sent representatives to the conference that met at Paris in September, 1904, to plan a campaign of collaboration with the revolutionary parties.[7]

The policy of the Social Revolutionary party followed two contradictory lines. On the one hand, it called for the complete destruction of the existing order, as seen in this quotation from one of the party's pamphlets:

> Comrades, sound the tocsin. Long live the social revolution. Demolish the prisons and free the friends of the people, which socialists are. Seize depots of arms, go quickly to the villages and hamlets, assemble the people, arm them, and tell them that the hour has come, that the land of all Russia belongs to those who till it. . . . Rouse yourselves, brothers, to struggle for a better future, for an equitable order, for land and liberty. Join the socialists who have long been fighting for the people's cause! Attack with a united front those who have always been our common enemies; sweep them away as a hurricane does dust, and on the ruins of their power, which is fatal to the people, let us erect the kingdom of equality and fraternity. Down with the Tsar and his government. Long live land and liberty! Long live socialism![8]

At the same time, to attract the support of the liberals, party members were at great pains to be present at liberal meetings, which were used as a sounding board for party views calling for a constituent assembly on the basis of universal, equal, direct, and secret suffrage.[9] This common cause made by the revolutionary groups with the moderates swept almost the whole of Russia. In this way they were parties to the movement that led to the establishment of the Duma, while holding in reserve a program of terror to which they were ready to resort. The government began to feel, as it entered the year 1905, that it was faced with the combined opposition of all parties.

The event that finally fanned the discontent into an intensity almost unparalleled occurred on "Bloody Sunday," when a

[7] Spiridovich, *Histoire*, 193.
[8] *Ibid.*, 199–200.
[9] *Ibid.*, 201–202.

procession of workers from the Vyborg Quarter was intercepted on its way to the Winter Palace and scattered by heavy
machinegun fire from the police. The massacre does not appear
to have been planned, but was the result of almost criminal
inefficiency and bungling.[10]

The immediate result of "Bloody Sunday" was to redouble
the terror, which in turn provoked violent measures of repression. On February 4, 1905, the Grand Duke Sergei Aleksandrovich was assassinated in the Kremlin.[11] An accidental explosion of a bomb in an apartment just across the street from
St. Isaac's Cathedral, on February 6, led to the death of a number of the Social Revolutionaries, and gave the government
much-needed clues to run down the members of the group,
most of whom were arrested on the nights of March 16 and 17.[12]

During the spring of 1905 contacts were made with various
socialist groups among the national minorities. This was done
on the initiative of Father Gapon.[13] There were hints of treachery in the numerous arrests in St. Petersburg and Nizhni Novgorod, and commissions were named to interrogate and investigate two members of the "Fighting Organization," Tatarov
and Azeff. Azeff was cleared, but Tatarov was condemned
to death on October 13, 1905, which was four days before
the promulgation of the constitution.[14]

The horror of "Bloody Sunday" unnerved the government
and stirred public opinion almost to a frenzy. The revolutionary
parties redoubled their efforts to create confusion and chaos.
The various legal organizations, such as the Union of Zemstva,
the Union of Municipalities, and the Union of Liberation, as
well as the associations of various professions, held feverish conferences to discuss the demands they would press on the government. Even the peasants in the All-Russian Union of Peasants demanded a calling of the Constitutional Assembly, in

[10] Gessen, *V dvukh Vyekakh*, 191–95.
[11] Spiridovich, *Histoire*, 241ff.
[12] *Ibid.*, 246ff.
[13] *Ibid.*, 251ff.
[14] *Ibid.*, 257.

support of similar demands made by fourteen different professional organizations, as well as by the so-called "Union of Unions." The constant strikes and demonstrations of the workers and agrarian disturbances of the most violent and destructive kind reduced the country to chaos, and on August 6 the government took the first step toward restoring tranquillity by a proclamation of the "Statutes of the Duma of the Empire," inspired by the minister of the interior, Bulygin, and usually referred to as the Bulygin Duma.

To the revolutionaries and liberals who had been demanding the summoning of a constituent assembly, this halfhearted concession made no appeal, nor was it able to calm the feverish atmosphere of St. Petersburg and Moscow. Discontent among the railway workers finally culminated in a great railway strike on October 15, which completely paralyzed the country.[15] Finally the Tsar, in desperation, turned for counsel to Count Witte, who had been dismissed so ingloriously two years before, and on the latter's advice issued a proclamation granting, not a constituent assembly, but a Duma which would, with himself and the state council, constitute the legislative branch of the government. The new Duma was to be elected on a broad franchise, with, however, a property qualification; the election was to take place in the winter, and the Duma to meet in the spring. Count Witte was appointed to the newly created post of prime minister.

The first Soviet Workers' Deputies was called into existence in St. Petersburg on October 13, 1905, with one delegate for every five hundred workers.[16] It authorized the publication of an official organ, *Izvyestiya*. It was this Soviet that was active in promoting strikes among the railway and other workers in October and again in December.

The central committee of the Social Revolutionary party apparently found itself dragged along by the Soviet in its pro-

---

[15] *Ibid.*, 206ff. For an excellent description of the wave of strikes that swept the country see James Mavor, *An Economic History of Russia*, II, 479–98.
[16] Spiridovich, *Histoire*, 263.

gram of promotion of strikes. A general strike ordered for December 7 was widespread and brought violence in Moscow, although the revolutionary movement was suppressed in St. Petersburg. All through December, disorder reigned along the railways and in the various scattered localities.[17]

The first congress of the party met at Imatra, Finland, from December 29, 1905, to January 4, 1906.[18] A desultory program of terror had been conducted throughout the autumn of 1905, which now developed into an official campaign. Nevertheless, the Social Revolutionaries decided at the congress to take no part in the elections but to continue their program of terror and plan further attempts at assassination.[19]

The Social Revolutionaries played some role in the work of the first Duma, but they were generally overshadowed by the Kadets and the so-called workers' party, the *Trudoviki*. After the dissolution of the Duma on July 9 and the issuance of the Vyborg Manifesto, the central committee of the party appealed for a general rising in a special proclamation to the organizations of the party—a manifesto to the peasants called for violence in the countryside, the seizure of lands, and the expulsion of officials by revolutionary committees. An attempt also was made to seduce the troops from their allegiance. In each town it was urged that Soviets of Workers' Delegates take the initiative.[20] Vast underground activity went on all over the Russian Empire. Propaganda directed at the military services led to mutinies in the Baltic Fleet at Sveaborg, which were only put down by severe measures. The mutiny at Cronstadt, which was to accompany the outbreak at Sveaborg, was a failure. Outbreaks also occurred in the Black Sea, where the cruiser Potemkin was seized by her crew, who then endeavored to win over the rest of the fleet.[21] In this, however, they did not succeed.

The "Fighting Organization" began elaborate preparations

[17] *Ibid.*, 270–71.
[18] *Ibid.*, 289.
[19] *Ibid.*, 354–55.
[20] *Ibid.*, 317.
[21] *Ibid.*, 330–35.

for the assassination of the new prime minister, Stolypin, and on August 12, 1906, his villa on one of the islands in the Neva was blown up, causing the death of thirty-two persons and wounding many others, including members of Stolypin's family. The Prime Minister himself, however, escaped.

Another blow struck was an armed robbery carried out in October, 1906, which resulted in the "Fighting Organization's" obtaining 600,000 rubles which were being transported from the port customs' office to the state treasury. However, this money did not all accrue to the party itself, and there was common talk that the robbers kept a considerable sum for their own dissipation, which brought some discredit on the "Fighting Organization."[22]

On November 9, 1906, Stolypin inaugurated, by administrative decree, a scheme for the dissolution of the village commune and the establishment of a class of individual peasant proprietors. This work ran counter to the philosophy of the Social Revolutionaries, and they immediately urged the peasants not to take advantage of this, arguing that the matter should be settled by a constituent assembly to be called after the coming revolution.[23]

The Social Revolutionary party decided to participate in the elections, although it reserved the right to use the Duma, as before, as a sounding board for its views.[24] One of the problems that agitated the Second Duma was that of terrorism. The members of the Duma sought to condemn the government's violent measures to repress disorders. Some of the moderate deputies felt that the resolution should also condemn the methods of terror, but this was not done. Actually, the party continued its preparation for further acts. The year 1907 saw the culmination of the campaign of terror. Plots were organized against the Tsar, the Grand Duke Nikolai Nikolayevich, and Stolypin. However, the government, under Stolypin, made in-

[22] *Ibid.*, 400ff.
[23] *Ibid.*, 350.
[24] *Ibid.*, 415ff.

tensive efforts to cope with the growing disorder, and the ensuing trial of strength between the party and the *Okhrana* finally turned in favor of the latter.

Actually, the "Fighting Organization" had embarked on an independent program of its own, and refused to admit the control of the Central Committee. The latter, as well as the parliamentary group representing the organization in the Duma, endeavored to disavow these acts.[25]

Autonomous groups, as well as transitory detachments, sprang up all over the country.[26] Vast organizations sought to seduce the armed forces, but the government expanded, organized, and increased its activity, and the arrests continued.[27] In 1908, Azeff constituted himself the practical leader of the "Fighting Organization," and together with Savinkov and Karpovich planned the assassination of the Tsar on the occasion of the visit of King Edward VII to Reval on the last day of May.[28] This attempt on the Emperor on the cruiser *Rurik* failed, possibly because of the information furnished to the police by Azeff himself.[29]

During 1908, suspicions with regard to Azeff were rife in the party. As a matter of fact, Madame Breshkovskaya had begun to have doubts of his loyalty back in 1906, but had never been able to get others to share her suspicions.[30] The matter dragged on, and it finally fell to the lot of Burtsev to settle the question. Burtsev became convinced of Azeff's guilt, and spent the year 1908 trying to unmask him.[31]

The Central Committee finally appointed a commission to "explore all the rumors regarding provocation within the party."[32] But this commission completely vindicated Azeff. A new factor arose, however, when Burtsev encountered Lo-

25 *Ibid.*, 450ff.
26 *Ibid.*, 473.
27 *Ibid.*, 489.
28 *Ibid.*, 506ff.
29 *Ibid.*, 507.
30 *Ibid.*, 373.
31 *Ibid.*, 537–38.
32 *Ibid.*, 537.

pukhin, the former minister of police, and managed to pry from him the fatal secret that Azeff was in the pay of the government. The result was that the commission immediately named a court, consisting of old and trusted revolutionaries, to hear the evidence and interrogate Azeff. Azeff fled in a panic to St. Petersburg to silence Lopukhin, but the latter had already gone too far, and apparently made further damaging disclosures. However, Azeff still tried to carry things off. He returned from St. Petersburg, giving out that he had been in Berlin. The Central Committee invited him to submit to questioning, but he fled, and on January 9, 1909, he was denounced by the Central Committee, and at a special session plans were made to kill him. These plans miscarried, and Azeff discreetly disappeared for a time. However, the disclosure of this double treachery within the Social Revolutionary party shook the morale of that organization and created what was not too far short of a panic in the public.

The campaign of violence did not end with the disappearance of Azeff from the scene. On September 1, 1911, the prime minister, Stolypin, was shot and fatally wounded in a theater at Kiev; the Social Revolutionary party hastened to disavow the act, carried out apparently by an irresponsible individual.

This long reign of terror left deep traces on Russian life. Although terror was the work of the Social Revolutionaries, and the Social Democrats condemned it as a weapon of revolution, they did so not on moral grounds but merely because of its futility. The post-revolution record of the Bolshevik regime affords ample proof that neither of the factions of the Social Democratic party would shrink from the most frightful means of terrorizing the population.

It may not, perhaps, be fruitful to consider whether the Russian people as a whole are less humane than others—perhaps because of their heritage of Mongol rule. Yet the question must be asked. There are so many things in Russian life that run counter to our ideals.

In the latter part of the eighteenth century, an incident of the Russo-Swedish War brought about a sharp disagreement between two persons who recounted it—one an Englishman, the other a Russian, both members of the Billings expedition. Martin Sauer, in his account of that expedition, recalls the visit of a Swedish privateer to the North Pacific for the purpose of raiding the Russian posts. Landing on a Russian-held island, the captain discovered the inhabitants in such extremities that he relieved their distress out of his own ship's stores. In telling of this, Sauer commented, "Nothing in the world can astonish a Russian more than disinterested liberality." His shipmate, Sarychev, who published his own account some years later, resented this wholesale impeachment of his countrymen. One cannot but sympathize with his natural indignation.

It is probable, as the latter contended, that the Russians have their fair share of the milk of human kindness. As the author has already recounted,[33] under the benign influences of the humanitarianism of the eighteenth century, the Russian masons were full of good works on behalf of the unfortunate. But even then private philanthropy was not looked on with favor by the government, which apparently regarded the relief of distress as its own peculiar affair. When Pinkerton, in the time of Alexander I, toured Russia on behalf of the British and the Foreign Bible Society, his practice of visiting the prisons in the various provincial towns and reporting on their condition undoubtedly reflected the broad humanitarian aims of the evangelical movement then prevailing in England, which he represented. Since he traveled under imperial patronage, his activities were never openly resented, but one feels that the average provincial governor regarded him as an officious busybody.[34]

But the spirit of charity withered under the fierce revolutionary passions of the nineteenth century. Even the distress caused by famine, which one would assume would have rallied all classes in a spontaneous surge of pity and benevolence, served but to occasion acrimonious exchanges between the government

[33] *The Russian Mind*, Chapter IV.
[34] Robert Pinkerton, *Russia*.

and the revolutionaries. Plekhanov urged his followers to have nothing to do with famine relief in 1891. An interesting article in *Iskra* in October, 1901, entitled "Efforts to Combat the Famine," reflects the attitude of complete indifference of the Social Democrats to individual suffering. They saw in the famine only occasion for stirring up discontent against the government; on the other hand, the government saw in the officious efforts of well-meaning persons like Leo Tolstoi and his fellow philanthropists the purpose of bringing discredit on the government.[35] As Dostoyevskii said, the revolutionist was inclined, in his concern with the sufferings of humanity in the abstract, to look with indifference on the sufferings of his next-door neighbor.

[35] *Iskra,* October, 1901.

11. Liberalism

IT might well be asked whether the political field had been entirely pre-empted by revolutionary parties. Was there any informed public opinion in favor of reform by less violent means than those advocated by the socialist parties? What had happened to the earlier demands for a constitution? Was there a so-called "liberal" movement in Russia at the turn of the century?

Before we can answer these questions, we must clear some of the ground. We are inclined to use the term "liberal" casually, as if we knew exactly what it means. It is sometimes associated with the *bourgeoisie*, as though the middle class had a monopoly on "liberalism." It may at times be equated with radicalism, or even with socialism. To understand what the Russians meant by the term "liberals," or moderate reformers, we must go back not only to the time when the terms themselves, as it were, passed as coin of the realm, but to an earlier day when the ideas they stood for first became popular.

The word "liberal" was best known in early times as applied to education, where the "seven liberal arts" were the sum total of that learning that was suited for the free man. But it is probably to England that we owe its original application to politics. Here, in the wake of the French revolutionary wars and the

Industrial Revolution, social and economic changes brought new political forces to the front. The Whigs, long out of office, sought to meet the new conditions by joining forces with the Radicals in Parliament, to champion the cause of the still disfranchised industrial capitalists and the new industrial towns not represented in Parliament. This coalition, whose members still retained the name of Whigs, later took under its wing the move for the repeal of the Corn Laws, which gradually broadened into an agitation for freedom of trade. They thus became identified with the ideas of the Manchester school and with the program for removal of all restrictions on trade and industry, a policy eminently in the interest of the rising middle class. After the Crimean War, the combined party fused with the remnants of the Tory group which had supported Peel in the repeal of the Corn Laws, and thus the Liberal party came into being as a party whose interests were bound up with trade and industry and the great urban centers, in contradistinction to the Tory party, which had been, and to some extent continued to be, the "country party," representing the agricultural interests, with which Disraeli linked those of the urban proletariat, hitherto neglected by the liberals.

The extension of the use of the term "liberal" to the Continent, where the same conditions did not prevail, could not but result in some distortion of the original. Here, in the early nineteenth century, it came to be used loosely to apply to some of the new movements directed towards constitutional government. To perhaps a lesser degree, it carried some notion of relaxation of governmental control of economic activities and reduction of tariffs. Cobden and Bright and other myrmidons of the Manchester school tended to popularize liberal views on the continent. In the revolution of 1848, liberalism was in the field. Its representatives were not members of the industrial and commercial classes, or their spokesmen, but rather intellectuals and members of the professional class, little accustomed to the rough and tumble of political life. It was the failure of this class that drew from Herzen the words of scorn with which he always assailed the middle class. He managed to fix on the liberal the implications of the term *"myeshchanstvo"*—that collective term for the meanest and most despised of all the social strata in Russia. According to Semevskii, "The *myeshchane* are migrants, like gypsies, engaged in peddling and tinkering."[1] To this might be appended the comment of Von Haxthausen, who visited Russia in 1841: "For the formation of an honorable and numerous class of citizens, there is at present no hope. The people who represent it, artisans, shopkeepers, and small traders, are utterly demoralized."[2] Herzen used the word "liberal" in his works with a special meaning; for instance: "Already, in 1839, the liberals looked on us as on those who had wandered from the road. These liberals were people of the older generation to which Polevoi belonged."[3] Later, however, he became more critical, calling the liberal a *myeshchanin*, and speaking scornfully of his "conglomerated mediocrity."[4]

It would seem that Herzen, in stressing the negative side of the European liberals, ignored or turned his back on their positive side, i.e., their yearning for national independence and constitutional government. The first of these aspirations had less appeal to the Russian, whose empire formed a polyglot association of peoples; liberals as well as revolutionaries were perplexed about whether to gratify the national yearnings of their minority groups—and so sacrifice the unity of the Russian state—or to deny them the right to secede in the hope that they would be placated by participation in the task of forging a new society. There was, therefore, no unanimity on this question. To the second of these issues, constitutional government, Russia had been at times attracted. In 1730 there had taken place a serious attempt to reduce the role of the autocrat to that of a constitutional monarch. But this had been an effort to set up

[1] *Politicheskie i Obshchestvennye Idei Dekabristov*, 99.
[2] *The Russian Empire*, I, 51.
[3] Ovsyaniko-Kulikovskii, *Istoriya Russkoi Intelligentsii, Sobranie Sochinenii*, VII, i, 43–44. According to Herzen the younger generation (of his day) was interested in Saint Simon. This citation is from *My Past and Thoughts*.
[4] Ivanov-Razumnik, *Istoriya russkoi obshchestvennoi mysli*, I, 343–44.

a ruling oligarchy, in the spirit of the English revolution of 1688 or the Swedish constitution of 1720, and seems to have left little imprint on Russian tradition. The Decembrist Revolt of 1825 was the natural fruit of the rational spirit of the French Enlightenment, but its quixotic nature prevented its success, and its failure did little to further the cause of constitutional government. But it left behind, at least in the mind of Speransky, who had perhaps the greatest intellect of the age, the conviction that, even if not replaced by constitutional government, autocracy ought to have some limitations: "Every right, including the right of the autocrat, is right in so far as it is based on truth. Where truth leaves off and falsehood begins, right ceases and despotism begins."[5] As we have already seen, however, interest in constitutional government died down, and its place in the revolutionary calendar was taken by the movement in favor of economic reforms for the relief of the peasants. However, in the discussions that followed emancipation, we find among the gatherings of provincial landowners more than one that echoed the aspirations of the early nineteenth century. For instance, a resolution of the assembly of the Tver nobility read, "The assembly of elected representatives from the whole of Russia is the only means of reaching satisfactory solutions to the problems which have been raised but not solved by the decree of February 19, 1861."[6]

Similar issues were raised by the assembly of the Moscow nobles, one of whose spokesmen, Count Orlov-Davidov, is quoted as having said:

It is clear to me—and I consider it quite unavoidable—that after the institution of local self-government, which has just been introduced, shall have been sufficiently developed, the isolated local assemblies will feel the necessity of a common center.

[5] Tatishchev, *Imperator*, I, 70–71.
[6] A. A. Kornilov, *Obshchestvennoe divizhenie pri Aleksandre II*, (*1855–1881*), 90–92. These sentiments expressed in this resolution of February 1, 1862, brought down on its authors the severe punishment of the authorities.

Liberalism

There is no doubt that this center, in the form of a general assembly, will one day come to exist.[7]

To this demand, the Tsar gave a formal refusal, which actually was more like a promise: "No single class is entitled to speak in the name of other classes; no individual has any right to anticipate the continuous care of the Tsar for Russia; and what has already been done for Russian progress must serve as a token of what is to be accomplished."[8]

The nobility could be and was overawed by the administration, but with the establishment of the *zemstva*, organs of self-government, such sentiments could more readily find expression and it was not possible to muzzle these institutions entirely. While the *zemstva* took many years to become organized and accustomed to their new role, they had begun by the end of the century to master their métier, and could speak with confidence and boldness. That is the significance of the famous outburst of Nicholas II in reply to the address submitted to him by the *zemstva* in 1895, when he denounced their "senseless dreams" of a representative body for the whole of Russia.[9] But the aspiration for a constitutional regime would not die, and by the end of the century the *zemstva* had become the repository of what feeling for self-government there was in Russia. When the Union of Zemstva came into existence in 1904, there was a place where the opinions of the liberal-minded landowners could be heard, and it was among these members of the nobility and their employees that the liberal movement of the twentieth century came into existence.

The liberals had, as early as 1881, acquired an organ of their

[7] P. N. Milyukov, *Russia and Its Crisis*, 276.
[8] *Ibid.*, 283.
[9] "The revival of the liberal movement in the *zemstvos* is chiefly due to another event which happened a little later: namely the death of Alexander III . . . the *zemstvos* used the first opportunity for addressing to the new monarch their former demands. . . . The boldest wishes the *zemstvos* dared to articulate were that the voice of the *zemstvos* might be heard by the throne." Milyukov, *Russia and Its Crisis*, 325–26.

179

own, the *Free Word*, edited by the eminent writer Dragomanov. Throughout the eighties and the nineties, the movement
remained a purely intellectual one, dying down with the revolutionary movement and reviving at the turn of the century
like the latter. But the revival of *"zemstvo"* liberalism is to be
attributed in part to the growing experience and confidence of
the *zemstvo* assemblies, as well as to their officials in the conduct
of public affairs.

The other element in the so-called liberalism at the beginning
of the century belonged to a separate school. Its adherents were
mostly intellectuals, the most important of whom were recent
converts from Marxism. It happened that at this time the popular systems of positivism and Marxism (dialectical materialism),
as well as the subjectivism of Mikhailovskii, were brought under
close examination by some of the young Marxists and found
wanting. The stars of Kant and neo-Kantianism were in the
ascendant, and the result was a movement to restore to favor
once more ethics and individualism, which had been discredited
by the prevailing materialistic philosophies. This, of course,
struck at the roots of Marxism and *narodnik* philosophy. It also
provided a new basis for "liberalism."

The Marxist intellectuals involved were Peter Struve, N. A.
Berdyaev, and S. N. Bulgakov. Beginning in 1894 with the
publication of Struve's *Kriticheskie Zamyetky*, the foundations of dialectical materialism were slowly undermined by
Struve and Berdyaev, who together published in 1901 a book
entitled *Subyektivizm i Individualizm v Obshchestvennoi Filo-
sofii*. The new point of view in philosophy emphasized the objective nature of truth and the role of the individual in society,
and was frankly hostile to the subjective philosophy of Mikhailovskii and the orthodox Marxism of Plekhanov. Eventually it
restored the individual to the center of civilization and regarded
the all-round development of the individual as its purpose and
social organization as the means to that end. In this field, however, the philosophy of individualism and "democratism" (an

Aesopian term for socialism) and the new democratic liberalism
did not part company. But gradually this group of individual-
ists began to realize that the transformation of society from the
old form to the new is essentially a transformation of the real
in the direction of the ideal, and is to be carried on by spiritual
rather than by material weapons, thus emphasizing the role of
the intelligentsia.[10] Struve's further evolution carried him completely out of the camp of the orthodox Marxists into that of
the "liberals," although his liberalism was of a very intellectual
type. His views at the beginning of the twentieth century are
expressed in a more popular form in his book *Patriotica* (published in 1910). In 1902 he went abroad and started a periodical,
Osvobozhdenie, at Stuttgart, and his program rallied many former Marxists and other intellectuals to his side. The group
came to be known as the *Osvobozhdentsy*.[11]

The crisis of the summer of 1905 stirred public opinion
deeply. It was natural, therefore, for all persons of moderate
constitutional leanings to come together in a group of their
own. The desire to form some kind of an organization to advance the cause of liberalism led to the effort to unite all these
aspirations in a "movement of liberation." A congress was held
on October 18 for this purpose, and it brought together the old
followers of the *zemstva* and the *Osvobozhdentsy*, who moved
into the new organization in a body.[12] The new party members were popularly known as Kadets, or Constitutional Democrats, and it was decided to start an organ to be known as the
Ryech. The party undoubtedly had a wide following, and in
the period of the first and second Dumas played a great role
under the spirited leadership of Milyukov. It never quite recon-

[10] In the above we have followed the account of Ivanov-Razumnik's *Istoriya russkoi obshchestvennoi mysli*, II, Chapter VIII.

[11] It is interesting to observe that as early as 1894 Lenin and his wife,
Krupskaya, had already noted Struve's heretical tendencies toward orthodox
Marxism. Krupskaya remarks that they felt that he was not one of them
(that is, a true Marxist). See Krupskaya, *Memories of Lenin*, I, 22–23.

[12] Gessen, *V dvukh Vyekakh*, 211.

ciled, however, two conflicting schools of thought: that of the *zemstva* workers and that of the former Marxian intellectuals.[13]

It is hard to avoid the conclusion that liberalism in Russia was already a lost cause. At the very beginning of the modern revolutionary movement the goal of free institutions gradually receded into the background. As has been shown, the ideal of constitutional government, which was in the forefront of the Decembrist program, had ceased to interest man in the forties. Nikolai Turgenev, the spokesman of these years, admitted that he had lost interest in free institutions. In the period of reform after the emancipation of the peasants, the general public became embittered about the lot of the peasantry and was little inclined to take much interest in the new organs of local self-government or in the reorganization of the courts on the western model. Moreover, the few who championed such ideas—the liberals of that day—were denounced as being content with half a loaf when they might have had the whole one. The movements that grew up in the wake of the reforms were pledged to the overthrow of autocracy, and no mention was made of constitutional government except to rally the support of the faint-hearted persons who yearned for better conditions but were not

[13] The difficulties of reconciling the points of view is demonstrated in the memoirs of Maklakov. In his words:

One of the first enterprises of the *Soyuz Osvobozhdeniya* was the publishing of an uncensored organ abroad, *Osvobozhdenie*, which was edited by P. B. Struve. The "Movement of Emancipation" thus secured a mouthpiece to define its platform. On entering into a struggle with the power of state, it joined forces with all those who were arrayed in arms against it, even though they [were employing] other methods. The line between evolution and revolution became more and more blurred. Even Struve wrote in *Osvobozhdenie* that "if in the eyes of the authorities, 'the opposition' became identified with 'rebellion,' then 'rebellion' in Russia is only 'opposition.' Liberalism ought to admit its affinity with 'revolutionary trends.' " In line with such a view, there took place "a conference" of the revolutionary parties for "co-ordinating the activities of all groups who were in the field against autocracy." And the *Soyuz Osvobozhdeniya* took part in this "conference." Its members did not then understand that the famous Azeff was also participating. Any possible advantage of such tactical procedure at the given moment should not have made them lose sight of the fact that in the future "liberalism" and "revolution" would travel different paths, and that the liberals themselves were arming their own enemy. Maklakov, *Iz Vospominanii*, 309.

willing to exert themselves to overthrow the existing order. Liberalism was the creed that appealed to the noble landowners and the *zemstva* men, and came, therefore, to be tainted with the idea of landlordism, from which it was never able to free itself. The new middle class in Russia was quite insignificant in size and had negligible influence, providing almost no recruits for the liberal element. As Milyukov points out in his book *Russia and Its Crisis*, liberalism in the early twentieth century was purely intellectual. Contrasting Russia with the West, he says:

> In Russia alone it so happened that social teachings prepossessed the more active spirits at a time when the work of political liberalism had yet to be done; and the Russian socialists, not satisfied to consider this liberal work superfluous, went even so far as to deem it dangerous for the people. Indeed both in politics and in social life, Russian radicalism fancied Russia able to jump clean over what was thought to be a transient stage, to the highest requirements of the most advanced theory. Without knowing it, in so doing they had chosen the way of bitter disappointment and of sad political experience.[14]

He finds, therefore, that the place of liberalism lay between the conservative and the Social Revolutionary party. The newly founded institutions of local self-government, the *zemstva*, formed its headquarters; the men of liberal professions, its active army.[15] But it is to be noted that Milyukov's position in the period immediately preceding the grant of the constitution was so little "liberal," in our sense of the word, that his support was apparently solicited by both the revolutionary parties. His refusal to accept was explained in the following language:

> We must choose one of two alternatives; either, like the Social Democrats, to concentrate on the special economic interests of the proletariat and pay no attention to the task of emancipation

[14] Pages 281–82.
[15] Milyukov, *Russia and Its Crisis*, 281.

of the whole nation . . . or, on the other hand, seek part of every subordinate purpose until we have achieved our goal that embraces all classes. So all our strength should be concentrated on the task of obtaining political freedom for the country, without distinction between groups or classes.[16]

Milyukov's objective was to obtain political freedom, but the methods he proposed to attain this objective could hardly be called constitutional. He was, therefore, prepared to make common cause with the revolutionary parties in reaching his goal. In this respect, he was accepting as allies even the Social Democrats, for whom "it is not a question of there being no tsar, or of whether there should or should not be a constitution, but of such relations that one class should not suck the blood of another."[17]

The Kadets were, of course, not the only liberals in the Duma. Alongside of them were the members of the "Party of the 17th of October," called Octobrists for short. This group, not very influential, believed that the constitution had been granted in good faith and that it was the duty of the Duma to co-operate fully with the administration in making it work. On the whole the Octobrists supported the government as long as there was no direct violation of the rights promised in the constitution. While insignificant in numbers in the first Duma, their memberships increased in the second, and in the third they became the dominant party.

How the liberals were viewed by their associates in the Duma is revealed by the comments of Victor Chernov, himself a member of the Social Revolutionary party:

> Generally speaking, Russian liberalism of those days had quite a distinct cultural and zemstvo-constitutional program; it was distinguished by practicality, narrowness, and obscurity. But it did not have its own general ideology. It was, on the one extreme, simply the last flowering of *narodnichestvo*: Kavelin had di-

16 Chernov, *Pered Burei*, 71–72.
17 Chernyshevskii, *Polnoe Sobranie, Sochinenii*, I, 9–10.

luted Herzen; Kareyev [had diluted] Mikhailovskii and Lavrov. At the other extreme, there were backward looks at "bourgeois Europe," or at the doctrinaire Anglomania of Russian landlordism, or at the Slavophilism of the "boyars" of the *zemstva*, or at some indistinct pining *zapadnichestvo*. In the realm of philosophy, of ethics, of sociology, Russian liberalism did not have its own distinct character. Against the materialism and positivism of the left wing, the then right wing boldly raised the flag of religious orthodoxy and religiosity. The neo-religious trend towards idealistic metaphysics characterized by greater freedom of thought was in an embryonic stage, and had attached itself to no political party. The liberals also had made no serious attacks on it. They were too narrowly practical for this and from a "philosophical" point of view had no interest for us. And so, liberalism existed on an entirely different plane from us.[18]

[18] Chernov, *Burei*, 67.

12. The Dumas

THE winter of 1904–1905 had not been a happy one
for Russia. Early in January, General Stoessel had
been forced to surrender Port Arthur, with its garrison, to the Japanese. With the capitulation of the town
went what was left of Russia's Far Eastern Fleet, which not
even the heroic deaths of two admirals—Makarov and Vitgeft—
had been able to save.

In Europe, since 1901, the country had been plagued by
the twin endemic disorders—agrarian outbreaks, and strikes and
lockouts in the industrial cities. The assassination of minister
of the interior Sipiagin in 1902 had been followed two years
later by that of his successor, the hated Plehve. The new minister of the interior, Prince Sviatopolk-Mirskii, known for his
moderation, was of the opinion that the administration must
bend to the gathering storm, and when a *zemstvo* congress, an
institution never hitherto sanctioned, was applied for, he induced the government to raise the ban—or, at least, to look the
other way when it assembled.

During the years preceding the war, the police department
(*Okhranoe Otdyleenie,* or *Okhrana* for short) had struggled
with the rising tide of unrest, which found expression in a
number of ways. One of the chief areas of disturbance was the

186

labor movement, which pressed for the right to organize. An ingenious official, Zubatov, had conceived the idea of the administration taking over the movement. "Zubatov" unions had come into existence under official direction, and various persons in the confidence of the government had joined the labor movement, with a view to controlling it. Among these was Father Gapon, a priest of the Orthodox church. The unrest in the capital had welled up to the point where the workers were determined to do something to obtain redress of their grievances. They were induced by Gapon to undertake a march on the Winter Palace to present their grievances to the Tsar. The authorities seemingly acquiesced in the plan, but when the workers streamed over the bridges of the Neva and crossed the Nevskii Prospect, sweeping aside a police cordon stationed at that point, the authorities became panic stricken and decided to disperse the demonstrators by firing on them. Who actually gave the order was never known, although General Fulon, the chief of police of the city, was ultimately responsible. There were hundreds of casualties. The workers broke in terror, leaving their fallen comrades in the snow. Father Gapon, by flinging himself on the ground, survived, to turn in apparent bitterness on the blundering government.

The massacre of January 9 shocked and outraged the public. Six weeks later, on February 17, the Grand Duke Sergei Aleksandrovich, held to be responsible for the government's reactionary policy, was assassinated in the Kremlin by Kalyaev. To this the government responded with a *ukaz* promising concessions to the popular demands, including the right of petition and a reform of the government; a *zemskii sobor* with deliberative powers was also granted. But the disorders spread to many cities in spite of these conciliatory moves. The workers were urged on by Father Gapon. But the true explanation of the rapid spread of these disturbances was that all classes of the community made common cause with the revolutionaries, and the administration found itself faced with a united front. The news from the theatre of war continued ominous. In March, the battle before Mukden ended in defeat and the withdrawal northward of the Russian Army. In May, the Baltic Fleet, after completing a voyage halfway around the world, entered the Sea of Japan to challenge Japanese naval power. It was attacked by the main Japanese fleet in the Straits of Tsushima and all but annihilated. Russia's plight, with near anarchy at home and humiliating defeat abroad, was desperate. To sue for peace was the only course open. A treaty was signed at Portsmouth, New Hampshire, between the Russian delegation led by Witte and that of the Japanese under Komura.

But peace abroad did not bring tranquillity at home. Disorders increased in number and scale throughout the summer, even while peace was under negotiation, and on August 19 the government bowed to the storm by the grant of the so-called Bulygin Constitution, issued on the initiative of Bulygin, minister of the interior. This provided for a body purely for consultative purposes. The reply of the public was not long in coming. The *zemstvo* congress, meeting in September, demanded that the new representative body be granted legislative powers. Peasant and student congresses swelled the chorus. Demonstrations in the cities, and peasant disorders reinforced the lesson, and in October came a paralyzing general transport strike. The armed services were plagued by mutiny and unrest. The *Knyaz Potemkin*, in the harbor at Odessa, was seized by her crew and put to sea in defiance of orders. Mutinies and armed risings occured at Sveaborg, Kronstadt, Reval, and Sevastopol. Frightened by the lack of discipline in the armed forces, the Tsar finally swallowed his pride and invited Count Witte, newly returned from his successful mission in America, to recommend measures to calm the storm. The result was the manifesto of October 17, granting an elective body with legislative powers.[1] The edict guaranteed the usual constitutional rights—inviolability of person, freedom of conscience, of meeting, of speech, and of association; it granted the franchise to

[1] See Maklakov, *Iz Vospominanii*, 345–46. The text of the manifesto is given in F. Golder, *Documents in Russian History*, 627–28.

all classes (within certain property limits) and declared that the consent of the elective body—the so-called Duma—would be required for all legislation. A cabinet was constituted on November 1 under a president of the Council of Ministers; the censorship was lifted, and a general amnesty was promised. The three most unpopular ministers—Pobyedonostsev, Bulygin, and Trepov—were retired. Witte became president of the Council of Ministers, with the courtesy title of prime minister.

It will be interesting to pause for a moment to see how the various actors in the drama viewed the new institution called into existence. During negotiations leading up to the decree of October 17, Witte had an audience with the monarch, in the course of which he supported his recommendation for the grant of a constitution with the argument that the Tsar would find in a legislative body a needed support for his authority; "Do not talk that way to me, Sergei Yulevich," Nicholas is quoted as having said. "I know full well that I am not creating a helper but an enemy."[2] Witte may have believed at the time in constitutional government as an alternative to chaos, but his whole record indicates that he was insincere in his advice. Years before, in his book, *Samoderzhavie i Zemstvo*, he had opposed the extension of *zemstvo* organization to the Polish provinces, maintaining that local self-government was inconsistent with the principle of autocracy: "He who is master of the government must also be master of the whole administration. . . . This truth we must ever bear in mind . . . it is impossible to create liberal forms unless we fill them with a corresponding liberal content."[3]

We can assume, it seems, that the bureaucrats regarded the granting of the constitution as a maneuver to enable them to get through the period of disorder, rather than as the gratification of a long-standing desire which would enable the government and the people to work together.

[2] S. E. Kryzhanovskii, *Vospominaniya*, 66.
[3] Page 66. Witte cites Pobyedonostsev's famous aphorism, "Constitutionalism is the great lie of our time." Sir Bernard Pares, in conversation with me, recounted an occasion when he had an interview at this time with Witte, who spoke in terms of utter contempt of the "constitution."

189

How was the Duma regarded by the persons who had been clamoring for a voice in public affairs? The answer is found by reference to an interesting incident—the attempt of William Stead, the English journalist, to intervene. An account is to be found in the memoirs of Maklakov:

> At that time, William Stead arrived in Moscow. A gathering of a select Russian public was arranged for him as a distinguished foreigner. Stead gave an address in which he defended the Bulygin Constitution. He showed that, in spite of its defects, a real constitution could develop; that not only the boycott, but even the attempts to disrupt the Bulygin Constitution from within was bad politics. I remember the quiet speech of the old Englishman: "Everything is not given at once; practice puts a new content into old forms; life and work teach everything."
>
> But these ideas did not appeal to the reason of those present. They poured over Stead streams of real and eloquent protests. I recall an extraordinarily effective speech of F. I. Rodichev, which concluded with these words: "We are entering the State Duma as an ambush prepared for us by our enemies."[4]

Mr. Stead's biographer recounts Stead's persistent efforts to introduce between the warring elements an English, but most un-Russian, spirit of tolerance and accommodation:

> But the Russian liberals would not listen to him. . . . [They] became impatient and angry, and even those newspapers which were most favorably inclined to Stead grew critical and sarcastic.
> . . . Mr. Stead . . . was too "English" to understand Russian internal politics, and the task of reconciling Russian progressives and Russian reactionaries was quite beyond his power. . . . The rest was failure.[5]

Dr. Dillon, correspondent of the London *Daily Telegraph* and an experienced observer of Russian life and politics, later made

[4] *Vlast i obshchestvennost' na zakatie staroi Rossii*, II, 392–93.
[5] Frederick Whyte, *The Life of W. T. Stead*, I, 277. Mr. Stead's original references were to the Bulygin Constitution of August. Of course, they applied *a fortiori* to that of October 17.

the following somber comment: "If only the suggestions then made had been harkened to, all that has since happened would have been averted." M. Pinot, French journalist and author, agreed that "several of those Russian liberals who made mock of their English well-wisher in 1905 as a presumptuous busy-body admitted afterwards that his arguments were sound and wise."[6]

Without pursuing further the question of how the English would have acted in similar circumstances, let us investigate the question of how the Russians treated their newly won right to participate in legislation.

The electoral law of December 11, 1905, following that of August 6, divided the electors into four classes: landowners, city voters, peasants and Cossacks, and workers. There was a curious mixture of direct and indirect elections, landowners choosing their representatives to the districts and the latter in turn choosing their representatives to the provincial assemblies. Cities were divided into police districts which chose representatives for the provincial assemblies. The peasants holding communal land and the Cossacks had an intricate system of indirect election—from the *volost* to the *uyezd* to the provincial assemblies, which made the final selection of deputies to the Duma. Twenty-six of the larger cities elected their own members in the Duma. Some few modifications were introduced by the law of December 11 in the direction of greater liberality. Elaborate machinery was set up to supervise the elections.[7]

As a result of the elections, the party of popular freedom, the Kadets, marshaled 177 votes, becoming by far the largest group in the Duma. Their nearest rivals were the Octobrists—

[6] This and the immediately preceding quotation are to be found in Whyte, *Stead*, I, 277–78. The prevalent attitude of intellectuals is reflected in Astrov's *Vospominaniya*, where one of the leftists in the statistical department of the Moscow City Duma is quoted: "Don't you see in this game the most barefaced deception? Why, they are just presenting this constitution for show. That is not the way you must win your freedom."

[7] A. Levin, *The Second Duma*, Intro. The proclamation of October 17, 1905, merely defined the principles on which the constitution should be based. The new constitution was actually issued as a law April 23, 1906.

the party of the seventeenth of October—a group which accepted the constitution and was prepared to work within its limits. Next came the "monarchists," the party of law and order which stood for an unrestricted autocracy. The revolutionaries had a small representation, since they had in their congresses decided somewhat ostentatiously to boycott the Duma, but nevertheless had some of their members elected.[8]

The Duma opened its sessions on April 27, 1906, when its members filed in a long procession to the Winter Palace to sit in one of its spacious but crowded chambers to listen to the speech from the throne; from there they returned to the Tauride Palace to begin work, hearing first an address in reply to the speech from the throne. The "opposition" (as the Kadets called themselves) complained that the speech did not contain a practical program. As a matter of fact, the administration was somewhat taken aback by the resignation of Witte on the eve of the meeting. Actually, however, the government, albeit in most general terms, had in earlier *ukazes* foreshadowed a liberal program containing many reforms.

The scene in the Winter Palace is described by V. N. Kokovtsev, the minister of finance:

> St. George's room, the throne room, presented a queer spectacle at this moment and I believe its walls had never before witnessed such a scene. The entire right side of the room was filled with uniformed people, members of the State Council, and farther on, the Tsar's retinue. The left side was crowded with members of the Duma, a small number of whom had appeared in full dress, while the overwhelming majority, occupying the first places near the throne, were dressed, as if intentionally, in workers' blouses and cotton shirts and behind them

[8] *Ibid.*, Intro.: "The Social Democrats entered the fray late in the campaign and only eighteen of their number were elected. The more radical wing of the party, the Bolsheviki, chose to boycott the Duma as an organ which could win nothing and do much to corrupt the 'revolutionary consciousness' of the people." Gessen, *V dvukh vyekakh*, 229, speaks of "Social Democrats from the Caucasus" in the First Duma. Others talk in general terms of the "left" boycotting the Duma. Despite the boycott, the "left" was represented in the Duma.

was a crowd of peasants in the most varied costumes, some in national dress, and a multitude of representatives of the clergy.[9]

The Empress Dowager told Kokovtsev that she was unable to calm herself after having seen all these people filling the rooms of the palace for the first time: "They looked upon us as their enemies and I could not make myself stop looking at certain faces, so much did they seem to reflect an incomprehensible hatred for us."[10]

How the Duma appeared to a spectator is to be found in the description of S. E. Kryzhanovskii, deputy minister of the interior, not, it is true, a very sympathetic observer. Nonetheless, his account appears to be borne out by the facts.

It was enough to look around at the motley mob of "deputies" —and it fell to my lot to pass whole days with them in the corridors and in the garden of the Tauride Palace—to be horrified at the sight of what constituted the first representative gathering in Russia. It was a mob of savages. It seemed that Russia, inspired by hate and envy, had sent to St. Petersburg everything that was wild. If you were to assume that these persons actually represented the people and their "hidden desires," one would be forced to admit that for at least one hundred years, they would have to be held in control by sheer force and not inner compulsion, and that the only regime that could save them would be an enlightened despotism. The attempt to rest government on the "will of the people" was clearly doomed to failure, for the sense of social responsibility, and, even more, of a common public spirit, was quite stifled in this mass by hatred and class feeling; more truly, it was quite absent. Confidence in the intelligentsia and its cultural influence also decreased. The intelligentsia was a relatively small group in the Duma and clearly remained inert before the boiling energy of the black mass. The former believed in the strength of fine words, insisted on ideals that were quite alien and superfluous to the masses, and was able

9 *Out of My Past*, 129.
10 *Ibid.*, 130.

to serve only as a springboard for the revolution, without any constructive power.[11]

The tone of the newspapers of the time was generally insolent and inflammatory. For instance, one could read in the newspapers the announcement that "Nicholas Alexandrovich Romanov is now without a job and is looking for work." There were wild stories in the papers of governmental excess, of the Black Hundreds, and of governmental agents.[12]

As has been discussed, the single most powerful influence in the Duma was the Kadet party. From the first its members adopted a policy of uncompromising hostility to the administration. Their attitude towards the constitution was one of rejection. They demanded that the government recognize the authority of the people, as expressed by the Duma, by selecting a ministry responsible to it. They were opposed to the existing franchise, insisting on the so-called "four-tail" formula—the principle of universal, equal, direct, and secret suffrage—without which they claimed there could be no true representation. They emphasized laws safeguarding civil liberty and independence of the courts.[13] Somewhat belatedly, they stressed the right to control the budget—a right granted by the constitution which had already been violated by the negotiation of a loan with France.[14] The role played by the Kadets was largely determined by their assumption of the role of "opposition." That meant that they criticized and resisted practically every proposal put forward by the government. In that way they were able to block practically all legislation.[15] They were supported by a large body of the public in their efforts to undermine the power of the autocracy and force the calling of a constituent assembly. Indeed, many members of the intelligentsia regarded it as the duty of the Kadet party to wage war

[11] *Vospominaniya*, 81–82.
[12] Maklakov, *Iz Vospominanii*, 345–47.
[13] Maklakov, *Pervaya Gosudarstvennaya Duma*, Chapter IV.
[14] Kokovtsev, *Out of My Past*, 107–22.
[15] Maklakov, *Pervaya*, 47–48.

on capitalism. These revolutionary proposals were even discussed seriously by the Society of Advocates.[16] The attitude of
the Kadets was clearly demonstrated in the address in reply
to the speech of the Tsar, and the final adoption of that address
on May 6 was practically a declaration of war on the government by the party.

It appears that in bureaucratic circles there was considerable
vacillation on the advisability of accepting the principle of responsibility of the ministry to the Duma, Kokovtsev informs
us that on his visit to Paris in the spring of 1906 for the purpose
of negotiating a loan, Clemenceau, premier of France, took it
on himself to urge the Russian government to name a ministry
with Milyukov at the head. This suggestion from a foreigner
that coincided with the views of the Kadet party became an
important issue before the session was out. Maklakov recounts
in his book on the First Duma a whole series of negotiations that
began in the spring between Milyukov and Trepov (the palace
commandant) concerning the establishment of a ministry.
These negotiations went so far that a tentative list of ministers
was drawn up. The situation carried panic into bureaucratic
circles, but any possibility of accommodation between the government and the Kadet party was completely eliminated by
the party's stand on the peasant question, on which the Kadets
yielded to pressure from the left and championed the proposals
of the *Trudoviki*.[17] On this point, Maklakov had some trenchant criticism of the Kadet program for the peasants. The
defects which he discussed were by no means limited to the
Kadets, for it was an illusion shared by all members of society
that the proper solution of the peasant question was the redistribution of land held by private landlords or by the state.
This basic preference for violent seizure of private land to the
improvement of peasant agricultural methods had certainly
been one of the major features of the revolutionary movement,
and persisted right through the Bolshevik Revolution of 1917–

[16] Maklakov, *Iz Vospominanii*, 324–25.
[17] Maklakov, *Pervaya*, 129. See also Kokovtsev, *Out of My Past*.

20. However, as the session of the Duma wore on, it became more and more evident that on the land question there could be no compromise, since the government insisted on the inviolability of private property. The negotiations for a Kadet cabinet, according to Maklakov, finally broke down under Milyukov's insistence that such a cabinet consist entirely of Kadets, without any representatives from the bureaucracy.[18]

The Kadets' refusal to agree to any solution other than that of "compulsory alienation" (taking over of the landlord's estates) brought to a head the long series of disagreements on fundamental legislation and convinced the government that it was not possible to work with the Duma.

On June 20, 1906, the government issued a circular, published in the *Pravitel' stvennyi Vyestnik*, announcing contemplated legislation on the peasant question, to which was attached a statement that official policy precluded the possibility of confiscation of private property. Against this the Duma protested violently in an interpellation, coupled with an appeal by the heads of the various parties to the population to resist and defeat the government's purpose. This curious resolution was adopted on June 27 and constituted, of course, open defiance. As a result, the government decided to dissolve the Duma. The Decree of Dissolution came on July 18, concluding with these words:

> Let our subjects bear in mind that only in complete tranquillity and [public] order is a substantial improvement in the lot of the people possible. Let it be clearly understood that we will not tolerate open defiance or lawlessness, and will employ the full might of the state's power to compel lawbreakers to bow to our will. . . . With an unshakable faith in the benevolence of Providence and in the good sense of the Russian people, we will expect from the members of the new Duma the fulfillment of our anticipations and the enactment of [measures] to meet the needs of regenerated Russia.[19]

[18] Gessen, *V dvukh vyekakh*, 229–30.
[19] Maklakov, *Pervaya*, 223.

Although not unexpected, the Decree of Dissolution struck panic among the members of the Duma, and, led by the Kadets, they determined to make a protest and to appeal to the public for support in defying the government. They, therefore, withdrew to Vyborg, Finland, where they unanimously adopted a proclamation calling on the people to refuse to pay taxes and provide recruits for the army, and to adopt other measures to paralyze the administration. But the Vyborg manifesto went almost unnoticed, and the deputies who signed it were indicted for defiance of the government upon their return to Russia. Being under indictment, they were excluded from becoming candidates in the new election.

A decisive step taken by the government preceding dissolution was the replacement of Goremykin, the president of the Council of Ministers, by P. A. Stolypin, who had been minister of the interior in the recent cabinet.[20] On taking office Stolypin set about the task of securing the election of persons to the new Duma who could be counted on to support the government. Kryzhanovskii, in his memoirs, recounts the statement of the Spanish ambassador to Stolypin at this time:

> I cannot understand why you are disturbed. With us everything is quite simple. The mayors are controlled by the government and, as presidents of the elective bureaus, at the right time they slip into the ballot boxes as many ballots for the party favorable to the government as are needed to win, and then dismiss the voters. They get a majority necessary to the government and everyone is satisfied.[21]

It is not recorded whether Stolypin consciously adopted the Spanish system, but there can be little doubt that the government's full resources were thrown into the attempt to secure a favorably disposed Duma.

The new Prime Minister put the interim between the two Dumas to good use by putting through a whole series of laws,

[20] Levin, *The Second Duma*, Intro., 19.
[21] *Vospominaniya*, 99.

the most significant of which were those of October 5, 1906, granting the peasants equal rights with the rest of the population, and of November 9, allowing the peasants to withdraw from the communes. These decrees were issued under the authority of Section 87 of the Fundamental Law, which allowed the Tsar to proclaim laws in the intersession if urgent.[22] Other reforms were introduced in the interests of the peasants. (Incidentally, in October of the previous year, Witte had cancelled all redemption dues payments from January 1, 1906.)

The campaign for election to the new Duma differed somewhat from the earlier campaign. The Social Democrats and the Social Revolutionaries both decided to participate. The Kadet party was at some disadvantage. Like all the parties (except the Union of the Russian People) it was not officially recognized outside of the Duma; its status was still pending when the Vyborg manifesto settled the matter. The Kadets were again refused recognition, and their members who had signed the Vyborg manifesto were again under indictment. The candidates they put up, therefore, were not of the highest caliber. Moreover, in the complicated electoral system, it was to the advantage of the factions to work out agreements among themselves. Some of the factions did this, but the Social Democrats absolutely refused to do so. There were bitter recriminations, feuds, violent diatribes in the press, and, over all, relentless pressure from the government through local agents and election officials. Kryzhanovskii records:

> With the appointment of P. N. Durnovo as minister of the interior, the government endeavored to pass from a merely passive attitude to an active one, and to use its influence in determining the course of events. Durnovo, in this matter, ap-

[22] Maklakov, *Vtoraya Gosudarstvennaya Duma*, 30. Gurko, *Features and Figures of the Past*, 499, takes some credit for this. Actually, the scheme was that of Witte and was the outcome of the work of his committee on the peasant question, created in 1902. See "Diary of Polovtsev," *Krasnyi Arkhiv*, II, 126, for the formation of the committee. For the work of the commission, see S. Yu. Witte, *Zapiska po krest'yanskomu dyelu*, especially his conclusions, 104–32.

pealed to Count Witte in a letter. Witte, without denying that it was desirable that the government intervene in the elections, correctly pointed out that time had already run out and it was probably impossible to do anything, and so it was not worthwhile to compromise the government by useless measures of pressure. Nonetheless, Durnovo decided to make an attempt at his own risk.[23]

The results of the election were somewhat unexpected. The revolutionary parties secured a powerful representation, though this was well divided among them. The so-called center groups —the Kadets and national groups—were considerably reduced in size, the Kadets especially so, since they lost half their representation. The parties of the right had added to their strength. The government, therefore, could hardly contemplate the coming session with equanimity.

The session opened on February 20, 1907, and proceeded to organize itself, naming as president a Kadet, Golovin, a somewhat colorless individual. After adopting rules of procedure, it heard the address of the president of the Council of Ministers, P. A. Stolypin (which took the place of the speech from the throne). Stolypin reviewed the land measure introduced some weeks before and foreshadowed further sweeping reforms. His proposals were received in silence and without enthusiasm.

The address in reply to the Stolypin speech precipitated a violent attack on the government by the Social Democrats. The Kadets joined in the attack and proposed the adoption of a bill of no confidence: "Having heard the statement of the chairman of the Council of Ministers on the introduction of the bills, the Duma passes to the regular order."[24] This affront to the administration provoked a sharp reply by Stolypin, in which he announced that the government proposed, in spite of all incitements to the contrary, to firmly enforce law and order. "You

---

[23] *Vospominaniya*, 76. These methods are described in some detail by Kryzhanovskii, although before the examining commission of 1917, he denied them. See *Padenie Tsarskogo Rezhima*, V, 399.

[24] Levin, *The Second Duma*, 119.

will not frighten us," he concluded. The Kadet proposal, however, was adopted.

The appointment of standing committees, especially those dealing with famine and unemployment, precipitated the first of a long series of bitter debates. It is impossible to read the accounts of the proceedings and fail to be struck with the extraordinary callousness with which measures for relief were treated. The first of these measures—that concerning the famine—precipitated a dispute over the relative spheres of the legislative and executive branches. The use made of this issue by the Social Democrats throws light on their tactics. They proposed that the legislative branch take the whole question of relief and of the food supply out of the hands of the administration and send out its own agents to secure information for themselves. More significant, however, was the statement that measures of relief were of less importance than propaganda; in the words of Dzhaparidze: "We shall not feed the peasants but we will give them something more important than mere food. We will furnish a broad strata of the population with a political education."[25] Much the same sort of oratory greeted the administration's proposals to deal with unemployment.[26]

The agrarian question proved to be one of the most controversial, as it had in the first Duma, despite the fact that Stolypin's land reforms had gone into effect. All the revolutionary parties had a considerable stake in the issue, and each had its own proposal to take the place of Stolypin's. Most crucial was the attitude of the Kadets, who came out for the principle of compulsory expropriation of land held privately by the landlords—a stand which challenged not only the program of Stoly-

[25] Maklakov, *Vtoraya Gosudarstvennaya Duma*, 100.
[26] *Ibid.*, 104–105.
[27] Not much could be said in defense of the budget, which was set up on antiquated principles laid down in the nineteenth century. There had always been considerable juggling of the ordinary and extraordinary budgets, with the result that the budget hardly revealed the condition of the state's finances. There was almost complete ignorance on this subject, and the fact was entirely overlooked that the resources available to pay taxes were strictly limited and that taxation could not but be oppressive to the peasants.

pin but the attitude of the Tsar, who had come out squarely in defense of the rights of private property.

Another issue that led to acrimonious wrangling was the budget, defended somewhat lamely by Kokovtsev.[27] The real issue here was, of course, the highhandedness of the government in overriding the Fundamental Law, which allowed the Duma some voice in the budget's control.

An inflammatory attack on the army by Zurabov roused the government and did much to determine the fate of the Duma.[28]

The situation was finally brought to a climax by an investigation of an alleged conspiracy involving the Social Democrats. The rather complicated story concerns a meeting alleged to have taken place between members of the Social Democratic party and representatives of the garrison, at which a list of "instructions" were drawn up and handed to the soldiers, setting forth plans for carrying on subversive propaganda and other activities in the garrison. While the soldier delegation was not apprehended, the police took into custody a number of Social Democrats, including some deputies. The deputies were detained, but later, on the demand of the public prosecutor, Kamyshanskii, released for lack of proof of criminal intent. This incident led to an interpellation on May 7, the Social Democrats stoutly denying complicity in any conspiracy. However, further searches and the assembling of additional material led the government to denounce the whole party for subversive activity and to demand the immediate withdrawal of the legislative immunity of its members. The matter was turned over by the Duma to a committee, a step which the government regarded as an effort to protract the matter and so thwart the government's purpose. Hence, on June 3, no action having been taken to carry out the wishes of the government, the Duma was dissolved. With the dissolution, the immunity of the Social Democrats automatically expired, and all members of the party who were not successful in disappearing were at once arrested and held for trial.

[28] Kokovtsev, *Out of My Past*, 180–81.

Shortly after the dissolution, a manifesto was issued by the monarch altering the electoral law in such a way as to give the government further control over the elections.[29] The new law, without fundamentally altering the existing system, gave a preponderant voice in the provincial assemblies to the representatives of those landholders who had not less than the property qualification needed to vote for the *zemstvo*.[30] Kryzhanovskii admitted that the promulgation of this decree was a direct violation of the fundamental statutes, but insisted it was the only alternative to abolishing the Duma and setting up a dictatorship. The government brought all the influence at its command to bear to secure the election of persons of known loyalty and political reliability, either through subsidization of the press in the capitals and in the provinces or by financial assistance to loyal organizations such as the Union of Russian People.[31]

The Third Duma opened on November 20, 1907. It was the first one to live out the normal term of five years, being formally dissolved by the Tsar on June 12, 1912. The election returned some eleven "fractions" (as they were called) to the new Duma, with the rights and the groups favoring moderate reforms having the largest share of the representation, the Kadets and moderate "leftists" a smaller share, and the extreme leftists a bare representation of thirty-three. Hence, Stolypin had less to fear, and the sessions were somewhat uneventful. Perhaps most serious was the constant sniping from the Kadets on the matter of the budget. Actually the debates were uninteresting and fruitless, and the Duma was on the whole colorless.

The country soon had other things to engross its attention. Abroad, diplomatic affairs more and more occupied the atten-

---

[29] Kryzhanovskii insists that the law was not issued under section 87 of the fundamental statutes (which would have required subsequent ratification by the State Duma and the State Council), but was a constitutional act emanating from the "highest authority"; i.e., the Monarch. Kryzhanovskii, *Vospominaniya*, 114.

[30] *Ibid.*, 108.

[31] *Padenie Tsarskogo Rezhima*, V, 403.

tion of the government. More and more the administration returned to the old procedure of debating matters in the Council
of Ministers, with the monarch issuing an *ukaz* to the Senate for
the necessary administrative order. Issues were debated in the
Duma and the Council of State, but legislation seldom resulted.
The one constructive measure which the Third Duma had to
its credit was the confirmation of the decrees of 1906, which
gave the peasants the right to withdraw from the communes
and bestowed on them full civil equality with other classes.[32]

In 1909, the whole country was stunned by the discovery
that the renowned revolutionary leader Azeff had been in the
pay of the police. Azeff had entered the employ of the government while a student in Berlin in 1894. On the formation of
the Social Revolutionary party, he had joined and become
a member of the "Fighting Organization," in which capacity
he had arranged the killing of Plehve in 1904, had participated
in the death of Grand Duke Sergei Aleksandrovich, and had
continued to advocate and plan further assassinations. Though
long suspected by certain individuals, he remained in good
standing with the leading figures in revolutionary circles, whose
suspicions he was constantly able to lull by throwing his enemies off the scent with tortuous methods and clever tricks.
Eventually he was run down by Burtsev and effectively discredited.[33] It seems incredible that a man could play so dangerous a double role for fifteen years without being caught, en-
joying, right up to the end, the confidence of the most experienced and trusted of the revolutionary leaders, which enabled
him on more than one occasion to turn the tables on his ac-
cusers and place them under suspicion.

The "unmasking" of Azeff demoralized the Social Revolu-

[32] See Pavlovskii, *Agricultural Russia on the Eve of the Revolution.* Also
Launcelot Owen, *The Russian Peasant Problem, 1900–1917.*

[33] The story is told by Nicolaevsky in *Azeff the Spy.* Also by Burtsev,
Borba Za Svobodnuyu Rossiyu. The latter, on page 263, lists the crimes with
which Azeff had been associated. It is a formidable list. The wonder is not
that he avoided detection so long, but that any one of his associates could
be found to cast the slightest doubt on his devotion to the revolutionary cause.

tionary party. The commission it named to report on the matter rather lamely whitewashed the party organization, and at the same time made the claim that the unearthing of this traitor left the party free from suspicion of harboring *agents provocateurs*—a claim that was far from the truth, as Azeff was only one of a number of secret government agents in the organization. Moreover, by using the term "expropriation" as a euphemism for armed robbery, the party sought to give an air of respectability to its crimes by attributing to their perpetrators revolutionary motives. But the temptation to which they were exposed by large sums of money in their possession was too great, and many of the "expropriators" took to lives of dissipation; the proceeds of the robberies, in many cases, were never accounted for.[34] The story of duplicity and of conspiracy within conspiracy is almost bewildering and indicates a condition of moral anarchy in which there seemed to be no principles, moral or otherwise. The world seemed divided into two opposing camps of antagonists—the administration and the revolutionaries—engaged in a kind of warfare for mutual extermination, in which there was no quarter and no rules of war. Each side resorted to force and to misrepresentation and distortion of the truth, and neither would make concessions or commit itself to any solution or compromise. There seemed to be good faith on neither side. To this situation were added other unhealthy phenomena in Russian life which we shall now describe at some length.[35]

The adoption of the electoral law of June 3, 1907, is regarded by Russian writers as the end of the so-called "revolution" of 1905. At any rate, after that date most events seemed to be anticlimactic. The new Duma was docile and, except for Milyukov and one or two of the more radical members, undistinguished. The "unmasking" of Azeff afforded a glimpse into the depths of official infamy that shocked the public and

[34] Spiridovich, *Histoire du terrorisme russe, 1886–1917*, 606.
[35] See E. J. Dillon, *The Eclipse of Russia*, 158, for a picture of this demoralized state of Russian society.

did the government no good; but on the other hand, the strong likelihood that the revolutionary movement continued to be infiltrated by agents of the government and persons using their revolutionary connections to cover up for ordinary bank robbery lowered the prestige of the parties and undermined morale. The Social Revolutionaries who were most closely linked with Azeff, practically ceased operations to take stock and purge their ranks. Acts of terror did not, however, come to an end. On January 3, 1910, Colonel Karpov, head of the *Okhrana* in St. Petersburg, was assassinated by Petrov, a school teacher, and on September 1, 1911, the prime minister, Stolypin, was murdered in a theater in Kiev. Both of these acts were disavowed by the central committee of the Social Revolutionary party, although the assassin of Stolypin at his trial claimed to have been a member of that party.[36]

But the most startling evidence of the utter demoralization that had overtaken Russian society was furnished by the appearance on the St. Petersburg scene of the notorious monk, Rasputin. He was but the last of a number of charlatans who had found entrance to the imperial circles, the key in his case being the almost hypnotic power with which he calmed the young heir apparent in his seizures and brought comfort to his distracted mother, the Empress.[37] It is not necessary to put the worst interpretation on his intimacy with the imperial family or with its entourage. But it is distressing to have to record that ladies of high rank hastened to pay court to him and that those close to the imperial couple, such as the Grand Duchess Militsa and her sister, did not hesitate to make use of him. His close links with the church are understandable, but the fact that one or two members of the hierarchy stooped to court him for his influence did little credit to the Orthodox clergy.

[36] For the murder of Karpov, see Spiridovich, *Histoire*, 597; for Stolypin's death, see 628. Petrov had emulated Azeff and entered into secret negotiations with the *Okhrana*, though with the consent of the party. But this merely underscores the moral anarchy and the conflicting loyalties which were demoralizing Russian life.

[37] Others were the French doctor, Philippe, the monk Iliodor, who introduced Rasputin, and the Buddhist Lama Badmayev.

From his first appearance in the capital in December, 1911, his behavior in the company of persons of high position and rank was insolent and familiar, but he continued by his "odor of sanctity" to impress those who were easily fooled and to conciliate those who were more discriminating but chose to overlook his escapades and vulgarity for personal advantage. From the very first, he was a cause of deep embarrassment to the administration, which was struggling to maintain at least the appearance of decorum and decency in the conduct of those in high positions, to give the lie to the revolutionary parties which proclaimed the utter bankruptcy of the existing order. But if his presence in the capital disconcerted and outraged the administration in peacetime, at least it was not dangerous. But in the tragic atmosphere of war and the period of intense heart searching that followed, his presence was nothing but an unmitigated disaster for Russia. No enemy of the Russian Empire could have conceived in his wildest dreams an influence so calculated to undermine the whole structure of the administration and carry consternation into the hearts of those struggling under the blows of war. Rasputin was an ill omen for the autocracy. In the words of Guchkov, Russia was "mired in a swamp."[38]

Perhaps something should be said about the means which the administration took to combat revolutionary influences. Its support of the Union of the Russian People, the only legally recognized Russian party, was well known; its support of the "rightist" press was openly admitted by ministers and their agents. To what extent it condoned the questionable measures of local officials or the acts of violence directed against members of the revolutionary parties—Jews or merely persons who were an embarrassment to the government—is not known. Kryzhanovskii, who makes the best case for the administration, emphasizes the complete lack in Russia of responsible agents of local administration. Control of the central government over its

[38] Kokovtsev, *Out of My Past*, 278. Telegram from Guchkov to *Novoye Vremya*, September 10, 1911.

agents was loose, even in the case of the police, and many of their acts were unauthorized.[39] Gessen records that some of the servants in the Winter Palace carried firearms.[40] The violence of the mobs in the city and the country was matched by the violence of the Black Hundreds, who were apparently in touch with the police and were openly encouraged and whose excesses were tolerated, even the pogroms of the Jews. Kokovtsev records that he personally intervened after Stolypin's death, with the Tsar's approval, to end this state of affairs, although the harm had already been done.

The Third Duma, as noted above, dissolved on June 12. The elections were held in the autumn of 1912, and the Fourth Duma convened on November 1 and was dissolved on February 26, 1917.

Russia's experiment with constitutional government invites some speculation as to the cause of its failure. The writer V. A. Maklakov, himself a Kadet, lays the blame on the leaders in the Duma and his own party. His criticism is that the members of the Duma ignored the only possibility of making constitutional government work—by some form of collaboration with the administration, in order not only to restore order but to introduce a regime of law. But when the Kadets and most of the liberals made common cause with the revolutionary parties to force the government to bow to what they called "the will of the people," and made the most extreme demands on the administration for further concessions—refusing to be satisfied with half a loaf—they abdicated their true function of facilitating the transition from autocracy to an ordered constitutional regime. This forced the government to take an equally uncompromising stand, in what was to be a trial of strength between two quite contradictory policies which allowed no middle ground. In such a struggle, the party that appealed to the worst passions and was most extreme in its demands had an immeasurable superiority; and, although reduced in numbers in

[39] Kryzhanovskii, *Vospominaniya*, 100.
[40] Gessen, *V dvukh vyekakh*, 245.

later Dumas, the revolutionary groups inevitably made rapid progress in winning popular support, to the disadvantage of the Kadets and other liberal parties whose programs were hardly to be distinguished from that of the revolutionaries. This analysis of Maklakov's may be "hindsight," but one must share the feeling that it was more important to introduce the reign of law than it was to carry out the visionary programs of the revolutionary parties. But since the time of Speransky, no Russian public figure had shown any enthusiasm for law or a passion for justice. According to the Russian revolutionary psychology, the workers and peasants had suffered for centuries from the exploitation of the privileged classes, and, like the primitive man who believes that wrongs can only be righted by vengeance on their perpetrator, the revolutionists demanded reversal of this position.

13. Vyekhi

THE end of the nineteenth century brought into sharp focus not only a number of conflicting political programs, as we have seen, but behind these programs a number of sharply opposed philosophies which arose to give significance to them. If Hegel and Marx dominated the thinking of Social Democrats; Comte, Lavrov, and Mikhailovskii, that of the Social Revolutionaries; and Mill and Spencer, that of the liberals, there were other active minds to which none of these made an appeal. This unsatisfied minority found its spokesman—and at the same time its leader and teacher—in the powerful figure of Vladimir Solov'ev, whose work lies in the two decades from 1880 to 1900.

Solov'ev was the son of one of Russia's greatest historians, S. M. Solov'ev, whose twenty-nine-volume *History of Russia* forms one of the major landmarks of modern Russian historiography. He was born in 1853, reared in a pious Orthodox household, entered the Moscow Gymnasium at the age of eleven, and was admitted to the University of Moscow in 1869. His formal education was somewhat varied, but he submitted and brilliantly defended his master's thesis at the University in St. Petersburg in 1874. His career as a teacher in academic institutions (Moscow and St. Petersburg) began shortly afterwards and continued until 1881, when he resigned as the result of public statements made in the aftermath of the assassination of Alexander II. He then devoted himself entirely to a career of independent study and writing on philosophical subjects. But many of his articles dealt with current social and political problems.

> While Solov'ev had in his youth been an ardent socialist and materialist, even a first acquaintance with Solov'ev's works impresses one with the fact that he has turned his back on the whole tendency of modern philosophy, i.e., radical autonomism, the purely secularist orientation so characteristic of modern times.[1]

Although Solov'ev's philosophy is difficult to concentrate in one all-embracing statement, it places religion, especially traditional Christianity, at the center of his system. Religion is necessary for an understanding of the world or for formulating any explanation of history or any program for the arranging of human affairs. He challenges socialism for basing everything on a materialistic foundation. (He criticizes the capitalist world for the same vice.) In his introduction to the work, "Justification of the Good," Solov'ev thus propounds the question:

> Has our life in general any meaning? If it has, is this meaning moral, is it rooted in the realm of ethics? And if it is, what does it consist of, what would be a complete and accurate definition of it? It is impossible to evade these questions, regarding which there is no agreement in the present-day consciousness. Some deny any meaning to life; others assert that the meaning of life has nothing in common with morality, that it is by no means dependent on proper and right relations with God, with man, and with the whole world; a third group, finally realizing the significance of moral standards for life, defines them in different ways and becomes involved in controversies which demand an analysis and a solution.
>
> In no case is it possible to consider such an analysis superfluous. In the present situation of human consciousness, even

[1] V. V. Zenkovsky, *A History of Russian Philosophy*, II, 487.

those few who have their own private fixed and final solution to the meaning of life ought to justify it to others; the mind that has resolved its own doubts does not render the heart indifferent to the errors of others.[2]

To these questions Solov'ev gives his own answer:

The moral meaning of life is originally and finally determined by good itself, which is accessible to us internally through conscience and reason, as far as these are freed by moral accomplishment from enslavement to passions and from the limitation of personal or collective self-love. . . . Man, in principle or by destiny, is an absolute inner form for good, as an absolute content. Other things are conditional and relative. Good itself is not conditional but conditions everything of itself and is created through everything.[3]

This leads him to discuss the relation of the individual to society (the question that is the chief preoccupation of the socialists). On this he makes a significant point: "The degree of the subjection of the individual to society ought to depend on the degree of subjection of society itself to the moral good. Without this the social environment exercises no rights whatever on the individual person."[4]

Solov'ev proceeds to a discussion of law, which he distinguishes from morality as "the requirement (backed up by force) that an exact minimum standard of right and wrong be maintained." Morality then goes beyond this minimum.[5] He justifies the use of force to back up law by citing the case of the peasants of early Rus' who suffered at the hand of the raiding Polovtsy:

The peasant goes out to the country to plow his fields, a Polovtsian leaps on him, kills him, drives off his horse; the Polovtsy then reach the village in a mob, slaughter all the peasants,

2 Vladimir Solov'ev, *Sobranie Sochinenii*, VIII, 8.
3 *Ibid.*, VIII, 22.
4 *Ibid.*, VIII, 290.
5 *Ibid.*, VIII, 409.

burn their houses, and take their wives off into slavery, while the princes are occupied the whole time with their own feuds.

Pity for these peasants, not to confine itself to mere words of sympathy, ought to have led to the organization of a single strong power in the state; strong enough to protect the peasants from the princely quarrels and the raids of the Polovtsy.[6]

With regard to socialism, Solov'ev has this to say:

> For a man who takes a stand on moral principles . . . it is impossible . . . to remain indifferent to the material well-being of his neighbor. If the elementary feeling of pity, which has received its highest sanction in the gospel, requires him to feed the hungry, to give drink to the thirsty, to warm him who is freezing, this command does not lose its force when the hungry and freezing are counted by the millions.[7]

But at the same time, he gives this warning:

> In their criticism of the existing economic order, in their declamations against the inequality of property, against selfishness and inhumanity, the socialists take their stand on the moral law and are inspired by a noble feeling of pity for those that labor and are heavy-laden. But if we turn to the positive side of their views, we will easily see that at first they are equivocal and later turn into a hostile attitude towards moral principles.[8]

Solov'ev makes the following significant comment on the principles that should guide government:

> Hence the two main principles of government—the conservative and the progressive—maintain the foundations of social life, without which mankind could not exist, and then improve the conditions of its existence by assisting in the free development of all mankind's powers, which should be the bearer of the future perfect condition. Without the conservative activity of the state,

[6] *Ibid.*, VIII, 486.
[7] *Ibid.*, VIII, 362.
[8] *Ibid.*, VIII, 368.

mankind would disintegrate and no one would be able to enter into the plenitude of our life; so without the state's progressive activity, mankind would forever remain at one stage of the historical process, would never attain the ability to accept or reject the Kingdom of God, and consequently, people would have nothing to live for.[9]

Enough has been quoted from the works of Solov'ev to show that while he sympathized with the humanitarian aspirations that lay at the basis of modern socialism and could be critical of capitalism, he insisted that the true basis of all government and society had to be moral and completely rejected the materialistic and secular foundations of the prevailing philosophy. His influence was great in his lifetime, but it was only after his death that the full impact of his thought contributed to the establishment of a whole school of thinkers and writers, whose influence has been felt in the religious rather than the political sphere.

This thoughtful trend which endeavored to base the approach to modern social and political problems on sound philosophical principles made slight appeal to those members of the various factions of the intelligentsia who sought to array the tumultuous forces of social unrest under their special banner. Yet even among the most ardent revolutionary leaders there were those of unimpeachable integrity who were prepared to subject their views to the most exacting test in order to verify or reject them. Thus the ranks of the extremists began to be thinned by the defection of a considerable number of individuals who had been forced to revise their former views in a conservative direction. As the revolution ran its course, this trend took on the character of a definite movement.

Finally, in 1909, there appeared at Moscow a book called *Vyekhi (Signposts)*, which consisted of a series of essays by well-known writers. The editor, who wrote the introduction and contributed an article, was M. O. Gershenzon. The writers

[9] *Ibid.*, VIII, 496–97.

were mostly members of the Kadet party, and before its formation had been *Osvobozhdentsy*. Their names were N. A. Berdyaev, S. N. Bulgakov, A. S. Izgoev, V. A. Kistyakovskii, P. B.
Struve, and S. L. Frank.

A number of these men were important later in the field of
philosophy rather than in politics. Berdyaev was for many years
the spokesman for the anticommunist, religious (not necessarily orthodox) group of *émigré* Russians in Europe. Bulgakov,
later a priest of the Orthodox church, wrote on religious subjects. Frank made important contributions in philosophy. Gershenzon, a talented writer, wrote many important books on
Russian social thought. Struve, we have already met as an ardent
follower of Marx and associate of Lenin. Izgoev was a member
of the Kadet party, whose contribution to *Vyekhi* was seen as
hardly short of treason. Kistyakovskii, less well known perhaps,
was still an important figure in the intellectual and political
world. At least three of them—Struve, Berdyaev, and Bulgakov
—had been Social Democrats and were now condemned as
renegades.

The book was an expression of disillusionment with the revolution (now regarded as ended), and the authors called for a
reappraisal of the revolutionary movement and of the future
of Russia. The general tone was struck in the introduction by
Gershenzon:

> The persons who have here co-operated in a common task
> differ, to some extent, in the fundamental questions of "belief,"
> as well as in their practical aspirations; but in general there is
> no disagreement among them. Their common platform is a rec-
> ognition of the practical primacy of spiritual life over the
> external forms of society, in the sense that the inner life of the
> personality is the only creative force in human life and that it,
> and not the self-sufficient principles of the political order, is the
> only solid foundation of any social structure. From this point
> of view, the ideology of the Russian intelligentsia, which rests
> on quite the opposite principle, is presented by the collaborators
> of the book as inherently false, as contradicting the nature of

the human soul, and, in a practical sense, sterile, incapable of leading to that end which the intelligentsia proposed for itself —the emancipation of the people.[10]

These words were so resounding a challenge to the Russian attitude of the preceding half-century and so complete a reversal of the prevailing trends of thought that they call for some comment.

Russian society had long pondered on problems concerning the individual and his relation to his environment, his relation to society, and his place in history. Byelinskii, Herzen, Chernyshevskii, Lavrov, and Mikhailovskii had all wrestled with them; in Dostoyevskii and Tolstoi they received artistic expression. Chernyshevskii's book, *What Is to be Done*, gave that author's ideas of man's place in the world and his subordination to his environment. The enormous vogue that this book had among the young Russians of the sixties is evidence that it struck a responsive chord in their minds. The natural yearning for a better world, kindled by contacts with the West and the works of western socialist writers, was now channeled into the examination of social environment, in the belief that it was in its improvement that man's salvation was to be found. This theory having been all but universally accepted, it was merely a question of the proper alteration to be made in the environment. On this point there was a violent clash between the *narodniki* (later the Social Revolutionaries) and the Social Democrats. But these two groups did not entirely dominate the field.

In the gradually increasing material well-being, there developed a philosophy of skepticism, of disillusionment with all higher moral values, perhaps even of satiety, without any spiritual vision. This spiritual vacuum, which the church did little to fill, could not be filled by the dry, formal teaching of Marx— even when fired with hatred kindled by class warfare—especially for the more sensitive souls to whom the world cannot be reduced to a material basis, to a group of warring classes strug-

[10] M. O. Gershenzon (Ed.), *Vyekhi: Sbornik statei o russkoi intelligentsii.*

gling for a greater share of the world's production. Through the *Sturm und Drang* of the late nineties and the earlier years of this century, members of the Marxist group, such as Struve, Berdyaev, and Bulgakov, were feeling their way towards something more satisfying. Legal Marxism, economism, and revisionism were stages along the road of their evolution. It was impossible for persons roused by the great works of Dostoyevskii and Tolstoi to accustom themselves to the intellectual strait jacket into which the votaries of Marxism had to be fitted and to the rigid discipline which the Social Democratic party sought to impose on its members. Madame Krupskaya, who met Struve in St. Petersburg in 1895, recorded her distrust of him as not "one of ourselves."[11] He was, at that time, of course, a very young man who had donned Marxism as a fashion in clothes.

The government tolerated "legal Marxism" because of its opposition to the terror of the Social Revolutionary party, although the latter group, which appeared on the surface to be more dangerous, could never match the "legal Marxists" in fanatical devotion and singlemindedness, as the government was later to discover to its cost. Lenin was disquieted by the tolerance extended to "legal Marxism" by the state, considering it of greater danger to the movement than persecution. He also reacted against the stream of revisionism at that time flowing into the party from Germany. He perceived the final fruition of the intellectual travail of the intelligentsia, which after four decades had found a program which seemed to meet the requirements of the revolutionary-minded, and he could not see any sense in re-examining any questions to which Marxism had found an answer and taking a chance on unsettling the minds of its devotees. The whole revisionism movement was as alien to him as to other Marxists. The former Marxists thus drifted away from their moorings. They finally founded the *Soyuz Osvobozhedeniya*, which published the illegal organ *Osvobozhdenie* at Stuttgart. As we have already seen, they moved almost

[11] Krupskaya, *Memories of Lenin*, I, 22–23.

as a body into the "Movement of Liberation," as the Kadet party was called, and became perhaps its most important members.

The first fruits of this movement began to appear as early as the turn of the century, when Struve published articles attempting to reconcile Marxism with the prevailing trends of the new western philosophy which emphasized the role of the individual. Berdyaev began to publish in 1901 a criticism of Mikhailovskii. These early signs of a change were perhaps not very distinct but nonetheless were extremely significant. As Ivanov-Razumnik says:

> There began a new era in the history of Russian philosophical thought, a new stage in the evolution of the Russian intelligentsia; the old ideals received a new basis of support, took on a new form, and shifted their center of gravity. New critical ideas dealt crushing blows to orthodox *narodnichestvo* and orthodox Marxism, and having overthrown their poorly armed enemies, continued their further internal evolution.[12]

The full effect of these new forces began to be felt when Struve started to publish in 1905 the series of articles that make up his *Patriotica*. Struve claims that the revolutionary intelligentsia was the spiritual heir of the great revolutionary leaders of the seventeenth and eighteenth centuries—Sten'ka Razin and Emelyan Pugachev. As for the modern intelligentsia, which he claims came into existence in 1862, he maintains that its chief characteristic was its "apostasy," by which he evidently means its revolt against authority, which he says was both absolute and relative.

The absolute sense of this is seen in a complete denial of all government, as in the anarchism of Bakunin and Kropotkin; the relative in the different forms of Russian radicalism, as, for instance, socialism. Marxism is a complete expression of that apostasy in its view of government as a class institution. But it is more than that; it is antireligious. From the first, Russian

[12] *Istoriya russkoi obshchestvennoi mysli*, II, 456–57.

positivism has been antireligious. Struve believes that this is a distinguishing mark of the Russian intelligentsia. Some claim that socialism can be a sort of religion, but Struve says this is impossible. Religion teaches that good and evil are not relative to the outer world but that moral values are inner; "The Kingdom of God is within you." The Marxist believes that moral values are determined by external circumstances.[13]

Struve also notes the sharp differences between the revolutionary writers and the great figures of national literature—Pushkin, Lermontov, Tolstoi, and Dostoyevskii (whom he claims were not members of the intelligentsia). His most trenchant criticism is directed against positivism, which, in his words, is a philosophy which has made "dogmative assumptions which have promised much more than it can fulfill." The positivists characterize "the category of causation as the highest principle of universal explanation," and "trace the ought to this source"; "they abolish freedom and these basic ideas of morality as self-evident concepts."[14]

Tolstoi had joined the chorus in denunciation of the state as an instrument of force: "The cause of evil from which we all suffer is not in people but in the false organization on a basis of force, which people believe indispensable."

To this Struve replied:

> As the Kingdom of Heaven is within you, so is the Kingdom of the Devil within you. . . . The most fearful phenomena of human life—crime and prostitution—are simply not traceable to individual ignorance or "the social milieu" [environment]. It is not simply that people are not able to arrange their life . . . they are undoubtedly weak.
>
> When I realized this . . . I ceased to be a Socialist; I ceased to believe in the external arrangement as a decisive factor in man's life, whether it is a matter of propaganda or force.[15]

[13] *Patriotica*, 339.
[14] *Ibid.*, 327.
[15] "Rokovye Vroposy," *Russkaya Mysl*, 1909. The citation from Tolstoi is not identified.

In another passage, Struve puts his finger on what he considered basic lacks in Russian life; namely, the absence of two vitally related tenets—the belief in personal responsibility and the belief in freedom. He maintained that the superiority of the English workman (over the Russian) was due to his greater efficiency; in the same way, the superiority of the German was due to his *Tüchtigkeit*, which Struve implicitly ascribes to his highly developed sense of personal responsibility. On the other hand, in the eyes of the intelligentsia, any outstanding merit of the individual was suspect, since it ran counter to that ideal of "equality" which had become a fetish, with personal responsibility relegated to a secondary place. Struve maintains that individual fitness is the real basis of capitalism and not (as alleged by the intelligentsia) "unequal distribution," "stealing," or "grabbing." Marxism had gone beyond the *narodniks* in ignoring the factor of personal responsibility. Modern socialism was an antireligious, mechanistic rationalism, which refused to recognize that the problem of improving the lot of mankind is essentially a religious one.[16]

Turning now to *Vyekhi*, we find a severe indictment of the revolutionists in the article by S. L. Frank, "Etika nigilizma" ("The Ethics of Nihilism"). Frank finds that the revolutionists are "amoralist," that they hold there is no absolute objective good and that standards of right and wrong are only related to an individual's subjective desires:

> Nihilist amoralism is the fundamental and most distinctive trait of the spiritual physiognomy of the Russian "intelligent"; from denial of objective values [naturally] flows the deification of the subjective interests of one's neighbor ("the people"), whence follows the recognition that the highest and only task of man is in serving the people; and from this, in turn, follows ascetic hatred of everything that stands in the way of, or even merely does not advance the realization of that task. Life has no objective inner meaning; the only blessing in it is material comfort, the satisfaction of subjective needs; hence, man is bound

[16] *Patriotica*, 362–69.

to devote all his energies to the improvement of the lot of the majority, and everything that distracts him from this is evil and ought to be ruthlessly discarded—such is the extraordinary chain of judgments, without logical foundation but firmly welded together, which guides every act and every evaluation of the Russian "intelligent." Amoralism, atheism, fanatical ruthlessness of moral demands, lack of principles in the metaphysical sense—this is nihilism. It is a denial of any moral judgment and objective distinction between good and evil.[17]

Frank defines the member of the intelligentsia as "warrior monk," with a nihilistic religion of earthly happiness:

> The intelligentsia is, as it were, a self-contained state, a special small world of its own, with its own severe and powerful traditions, its own etiquette, its own morals, its own customs, almost its own culture; and one can see nowhere but in Russia so unshakably solid a tradition, such definiteness and severity in the regulation of life, such downrightness in passing judgment on persons and conditions, such fidelity to its corporate spirit, as in this all-Russian spiritual monastery constituted by the Russian intelligentsia.[18]

Perhaps the most influential and productive of these writers was Berdyaev, who long afterwards became the pillar of anticommunist thought in Europe. In his article "Filosoficheskaya istina i intelligentsaya pravda," he attacks the intelligentsia for its perverse indifference to truth.

> The intelligentsia was ready to accept as truth any philosophy on the one condition that it sanctioned its social ideals; and it uncritically rejected every one, even the profoundest and truest philosophy, if it suspected it of an unfavorable or critical attitude towards the group's traditional predilections and ideals. . . . the intelligentsia . . . required of truth that it serve as a weapon of revolution. . . . the basic moral judgment of the intelligentsia

[17] *Vyekhi*, 156.
[18] *Ibid.*, 174.

is embraced in the formula, "Let truth perish if from its death people will live better, if they will be happier; away with truth if it stands in the way of the traditional watchword, 'Down with the autocracy.' "[19]

Berdyaev has hit on one of the most abiding prejudices of the Russian intelligentsia—that a thing is true or false only in so far as it promotes the cause of socialism or retards it. An equally baseless prejudice is that a positive or materialistic philosophy is by its very nature progressive, just as any form of idealism is necessarily reactionary.[20] Berdyaev concludes that "What we need most at the present time is a recognition of the value of truth in itself."[21]

Struve's contribution to *Vyekhi* was little more than a re-iteration of the message contained in *Patriotica* and a plea for re-examination of the basic assumptions of the socialist:

It is absolutely essential for the intelligentsia to re-examine its philosophy and in that category to subject its cornerstone—the socialists' denial of personal responsibility of which we spoke above—to drastic reconsideration. With the removal of this cornerstone—and it ought to be removed—the whole structure of this philosophy will crash.[22]

Kistyakovskii discusses the intellectual's attitude towards law and freedom. In this connection he cites Mikhailovskii:

Freedom is a great and attractive thing but we do not want freedom if, as has been the case in Europe, it only increases our age-old debt to the people. . . .
Skeptically disposed towards the principle of freedom, we are

[19] *Ibid.*, 6.
[20] Ivanov-Razumnik in *Istoriya russkoi obshchestvennoi mysli*, rightly protests against linking these things together. "Why should this realism in its noncritical form have the right to the term 'progressive,' and what could be more absurd than the recognition of a logical connection between idealism and reaction." II, 490–91.
[21] *Vyekhi*, 21.
[22] *Ibid.*, 142.

prepared not to seek any rights for ourselves, not to mention privileges, [but I do not want] even the most elemental paragraphs of what, in former times, was called natural law. . . . And all this for one possibility, to which our whole soul yearns—the possibility of passing over to a better, higher form of society, bypassing the intervening stage of European development, the stage of the bourgeois state. We have believed that Russia can blaze a new historical trail distinct from that of Europe.[23]

Kistyakovskii claims that this amounts to the rejection of a legal structure for the new society.

We thus find that the new philosophy born of the travail of the turbulent years of the revolution had come face to face with some of the underlying assumptions of the whole previous revolutionary epoch, and demanded that they be re-examined. These are:

(1) The belief that man and his institutions are the product of their environment and that no improvement can be made in man except through altering the environment.

(2) The application to philosophy as a criterion not the objective standard of truth or falsity but the applicability of the philosophy to revolutionary purposes.

(3) The amoralism that holds that standards of right and wrong are purely relative to the environment in which man lives and that there is nothing absolute.

(4) The indifference to law and personal rights.

These basic aberrations the writers believe lie at the root of most of Russia's troubles.

Despite the adverse criticism which it encountered, *Vyekhi* ran through five editions within four months.[24]

This political stocktaking undoubtedly made a profound impression, but it is questionable whether it had any effect on the course of events. N. Lossky, in his *History of Russian Phi-*

---

[23] V. A. Kistyakovskii, "V zashchitu prava," *Vyekhi*. The citation from Mikhailovskii is found in "Literaturnye Zamyetki, Septyabr, 1880" in *Sochineniya*, IV, 939–58.
[24] Gessen, *V dvukh Vyekakh*, 266.

losophy, says that "the authors of *Vyekhi* were right in what they said of the defects of the Russian intelligentsia but mistaken in thinking that the Revolution of 1905 was a failure." He further emphasizes the fact that while the violent revolutionary spirit of the First and Second Dumas came to an end in 1907 and was succeeded by a period of relative calm and co-operation between government and Duma, this did not signify the halting of reform; actually, there is reason to believe that the harsh, and perhaps unconstitutional, measures of the government in 1907 had a salutary effect. At any rate, Russia entered on a period of material prosperity which provided a poor seedbed for revolutionary ferment.[25] Gessen, himself a Kadet, deeply resented the efforts to discredit the whole revolutionary movement, which he thought had something of heroism in it. But he admitted the strong influence exercised by this appeal to the prevailing mood of disillusionment.[26]

The most trenchant criticism, however, was that of Ovsyaniko-Kulikovskii, who contributed an article to *Intelligentsiya v Rossii* in 1910 as a retort to *Vyekhi*. The fault of the *Vyekhi* according to Kulikovskii, was that the time was past for this stocktaking. The ideologies of the Russian intellectual had been worked out by speculation on general philosophical and religious lines—much of it in the eighteenth century. Therefore these new speculations have had no meaning; the ideology had been accepted by the majority and theoretical questions had given way to practical ones, so that the effort of Struve to turn the clock back and re-examine the ideology was quite useless.[27] This comment, whether well founded or not, is an extremely important one. In theory, at any rate, man's progress often turns on his ability to re-examine the basic assumptions on which he has been working. In practice, however, it would seem that this is seldom done. Each generation builds on what has been bequeathed by a former one, without questioning the validity of

[25] Pages 173–74.
[26] Gessen, *V dvukh,* 265.
[27] Ovsyaniko-Kulikovskii, *Intelligentsiya v Rossii,* 218–19.

the assumptions. Nonetheless, it is a sad comment on the revolutionary movement that after having developed a program on a very shaky philosophy, it would not submit to fundamental questions, but felt compelled to proceed on the course that it had chosen. In this sense, therefore, the intelligentsia seemed impelled by forces beyond its control, and these forces were hurrying it to a crisis whose end could not be predicted.

Others who took up cudgels on behalf of the intelligentsia in this collection, *Intelligentsiya v Rossii*, were I. I. Petrunkevich, K. K. Arsen'ev, N. A. Gredeskul, M. M. Kovalevskii, P. N. Milyukov, M. A. Slavinskii, and M. I. Tugan-Baranovskii. In general, they sought to justify the role of the intelligentsia and made capital of the differences and inconsistencies in the views held by the authors who contributed articles to *Vyekhi*. Yet the replies were feeble and did little but repeat what had already been said a thousand times. The views expressed by *Vyekhi* were applauded by one churchman, Archbishop Antonii of Volhynia, who treated the book as a call of the world to repentance. This approval, it can easily be realized, was not welcomed by the authors.[28] Lenin dismissed *Vyekhi* as bourgeois, as an expression of Kadetism and counterrevolution.[29]

How did these assumptions affect the individuals immersed in the problems of daily life? In a recent work, Madame Kaidanova, a teacher, whose experience covered the revolutionary period at the beginning of the century as well as the period from 1917 to 1930, has made some shrewd and interesting observations. Madame Kaidanova was one of an army of devoted persons absorbed in the work of enlightening the masses and, of necessity, was thrown into contact with some persons in her profession who were revolutionarily inclined. She records that "after every meeting with them something in them definitely turned me against them. . . . I felt myself quite unsuited for revolutionary activity.[30] She saw with her own eyes the rise

[28] I. I. Petrunkevich, *Intelligentsiya v Rossii*, x.
[29] Lenin, *Sochineniya*, XVI, 106–21.
[30] O. V. Kaidanova, *Ocherki po istorii narodnogo obrazovaniya v Rossii i SSSR*, I, 70.

in the post-reform period of the revolutionaries, which she endeavors to explain.

In discussing the results of the reforms and the natural impatience of the public with the insignificant results attained, she records that some persisted in carrying on their public-spirited work, while others, becoming exasperated, came to feel that the only way to obtain quicker results was to destroy the existing system and the obstacles in the way:

> Revolutionary activity was surrounded with an aura of martyrdom; it drew to itself those who were prepared to sacrifice themselves for the general good. Passing over to a revolutionary attitude of mind in many cases was the immediate development from a religious attitude or philosophy (*Breshkovskaya*) from the reading of the lives of the saints to the underground literature. . . . In propounding the question of the means to be adopted in the struggle and the attainment of the new form of society, one general error was committed. . . . The significance of the universal practice of everyday life in Russia, which had just rid itself of serfdom and so was incomplete, was underestimated. It was the development of habits of social life of which Russia at that time stood in greatest need; meanwhile, the revolutionary movement itself served to distract people from the fostering of these habits.
>
> . . . Almost no one gave a thought to the question of what would happen the day after the revolutionary coup if they were successful in overthrowing the Tsar. "Just let us throw off our chains, just let us overturn the Tsar's throne. The people, once they are free, will know how to arrange things." . . . The question was never subjected to careful analysis; sufficient unto the day is the evil thereof.[31]

It is to be noted that Madame Kaidanova's experiences covered the first twelve years of the Soviet regime and her considered judgment was equally critical of the Soviet system and the

[31] *Ibid.*, II, ii, 9-11.

effects of its theories: "Life cries out against the class struggle, in that form in which it is put into effect in the Soviet Union."[32]

Perhaps the most mournful judgment passed on the revolutionary intelligentsia has come out of a concentration camp. A Finnish businessman fell into the toils of the Ogpu and was sentenced to a term of hard labor. During his imprisonment he encountered former Russian revolutionaries who opened their hearts to him, one of whom, named Bakhtiarov, committed suicide in despair at the low ebb Soviet life had reached.

> Bakhtiarov . . . often made me think of his views as to where the responsibility for the Russian tragedy lay. He thought the Russian intelligentsia had done more than anything else to bring the country under Bolshevist domination. . . . His indictment was directed against the intelligentsia. . . . The intelligentsia was the brains of the people. . . . It never gave a thought to what was going to follow the Tsar's regime. It did not understand the basic character of the Russian people. It had no notion how to govern them. It idealized the people and lived in a world of dreams.[33]

[32] *Ibid.*, II, ii, 83.
[33] George Kitchin, *A Prisoner of the Ogpu*, 214–15.

14. The Revolutionary Movement Evaluated

HAVING now recorded the progress of the revolutionary movement, the time has come to take stock of it as a whole and to make some generalizations concerning its character. The convulsions of 1917 that overturned the old regime make such an evaluation inevitable. In passing judgment, little help is received from Russian writers, who are inclined to accept the revolution either as its own justification or, if they are not sympathetic to the Soviet regime, to regard it as salutary but as having been corrupted in the hands of the present leaders of Russia. The thought of most of them moves within a framework of ideas beyond which they seldom look. Without stating so, they make certain basic assumptions, and it is perhaps these basic assumptions that need to be examined.

There is a belief, somewhat widely held, that the revolutions of 1917 were a natural and spontaneous rising of the people against a regime that was at once corrupt and oppressive and that there was no alternative to the destruction of the system unless the Russian people were to give up all hope of attaining any degree of well-being or happiness. The writers favored by the present regime generally accept this interpretation, but there is also a school of thought, mostly among *émigré* writers, that does not regard the revolutions as inevitable, but maintains that the war into which Russia plunged in 1914 slowed the natural progress of Russia towards an ordered constitutional government and disturbed the reorganization of Russia's basic industry, agriculture, on the basis of private property, as foreshadowed by the Stolypin reforms. For this latter belief there is some evidence that after the convulsions of 1905–1907, Russia had entered on a period of unusual prosperity.[1] The idea that Russia was about to emulate the countries of Western Europe in her economic development is a tempting one, but of course it is merely one of the "might-have-beens" of history. With regard to the view that it was the economic breakdown occasioned by the war which caused the revolution, we cannot do better than quote the words of M. Aldanov:

> Foreigners to whom everything in the February revolution is clear, arrange such neat patterns for it. The remote causes are sufficiently well known; the less cosmic [are assumed to be] nearer ones; defeats at the front, the food shortage in St. Petersburg, [scandals connected with the government about] Sukhomlinov, Rasputin. However, in these patterns, the nearer causes constitute the weakest side; Rasputin had been killed a full ten weeks before the revolution; with regard to Sukhomlinov, I suppose in February, 1917, they were still talking about him in the provinces, but in the capitals and at the front they had long since ceased to discuss him. As far as the food shortages in St. Petersburg are concerned, after 1920 it is absurd for the historian to write about them as a cause of the revolution. Some years ago in Germany I saw approximately the same food shortages. . . . Thus, the February revolution [can be explained] perfectly "without the nearer causes." We had been expecting it

[1] See Kokovtsev's review of Russia's economic development from 1904 to 1914 in his book, *Out of My Past*, Chapter XXXVII, 457–566; also Lyashchenko's *History of the National Economy of Russia*, Chapter XXXIII, for another view. For the view that the revolutions of 1917 were the outcome of forces let loose by the war, see Florinsky, *The End of the Russian Empire*; Pares, *The Fall of the Russian Monarchy*; and Walsh, *The Fall of the Russian Empire*.

228

for a hundred years, and yet it came on us unforeseen by the chief actors.[2]

When we attempt to make an appraisal of the view that the revolution was the natural outcome of the oppressive and corrupt nature of the tsarist regime and the hopeless stagnation of the economic life of the country, we find it difficult to accept this theory. Economically, Russia had been making, and was continuing to make, considerable progress, and there does not seem to be any ground for believing that the situation demanded drastic action. Statistics on the economic life of Russia were somewhat loosely prepared. Moreover, it was notorious that the offices of statistics were manned by "radicals." They may have been conscientious in their assembling of figures, but there is the strong suspicion that we should take a somewhat reserved attitude toward any conclusions based on these statistics.[3] One has a feeling that apart from the economic and social questions, certain views had developed among the Russian writers which caused them to put on blinders and to refuse to see any solution of economic problems other than their own. It would seem most profitable, for the moment anyway, to suspend judgment on the possibility of economic and social factors' being responsible for the revolution and to make some examination of the basic assumption of most revolutionary writers—that before any progress could be made the old regime had to be overthrown.

The Russian autocracy is generally held to have emerged in the sixteenth century, at the same time that the absolute monarchies in Western Europe were taking shape. However, there were certain marked differences between the absolutism of Western Europe and the Russian autocracy. The monarchs of Western Europe, in crushing the feudal class, made effective use of the support of the towns, whose financial resources went far in giving the monarchy a sound financial basis. But in the case of the Russian autocracy, it was quite different. There were

2 P. N. Milyukov; Sbornik Materialov, 23.
3 N. I. Astrov, Vospominaniya, I, 339.

229

no towns of any consequence in Russia, and the power of the autocrat was established at the expense of the whole boyar class, the monarch drawing on the support of a new class, which he elevated from the lower ranks of society and from which came his close intimates and supporters. Let us quote here the words of Ivan IV:

> From the beginning the Russian autocrat has held sway over all his lands and not just the boyars and grandees. . . . How shall he be Tsar unless he himself plan? Through God's mercy and the grace of the Mother of God and the prayers of our parents, the land is ruled by us, their descendants, and not by judges and generals . . . the rule of the many is like a woman's folly.[4]

The process of centralization was accompanied by the destruction of the institutions of local self-government. The effects of this are observable at frequent periods in the seventeenth and eighteenth centuries, more particularly at the time of the peasant risings. On such occasions the local representatives of the government, frequently without any power to back them up, were usually helpless and could not provide a rallying point for opposition to the revolt. In such cases it was necessary to organize and dispatch an army from the capital. During the nineteenth century an agitation developed to restore some degree of self-government. It was finally achieved in the establishment of the *zemstva* in 1864, but the latter were without experience and were frequently frustrated by government interference. It was not until the end of the century that they succeeded in taking over their proper functions and marshaling some measure of public opinion in the provinces behind them, but they still continued to be weak. The centralization of power in the capital and the weakness of all local organs meant that the government was always an alien element that intruded into the life of the community and hence enjoyed neither moral

[4] Letter of Ivan IV to Prince Kurbskii, in N. Popov, *Tatishchev i ego Vremya*, 68.

support nor active co-operation from the population. Its reliance was chiefly on force.

In this respect the local organs of self-government showed striking contrasts to their counterparts in England. While the English royal power in the Middle Ages struggled to weaken and destroy the feudal, it continued to retain various institutions of local government. These might at times become merely agents of the central government, but on the whole they kept alive a sense of participation in the political life—a factor of immense moral significance. There was seldom a sharp division between the royal government and the people. Occasionally this friendly spirit of co-operation broke down, but usually the crisis was surmounted by some form of accommodation.

In Russia there was a tendency for government and people to confront one another as two mutually hostile camps. The transition from an autocracy to a constitutional monarchy would be difficult in any case, but in Russia the weaknesses of all local institutions immensely aggravated it. However, there were other more subtle factors that seemed to make an understanding between the administration and the people impossible. Milyukov (writing at the beginning of this century) claimed that there had been two occasions in the latter part of the nineteenth century when it might have been possible to establish amicable relations between the sovereign and the people: the first in the sixties at the time of emancipation and the second in the eighties when the wave of revolutionary violence had spent itself in the assassination of Alexander II.[5] This claim has to be carefully examined before it can be accepted.

If we consider the first occasion, the era of the great reforms, we shall probably find it really a test case for this hypothesis. There is ample evidence that the official atmosphere of Russia was quite transformed by the accession of Alexander in 1855, from which was to date the great reforms. The period from 1855 to 1860 can be regarded as the honeymoon of this

[5] Milyukov, *Russia and Its Crisis*, Chapter on "The Liberal Idea," especially 278 and 323.

reign. Outwardly, there was nothing to mar the harmony that seemed to exist among all parties in the political situation. There was a relaxation of censorship, the restrictions on the universities were suspended; in fact, all the harsh regulations of the last seven years of Nicholas' reign were either abolished or allowed to lapse into desuetude.[6] But beginning in 1860 there was a marked change for the worse in the relations between the state and the public. The surface manifestations were the disturbances among the university students in 1861, the incendiary fires of 1862, the dissemination of inflammatory appeals addressed by revolutionary leaders and printed secretly in Russia, and the circulation of Herzen's *Kolokol* and other *émigré* literature designed to appeal to discontent. To these the government replied by suspension of the Sunday schools, the tightening of censorship through administrative action, and the introduction of oppressive measures into university life.

There is a tendency for writers on this issue to align themselves on one side or the other and to assign the blame to the opposite group. It does not seem to me that this is reasonable. The inability to attain any sort of harmonious equilibrium was a reflection of the political and intellectual life of the time and of the unique characteristics of Russia's life. In the first place, the idea that an autocracy can pass by easy stages to a constitutional monarchy does not seem to be practical, at least not in Russia. The attitude of most Russians when the government

[6] Following are some of the measures taken to relax the most severe of the regulations imposed by Nicholas during the closing years of his reign:

1. Universities were allowed to admit an unlimited number of students to all faculties.

2. Professors deprived of their pensions since 1852 had them restored.

3. The decision was made to open a university in Siberia, and a medical and a law school at Warsaw.

4. Permission was granted to young men to go abroad to train for academic posts.

5. Regulations were relaxed to allow Russians to travel freely abroad, and the tax on passports was reduced.

6. The *raznochintsy* were freed from their obligation to military service.

7. The excessively harsh rules imposing military service on Jews and Poles were abolished.

See *Obshchestvennoe dvizhenie pri Aleksandre II, 1855–1881*, 14.

made a generous gesture undoubtedly was that concessions were a sign of weakness and should lead to increased demands. One finds illuminating expressions of this at various times in the works of the revolutionists themselves. One of the best instances is found in a petition given by Nikolai Serno-Solov'-evich to the Tsar in 1864, in which occurs this passage:

> But in an absolute government, a series of concessions reveals that the interests of the government and the people are different and that the government is beginning to feel itself in difficulties. So every concession it makes invites new demands from the people, but each demand naturally arouses in the government the wish to repress or control it. Hence, a series of continuous vacillations and half-measures by the government and growing dissatisfaction among the public.[7]

Other instances could be quoted in support of this.

A second unfortunate attitude from which Russia was unable to free itself was that political struggles necessarily involve personal animosity, an attitude completely foreign to free governments, whose political battles may be likened to competition in the field of sports, which is carried on under certain rules that, at least in theory, preclude personal violence. An interesting illustration of the Russian attitude towards politics is afforded by a letter which came into the possession of the Third Section in 1862. This letter was addressed by one of the persons accused of spreading seditious propaganda, a man named Albertini, to the Marquis de Traverse. The latter, it seems, had agreed to work for Katkov on the *Russkie Vyedomosti*. The former protested in these words:

> You will not believe how shocked we were to receive news of your joining up with Katkov. Really, this association with Katkov, unless you are joking, explained to A. I. the defection of such people as his friends Evgenii Korsh and Ketcher, both of them at present the friends of Chicherin. This arises, according

[7] Lemke, *Ocherki osvoboditel'nago dvizheniya "shestidesyatykh godov,"* 214.

to him, from the fact that we have not as yet attained political sense and political honesty.

As you will see, I am entering the lists against you with all possible arguments. Your word of honor is dear to you. Your word of honor is very dear to me. This is the reason why you should not join Katkov. The time will come when to be leagued with Katkov will be just as dishonorable as to be leagued with Chicherin, because both of them are equally the foes of our movement. . . .

Whence comes your conciliatory spirit? You say all people are honest. Well, you ought to see that these men are scoundrels, to feel them such, to feel their villainy at the present moment, and then you will be against them with every fiber of your being.

Do you see now where this has led you—to seeing honesty in Chicherin and Solov'ev. Do you forget that apart from trades-man's honesty, there is honesty of another kind—political, the honesty of a public figure.[8]

Apparently, political honesty in revolutionary morals pre-cluded personal friendships with those in disagreement with you. Hatred of your opponent was the rule, and the person who endeavored to take a middle position was regarded as a traitor by both sides. To justify this challenge to the principle of a liberal tolerance, a specious appeal was made to history:

In knowledge and practice, where powerful forces come on the scene, the truth is never in the "golden mean" between them; neither in the warfare of paganism with Christianity, of Cathol-icism with Protestantism, nor in any other struggle between inertia and progress. A real force is true to itself and pursues its own end.[9]

The third factor that prevented a *rapprochement* was the

[8] *Ibid.*, 139.

[9] Dorovatskii and Chernuzhnikov, *Ocherki realisticheskago mirozryeniya*, Intro. The writers have conveniently overlooked the fact that Islam had to establish a *modus vivendi* with Christianity, which it was not able to destroy, just as Catholicism had to accept the Protestant revolt as a movement which it was powerless to crush.

tendency very deeply rooted to neglect all tradition. Milyukov quotes with approval the words of Herzen:

> A thinking Russian is the most independent being in the world. What, indeed, could stop him? Consideration for the past? But what is the starting point of modern Russian history other than an entire negation of nationalism and tradition. . . . On the other hand, the past of the Western nations may well serve us as the executors of their historic will. We share in your doubts but your beliefs leave us cold. We share in your hatreds but do not understand your attachments for the legacies of your ancestors. You are constrained by scruples, held back by adventitious considerations. We have none . . . we are independent because we start a new life.[10]

This lack of attachment to the past may have been due, as Herzen implies, to the complete break Peter made in the continuity of Russian life; it became extremely widespread in the nineteenth century. There was thus no respect among revolutionary thinkers or the public for national tradition. Milyukov, like other liberals, joined with the revolutionists in decrying any attempt to follow the past:

> So we ought not to deceive ourselves and others by fear of socalled treason to national tradition. If our past is linked with the present, it is only a kind of ballast that drags us down, though with less and less force each passing day. This lessened link with the past even nationalists admit without regret. From a demand that we be true to historical tradition they often pass over to the mournful admission that we have no real traditions.[11]

What strikes one in reading the Russian novelists is that there is (apart from the Slavophiles) no one, or almost no one, to defend the existing system. There was a passion among not only the intelligentsia but all well-informed people—even many in government circles—to profess, at least privately, complete

[10] *Russia and Its Crisis*, 363–64.
[11] N. M. Sokolov, *Ob ideyakh i idealakh russkoi intelligentsii*, 143.

scorn for the system under which they lived. The most violent radicals could always count on the secret sympathies of a vast number of highly placed persons. An example is found in the character of Stephen Verkhovensky in Dostoyevskii's *The Possessed*, who, while living a parasitic life of ease at the home of a member of the gentry class, is constantly professing the most radical views. Lev Tikhomirov, in explaining why he abandoned the *Narodnaya Volya*, comments on this situation in appealing to the older generation:

> I must turn to the older men, the upper classes who should realize the truth of the points I have made. On them lies the obligation to give a new direction. The obligation to make some contribution towards fashioning a positive and creative view lies especially on my contemporaries, wearied as much by "the revolution" as I, and who, like me, have been through much and therefore have come to think things over. Their experience and age, of course, have taught them much and aroused in them an urge towards soberness of thought. The same obligation rests on another part of our generation, who at one time were sufficiently skeptical to allow themselves to be attracted by any "movement" and who are now competent, often respected members of Russian society. The means for peaceful development of the country is in their hands. Finally, many pioneers will be found who have long blazed the trail of which I speak, but who have been working in isolation, not presuming to raise their heads and boldly declare that they are the real salt which preserves from spoiling the land torn by the struggle between the revolutionaries and the reactionaries.[12]

On this question of the break between the government and public opinion, Serno-Solov'evich, in his petition presented to the government in 1864, has this to say:

> Eight years ago you could have counted on the fingers of one hand the people who even dreamed of some kind of representative institutions; three years ago there were people who had

[12] Tikhomirov, *Pochemu ya perestal byt' revolyutsionerom*, 78–79.

no use for monarchial institutions, but the most extreme of them would have shrunk from the role of terrorists; but now, in all likelihood, time is already fashioning such people, but the preservation of old forms will soon multiply their numbers.[13]

The break between the two was signalized, as we have seen, by the restoration of many of the oppressive features of the old regime. It is customary to blame the government, or at least the bureaucracy, for the resumption of a policy of severity, but in reality there is every reason to believe that the government long hesitated to adopt these measures. The general tone adopted by the revolutionists with regard to the reforms was that they were designed as a trap to mislead the unwary public. We find Bakunin stating in a letter to Turgenev in 1862 that the much-talked-about project for judicial reform was designed merely to distract attention from martial law.[14] One of the controversial issues in this confused period was the closing of the Sunday schools, on the charge that they were being used for subversion. We find one of the revolutionary leaders, Ishutin, commenting on the use to which the Sunday schools could be put: "We will make revolutionists out of these youngsters."[15]

We have already seen that even during the honeymoon of the reforming period in the first years of Alexander II, the institutions of higher learning had been invaded by a spirit of unrest, and many persons were recruited and, as Pisarev pointed out, weaned away from serious occupation with learning. Their minds were entirely taken up with plans for a Utopia, and those plans involved the overthrow of the existing order. A curious incident is recorded in the evidence of Obruchev, one of the persons charged in the student revolts of 1861. Apparently on instructions from the Emperor, Obruchev was visited by the Prince of Oldenburg, with a view to discussing, if possible, the reasons for the discontent. The young man was brought before the Prince, who asked him about his personal life and his revo-

[13] Lemke, *Ocherki osvoboditel'nago*, 217.
[14] *Ibid.*, 170–71.
[15] Venturi, *Il populismo russo*, I, 544.

lutionary activities. In the midst of the conversation, Obruchev was interrupted by the Prince, who asked him what the revolutionists really wanted. "The press is free; people write what they want—why even Chernyshevskii is not restricted. What is it you want; is it a constitution?"[16]

It seems to me that these facts indicate reasonably honest intentions of the government to pursue the program of reform, with a view to meeting public opinion halfway, but Alexander found himself confronted with the irreconcilable hostility of the "intelligentsia" and found no support from public opinion for his program of moderation.[17] The only voices heard were those demanding the most radical changes, and the effort to find a solution that would be acceptable to all parties led Alexander to seek the support of the bureaucracy. This group was not disinterested and was certain to prejudice the program of reform in the eyes of the educated public. It would appear, therefore, that the government reached an impasse for which there was no solution, and that unless and until there arose in Russia a moderate and conservative faction, there was no element of the population on which Alexander could rely for support and co-operation (except the landowning nobility). This seems to have been the major tragedy of Alexander's life.

The inability of the government to attract into its service the best minds and the resulting gulf that developed between the bureaucracy and the intelligentsia are illustrated by the experience of Serno-Solov'evich, a young noble who served with the Provincial Committee on Peasant Affairs for the province of Kaluga and later in the Chancery of the State Council. Becoming disillusioned and disheartened at the opposition that his plans met in official circles, he resigned in 1859 and was arrested in 1861 on suspicion of being linked with the sub-

16 Lemke, *Ocherki osvoboditel'nago*, 386–87.
17 See also the conversation of Alexander with Golokhvastov, marshall of the nobility of Zvenigorod, in which the Emperor is quoted as saying he would gladly "bestow any constitution that would be useful [to the country] if he were not afraid that Russia would fall apart the next day." *Obshchestvennoe Dvizhenie pri Aleksandre II*, 134.

versive movement.[18] He was detained in prison for upwards of two years, and during this period he gave much thought to the problems of Russian life. He acknowledged in 1864 that he had changed some of his views and had come to the conclusion that what was most needed in Russia's political life was the co-operation of the thinking class of Russians with the government. He summed it up in these words: "A free man who seriously desires the good of his country must not separate himself from the government but keep closely in touch with it."[19]

The difficulty of Alexander in finding a class to which he could appeal is recognized by the author of *Obshchestvennoe Dvizhenie*, who says:

> So, having undertaken a series of broad, fundamental reforms, which assumed a liberal and even radical character in relation to the formerly existing regime, he still clung to the outmoded bureaucratic regime and could not make up his mind to trust either of the public trends and tendencies which had been roused and called into life by himself.
> Hence the insecurity and uncertainty of his position. Having surrounded himself with a group of courtiers and bureaucrats, he actually had no one to rely on—a fact of which he complained time and again. Hence the blind struggle which lasted through his reign and brought him finally to a tragic end.[20]

There was no apparent means by which the gulf between the sovereign and his people could be closed.

The second period mentioned by Milyukov as a possible time of reconciliation between the two opposing sides—the period of the eighties—presents a somewhat different problem. By this time the revolutionary psychology seemed to have been fixed, and the revolutionists seemed to be the victims of their intellectual theories. In 1885, Lev Tikhomirov, who had been secretary

---

[18] Lemke, *Ocherki osvoboditel'nago*, 185–86.
[19] *Ibid.*, 210–11.
[20] Page 85.

of the general committee of the *Narodnaya Volya,* which had planned the assassination of Alexander II, decided to break with his revolutionary colleagues, in particular with Lavrov, his fellow editor of *Vyestnik Narodnoi Voli.* During his years of exile Tikhomirov had taken stock of the revolutionary movement and had come to certain inescapable conclusions; one was that "in the Russian way of thinking there are two characteristic sides, the want of feeling or want of regard for the fact, and the opposite, an unlimited faith in theory and hypothesis."[21] This Tikhomirov ascribed to the immaturity of the Russian mind. Another thing he noted is that the revolutionary activists were for the most part recruited in institutions of learning, many of them in the Gymnasia (we have already noted this phenomenon dating from the Crimean War). The result was that young persons, carried away by the plausible arguments and the attractive Utopias of the revolutionists, were drawn into the movement before their minds were capable of forming sound views. Once in the movement they found it impossible to develop a critical attitude of mind or to question the fundamental ideas of their associates. The result was not only that they neglected to pursue the studies which might have made some contribution to Russian life, but that they found themselves caught in a machine from which there was no escape.

Tikhomirov deplored this misdirected energy and also challenged the usefulness of the thinking of these votaries, which was mostly concerned with impractical, fantastic projects which had little relation to Russian life. The weakness that we found back in the sixties was still prevalent in the eighties; i.e., the older generation either sympathized with the younger or at least feared to oppose any of its ideas.[22] The most serious charge, however, that Tikhomirov leveled against the revolutionists concerned their complete break with all established principles of morality. His own break with Lavrov was an extreme one. The latter refused to print in the valedictory any

[21] Tikhomirov, *Pochemu ya perestal,* 52–53.
[22] *Ibid.,* 58–59.

criticism of revolutionary ideas and apparently insisted that Tikhomirov, by his break, had put himself outside the revolutionary circle and was therefore to be treated as an enemy. This incident, one is tempted to say, is an early indication of the emergence in revolutionary psychology of a discipline imposed on its members, including a rigid censorship that refused to allow members the right to make up their own minds. Tikhomirov's condemnation of such a spirit has a tragic interest in view of the close discipline imposed later by the Communist party.

> In a moral sense I discover plainly that the ideas of Lavrov lead merely in some degree to a revival of a quite primitive, imperfect kind of morality. Instead of a universal brotherhood and a higher justice which governs all private interests (even those of his group), Lavrov revives the Old Testament group solidarity. According to this, within the group (or party) the closest relations develop, but all the rest, the outer world so to speak, consists of some goys and giaours; it comes about that they are looked on as enemies, as Nyemtsy, Nemy (the dumb), with whom the Lavrovs cannot make common cause (there is no common language). Doubtless this outer world they have in mind to "save," but in the first place, as a mass, as mankind, while individuals, who come under the heading of "enemies of socialism," have no right to expect justice. In their attitude towards the latter, as is evident from the above, the revolutionaries permit themselves to drop all ideas of honor. In the matter of "saving," neither honesty nor regard is shown the outer world.[23]

The whole spirit that had apparently come to dominate the revolutionary movement—that the individual did not have the right to an opinion of his own—admitted a strict censorship. The revolutionaries' moral code involved absolute renunciation of private judgment in the question of right and wrong—an obligation that was a contradiction to the party's own principles.

[23] *Ibid.*, 108–109.

In other words, the revolutionary movement attempted to apply a double standard, and, in view of the divisions of the world into two opposing camps, there was a reversion to primitive pre-Christian times. We have the logical outcome of the nihilism of the sixties. It amounts to nothing less than the introduction into the revolutionary movement of a moral code that outraged prevailing moral ideas; the revolutionists professed lofty ideals of liberty, of thought, of conscience, at the same time that they denied these things to their own members. Tikhomirov claimed that their purpose was "to silence the voice of reason and conscience," while the new order which they proclaimed took the country not forward but backward.[24]

We thus see that Milyukov's claim that the government alone was responsible for failure to secure the co-operation of all classes is not borne out by the facts. This inability to secure a middle ground between conflicting interests also hindered the so-called liberal movement at the beginning of the twentieth century. It was impossible, as we have seen, to find any basis of co-operation or compromise between the government and the Duma. Maklakov, in his reminiscences, poses the question in a very pertinent form. He assumes, apparently, a parliamentary system like that in England, where policy is made by compromises between the opposing interests. Maklakov says:

> Out of the conflict of interests of different professions, out of the duality of the nature of man, as from every antimony—there is one issue, their synthesis; that is, a compromise between them which would be acceptable to both. Every struggle ought to end in peace. But peace is an agreement between two former antagonists. On what basis can it come about in spite of diversity of interests? Not by the victory of the "strongest" and the forced submission to him [of the conquered]; not by the capricious "will" of the "majority." Voluntary agreement of former opponents can be based only on the recognition of the mutual

[24] *Ibid.*, 112–16. Tikhomirov quotes Lavrov as having said: "Comrades ought to shadow all members on the street to their bedrooms and severely punish all violations of rules."

interests of both, i.e., on justice. The existence of justice is known to all. The Romans called it "aequitas," which in addition to justice meant also equality. They expressed this in a more explicit formula, "Do not to others what you would not like them to do to you." "Justice" is a synthesis between renunciation of oneself for others and the animal nature which strives to take things away from others for oneself.[25]

A factor that militated against the attainment of any other solution than a violent one was the failure of Russian society to accept the rule of law as the basis of life. Farsighted jurists had advocated the inauguration of a system by which government would proceed in accordance with fundamental law, to which even the monarch would be subject, but Russian society showed a strange indifference to constitutional rights. In the eighteenth century, reformers had claimed that the great need of the peasants was to have their dues fixed by law, but this was forgotten in the general enthusiasm for more far-reaching reforms. We have seen that Turgenev lost interest in a constitution as a prelude to reform and that two of the most influential writers of the latter part of the century also indicated a profound indifference. Chernyshevskii, while admitting that the Western European countries were far ahead of Russia in matters of personal liberty and inviolability, claimed that liberty had done the poor people in those countries little good: "The present conditions for nine-tenths of the population of England and France is so abnormal and wretched that of necessity there must appear new tendencies by which the disadvantages of the former, one-sided ideal would be removed."[26] Somewhat later, Mikhailovskii claimed that he was not interested in securing privileges guaranteed by any law or constitution. One can well see why the reform of the courts in 1864 made scarcely a ripple on Russian life.

A unique feature of the revolutionary intelligentsia was their

[25] *Iz Vospominanii*, 381–82.
[26] *Izbrannye Ekonomisheskie Proizvedeniia*, I, 103–107. "New tendencies" is probably Aesopian language for "a revolution."

243

peculiar concept of truth. The Western world, through long intellectual travail, has passed from its reliance on myths for an explanation of natural phenomena and has come to accept the view that the world is best understood by eliminating from our thoughts all subjective experiences and taking a completely detached view, in which emotional factors play as small a part as possible. The early Greek thinkers pointed the way and revealed that the only universal language is that of reason. Mankind has been endeavoring, with varying success, to follow this path and to penetrate the secrets of the universe by observation and contemplation, in a spirit of complete detachment undisturbed by emotions or prejudices. In human affairs, however, this is extremely difficult, since our prejudices and preferences, our hopes and yearnings, are inextricably bound up with our mental process. As one Russian writer, Mikhailovskii, expressed it, "One cannot have a sociology at all without a Utopia." Western man has endeavored to reconcile the claims of pure reason with the need to humanize it by admitting some play of feeling in order to interpret experience. In general, therefore, pure reason in human affairs remains merely an ideal toward which we strive.

The Russian intelligentsia, however, has not been able to shake itself free from its earlier predilection for explanations that would satisfy its emotional needs. At an early stage in the nineteenth century it abandoned the belief that empirical science can give us a sound philosophy, that there are emotional needs that must be satisfied by philosophy. The most insistent of these needs concerned a romantic sympathy with the long-abused peasant, and it came to be regarded as self-evident that truth in human affairs must in some way or other promote the welfare of the common man. This was achieved by invoking a higher truth than that of reason, namely, one that took into account the whole of man's nature, for which the intelligentsia thought it found justification in Hegel. From this it was but a step to the belief that the pure truth discovered by reason must be superseded by a higher truth. For this assumption, the Russians could appeal to Engels, who said, "What is false in the formal economic sense may be true in the world historical sense."[27] This might be seconded by a reference to Aristotle, who stated that poetry has a higher claim to truth than history. Applied, however, by the Russians in their reckless way, this theory resulted in a topsy-turvy view of human affairs, where truth becomes that which one wishes to be true rather than what is actually true, a curious contrast to the claim of Russian writers that their literature is essentially realistic. This subject was discussed at some length by Berdyaev in his articles in *Vyekhi,* and he ends with the statement, written in 1909, that "what we need most at the present time is a recognition of the value of truth itself." Preoccupied as he was with the goal toward which he was working, the Russian thinker forgot or failed to see that he was no longer speaking the universal language of reason and to a great degree was diverging from the well-trodden road of western thought.

Russian thought, and hence Russian politics, in the latter part of the nineteenth century and the beginning of the twentieth century was dominated by the intelligentsia, and we have seen that it was a force with scarcely a parallel elsewhere. Western writers are inclined to confuse the intelligentsia with the "intelligent" in the sense of "educated" people.[28] Nothing could be further from the truth. Beginning with the relaxation of censorship and restriction on the universities that came in the wake of the Crimean War, there came into existence in many of the educational institutions in Russia, groups of persons dedicated to the overthrow of the existing order. These in time separated themselves from the rank and file of the students, as described by Pisarev. These groups multiplied, recruited wide-

[27] Cited by N. Pokrovskii in his *Leninizm i Russkaya Istoriya,* 304.
[28] *Origins of Russian Communism,* 16–17. "Western people would make a mistake if they identified the Russian intelligentsia with those in the west who are known as 'intellectuals.' Many Russian scholars and writers certainly could not be reckoned as belonging to the intelligentsia in the strict sense of the word. Our intelligentsia were a group formed out of various social classes, held together by ideas and not sharing a common profession or economic status."

ly, and came eventually to form conspiratorial circles with wide, though secret connection. Arrests, exiles, and executions in ordinary times might reduce their numbers; but only full concentration of the government's powers of detection and coercion would suppress them; relaxation allowed them once more to multiply. By the end of the century they had become almost a permanent fixture in all educational institutions above the elementary level. E. J. Dillon, describing the universities during the eighties, tells of "one [student] in particular who frankly admitted that he never opened a book nor attended a lecture but simply lived for and on the coming revolution."[29]

The predisposition of the Russian intelligentsia to seek extremes led its members to endow scientific hypotheses and philosophical theories with the character of dogmas. This is emphasized by Berdyaev in his *Origins of Russian Communism*.[30] This may be a relic of Russian religious past. It has given to all political and religious disagreements a character of savage intolerance that ill accords with the claims of revolutionary writers to be "scientific." We might cite as a parallel the religious sects, which have clung with utmost tenacity to their pacifist and non-violence ideas and have not hesitated to face the most brutal forms of coercion attempted by the government. The veneration in which basic principles are held is also illustrated by a pronouncement of Stalin in 1932 censuring the editors of *Proletarskaya Revolyutsiya* for having published an article by Sluitskii. He charged that "you [the editors] are resolved anew to draw people into a discussion on questions that are an axiom of Bolshevism."[31]

We can, perhaps, understand the attitude of the revolutionary groups whose program was one of war *à l'outrance* with the existing regimes. But the moderates were carried along with the stream and had to bid for popular support by equal intransigence.[32] In the revolution of 1905, the Kadets, who rep-

29 *The Eclipse of Russia*, 67.
30 Page 18.
31 Letter to the editors of *Proletarskaya Revolyutsiya*, *Sochineniya*, XIII, 85.

resented the liberal element, refused to accept the constitution and insisted on regarding themselves as "the opposition," claiming to represent the "popular will" and seeking to coerce the government into acknowledging their power by introducing far-reaching modifications into the constitution and allowing the party to take over control of the administration. Some would have gone so far as to turn the Duma into a constituent assembly with power to depose the monarch and usher in a republican regime. There was thus no possibility of compromise or collaboration between the government and the moderates. Since the fanatical leaders refused any middle ground, there was no place in the battlefield for the moderates, who were pushed ruthlessly aside.

We must not assume that the Russian people were all fanatics and radicals bent on sweeping away the existing order. There is another side to the picture. In her revealing book, *Outlines of the History of Education in Russia and the Soviet Union*, Madame Kaidanova has given us an insight into the lives of dozens of devoted persons in the field of education—men and women who had caught a vision of the ameliorative role of education in transforming human society and gave their lives and energies unsparingly to the spread of knowledge. These people accepted the existing regime as they found it and labored in the belief that the greatest and most enduring changes in man come through slow and laborious effort, often in obscure corners, and that fruitful ideas and creative efforts are essentially the work of the individual, the sum total of whose contribution makes human progress. But their sacrifices were given without thought of securing political power to force the pace. They were content with the slow transformation of the world by a process of evolution. Much the same might be said of the work of the *zemstva*.

But the Russian intelligentsia was not content with this kind

<hr>

[32] Berdyaev, *Origins*, 37. "The liberal tradition has always been weak in Russia and . . . we have never had a liberalism with moral authority, or which gave any inspiration."

of progress. Professing to regard the Western world as degenerate and effete, since its thinkers were content to project their Utopias to some distant time in the future,

That far-off divine event,
Towards which the whole creation moves,

the Russian insisted on attaining his Utopia at once by direct action, i.e., by forcing the world to conform to his pattern. There was some talk, perhaps, of human liberty, of law and constitutions, but it does not seem that the revolutionary writers had much confidence in the ability of man, either individually or collectively, to arrive at his goal without being cajoled, guided, or forced by some higher power—either an autocrat or an elite of some kind. At first they were content to rely on working through the autocrat, by persuasion or by terrorism, to inaugurate their Utopia; but in time this method gave way to the idea of replacing that legal power by the creation of an elite, and from the sixties on we see the slow molding of these groups (sometimes mutually hostile)—at first, perhaps, confused, toying with constitutional ideas, with mild reforms to speed up the processes of evolution, "to give history a push" in the words of Zhelyabov. But this gave way eventually to the idea of attaining the ideal state through violent seizure of power, to enable the intelligentsia to organize the ideal society to suit its aims, by ruthless suppression of the individual and by subordinating him to the purposes of the state. Such a creed finds an admirable foundation in the teachings of Marx.

Of these two trends, sometimes in sharp conflict, the second eventually won out and pushed the other ruthlessly aside. There were protests from time to time and appeals to return to the more peaceful method which, in general, had been followed by Western Europe. But the warnings, as we have seen in the case of Tikhomirov and the authors of *Vyekhi*, made slight impression. The influence of Western Europe was too weak, and force and direct action had a greater appeal to the Russian mind. The question that inevitably arises is, if these same trends are

applied on a world-wide scale, does not this very moderation
and tolerance, humanitarianism, and renunciation of coercion
and deception, which are generally the ideals of the West, ex-
pose it to a force free from these restraining influences? Can
civilization which relies on moral appeals avail with those who
accept none of the scruples of civilized men? In a world of
naked force, is the civilized man doomed to go under as the
civilized Roman went down before the relatively uncivilized
barbarian in the fourth century of our era?

Amid this clash of forces we can be sure of one thing—that
neither monarch, nor responsible official ever lost sight of the
need of force to hold together the enormous extent and polyglot character of imperial Russia. To rule this vast area, with
its diverse population won by long and ceaseless effort, has
constantly strained the resources of the government. Although
the Russians might listen to the siren call of reduced armaments
or play with the idea of relaxing the bonds by which the subject
races were held, no patriotic Russian could contemplate with
equanimity the loss of power to protect or expand their pos-
sessions entailed in such reduction or the final severing of the
bonds by which their polyglot empire was held together.

In February, 1917, these trends moved relentlessly to their
denouement. The final act was the refusal of the Tsar's brother,
Mikhail, to receive the crown which had fallen so ingloriously
and precipitately from the brow of Nicholas; the Kadet leader,
Milyukov, endeavoring to persuade the prince to accept it,
was aghast at the alternatives.

His head shining white like the moon, his face gray with lack
of sleep, his voice hoarse from making speeches in the barracks
and public meetings, he [Milyukov] did not so much speak his
words as croak them in a throaty rattle.

"If you decline . . . Your Highness . . . it will be the end.
Because Russia . . . is losing . . . its helmsman. . . .The monarch
is that helmsman. . . . The only pilot of the ship of state . . .
the Russian masses . . . around what else can they rally? If you

decline . . . there will be chaos . . . anarchy . . . rivers of blood.
. . . The monarch . . . is the single focus. . . . The sole one that
people know. . . . The only universally recognized concept of
power, so far in Russia. . . . If you refuse . . . there will be utter
collapse . . . horrible to contemplate . . . because there will be
. . . no force in oaths . . . there will be no government . . . no
Russia . . . there will be nothing."[33]

The account of the fateful meeting continues:

Milyukov seemed to break off. . . . He did not want to go on,
he could not, he hated to finish. This man, ordinarily so deferential and moderate, would let no one finish; he brushed aside
all those protesting, Rodzianko, Kerenskii, everyone. . . . In
the schoolroom of the twelve-year-old daughter of Prince Putyatin, V. D. Nabokov and B. E. Nolde sat down at a desk and
on a lined sheet of an exercise book wrote out the act of abdica-
tion ending a three-century-old dynasty. At four o'clock in the
morning, the Grand Duke sat down at the same desk and affixed
his signature. Pavel Nikolayevich [Milyukov] was not present
at that scene—the sight of the head of Hasdrubal was too much
for him. Without waiting for breakfast at Millionovna, he left
for home. He announced that he would not take part in the
government. In his soul was deep, impenetrable despair.[34]

Thus the Romanov dynasty passed into history, and Russia,
for the second time in a generation, plunged into a revolution
whose consequences no one could foresee.

[33] V. Shulgin, *Dni*, 237–38. Cited by M. Aldanov in *P. N. Milyukov,
Sbornik materialov*, 29.
[34] The last paragraph is Aldanov's own, based on the account of one of
the participants in the scene.

Bibliography

CHAPTER I

General Account of Reforms

Dzhanshiev, Grigorii Avetovich. *Epokha Velikikh Reform; Isto-richeskiya Spravki.* 2nd edition. Moscow, 1896 and 1898.

Tatishchev, S. S. *Imperator Aleksandr Vtoroi; Ego Zhizn i Tsar-stvovanie.* 2 vols. St. Petersburg, 1903.

Peasants

Byelokonskii, I. P. "Krest'yanstvo i Narodnoe Obrazovanie," *Velikaya Reforma,* Vol. VI.

Chernyshevskii, N. G. *Izbrannye Ekonomicheskie Proizvedeniia.* 3 vols. Ed. by I. D. Udal'tsov. Moscow, 1948–49.

Dietze, Constantin von. *Stolypinsche Agrarreform und Feldgemeinschaft.* Leipzig and Berlin, 1920.

Dorosch, Henry. *The Russian Agrarian Reform.* Philadelphia, 1937.

Druzhinin, N. M. *Gosudarstvennye Krest'yane i Reforma P. D. Kiseleva.* Vol. I. Moscow and Leningrad, 1946.

Dzhivilegov, A. K., S. P. Mel'gunov, and B. I. Picheta, eds. *Velikaya Reforma.* 6 vols. Moscow, 1911.

Engelman, Johann. *Geschichte der Leibeigenschaft in Russland.* Leipzig, 1884.

Haxthausen, A. *Studien Über die Inneren Zustände, das Volksleben*

251

und insbesondere die Ländlichen Einrichtungen Russlands. 3 vols. Hanover, 1847, Berlin, 1852.

Kornilov, A. A. *Krest'yanskaya Reforma.* St. Petersburg, 1905.

——. "Krest'yanskoe Samoupravlenie po Polozheniyu 19 Fevrala," *Velikaya Reforma,* Vol. VI.

Koshelev, A. I. "Obshchinnoe Pozemel'noe Vladenie," *Russkaya Besyeda,* Fasc. VIII (1858).

Kranikhfel'd, V. P. "Poreformennoe Krest'yanstvo v Belletristike," *Velikaya Reforma,* Vol. VI.

Kuz'min-Karatayev, V. D. "Krest'yanstvo i Zemstvo," *Velikaya Reforma,* Vol. VI.

Leont'ev, A. A. "Zakonodatel'stvo o Krest'yanakh Posle Reforma," *Velikaya Reforma,* Vol. VI.

Lyashchenko, P. I. *History of the National Economy of Russia to the 1917 Revolution.* New York, 1949.

Manuilov, A. A. "Reforma 19 Fevrala i Obshchinnoe Zemlevladenie," *Velikaya Reforma,* Vol. VI.

Maslov, Piotr Pavlovich. *Agrarnyi Vopros v Rossii (Usloviya Razvitiya Krest'yanskago Sosloviya v Rossii).* St. Petersburg, 1906.

——. *Krest'yanskoe Dvizhenie: Obshchestvennoe Dvizhenie Rossii.* St. Petersburg, 1909–12.

——. *Krest'yanskoe Dvizhenie v Rossii do 1905-g (Agrarnyi vopros v Rossii).* Moscow, 1924.

——. *Krest'yanskoe Dvizhenie v Rossii v Epokhu Pervoi Revolyutsii (Agrarnyi Vopros v Rossii).* Moscow, 1924.

Mavor, J. *An Economic History of Russia.* 2 vols. New York, 1925.

Maynard, John. *Russia in Flux: Before October.* London, 1941.

——. *The Russian Peasant and Other Studies.* London, 1942.

Owen, Launcelot A. *The Russian Peasant Movement, 1906–1917* Foreword by Sir Bernard Pares. London, 1937.

Pyeshekhonov, A. V. "Ekonomicheskoe Polozhenie Krest'yan v Poreformennoe Vremya," *Velikaya Reforma,* Vol. VI.

Robinson, G. T. *Rural Russia Under the Old Regime.* New York, 1932.

Semevskii, V. I. *Krest'yanskii Vopros v Rossii v XVIII i Pervoi Polovine XIX Veka.* 2 vols. St. Petersburg, 1888.

Stepniak (Sergiei Mikhailovich Kravchinskii). *The Russian Peasantry, Their Agrarian Condition, Social Life, and Religion.* London, 1905.

Bibliography

Tengoborski, M. L. *Études sur les Forces Productives de la Russie.* 4 vols. Paris, 1852.
Timoshenko, Vladimir P. "The Agrarian Policies of Russia and the Wars," *Agricultural History* (1943).
Vyetrinskii, Ch. "Kolokol i Krest'yanskaya Reforma," *Velikaya Reforma,* Vol. IV.

Courts

Davydov, N. V., and N. N. Polyanskii, eds. *Sudebnaya Reforma.* Moscow, 1915.
Dostoyevskii, F. M. *The Diary of a Writer.* 2 vols. Trans. by Boris Brasol. New York, 1949.
———. *Dnevnik Pisatelia.* 3 vols. Paris, n.d.
Kucherov, Samuel. *Courts, Lawyers, and Trials Under the Last Three Tsars* (Foreword by Michael Karpovich). New York, 1953.

Zemstva

Veselovskii, Boris Borisovich. *Istoriya Zemstva za Sorok Lyet.* 4 vols. St. Petersburg, 1909.
Witte, Count S. Iu. *Samoderzhavie i Zemstvo: Predislovie Cherevanina.* St. Petersburg, 1908.
Zak, L. S. "Zemstvo i Krestyanskoe Khozyaistvo," *Russkaya Mysl'* (April, 1901).

CHAPTER II

Alekseyev, N. A., ed. *Protsess N. G. Chernyshevskogo: Arkhivnye Dokumenty.* Saratov, 1939.
Carr, E. H. *Michael Bakunin.* London, 1937.
Chernyshevskii. *Polnoe Sobranie Sochinenii.* 15 vols. Moscow, 1939.
Dostoyevskii. *The Diary of a Writer.*
———. *Dnevnik Pisatelia.*
Engelhardt, Nikolai Aleksandrovich. *Ocherki Istorii Russkoi Tsenzury v Sviazi s Razvitiem Pechati, 1703–1903.* St. Petersburg, 1904.
Evgen'ev-Maksimov, V. *Sovremennik pri Chernyshevskom i Dobrolyubovye.* Gosizdat, 1936.
Herzen, A. *My Past and Thoughts: The Memoirs of Alexander Herzen.* 6 vols. London, 1924–27.

253

——. *Polnoe Sobranie Sochinenii i Pisem.* 21 vols. Ed. by M. K. Lemke. Petrograd, 1919–23.

Kaidanova, Ol'ga Vladimirovna. *Ocherki po Istorii Narodnogo Obrazovaniya v Rossii i S. S. S. R. na Osnove Lichnogo Opyta i Nablyudeniya.* 2 vols. Berlin, 1938.

Labry, Raoul. *Alexandre Ivanovic Herzen, 1812–1870: Essai sur La Formation et le Développement de ses idées.* Paris, 1928.

Lemke, Mikhail Konstantinovich. *Epokha Tsenzurnykh Reform, 1859–1865.* St. Petersburg, 1904.

——. *Politichiskie Protsessi v Rossii 1860-kh godov.* Petrograd, 1923.

Novich, I. *Zhizn' Chernyshevskogo.* Moscow, 1939.

Shelgunov, N. V. *Vospominaniia.* Ed. by A. A. Shilov. Moscow and Petrograd, 1923.

Tatishchev. *Imperator Aleksandr Vtoroi.*

Tikhomirov, L. *Russia: Political and Social.* 2 vols. London, 1892.

Venturi, Franco. *Il Populismo Russo.* 2 vols. Torino, 1952.

CHAPTER III

Brodskii, N. I., and I. N. Kubikov. *Russkaya Literatura: Sbornik literatur'nykh Proizvyedenii i kriticheskikh statei.* Moscow, 1934.

Byelinskii, V. G. *Sochineniia V. G. Bielinskago.* 4 vols. St. Petersburg, 1907.

Dobrolyubov, N. A. *Sochineniya.* 4 vols. St. Petersburg, 1876.

Dragomanov, Michail. *Michail Bakunins Sozial-Politischer Briefsechsel mit Alexander Herzen und Ogarow.* Stuttgart, 1895.

Engelhardt. *Ocherki Istorii Russkoi Tsenzury v Sviazi s Razvitiem Pechati, 1703–1903.*

Frank, S. L. (and others). *Vyekhi.* St. Petersburg, 1909.

Gogol, Nikolai. *Sobranie Sochinenii.* 6 vols. Moscow, 1952.

Herzen. *My Past and Thoughts.*

——. *Polnoe Sobranie Sochinenii i Pisem.*

Labry. *Alexandre Ivanovic Herzen.*

Ovsyaniko-Kulikovskii, Dmitrii Nikolaevich. *Istoriya Russkoi Intelligentsii, Sobranie Sochinenii.* 9 vols. St. Petersburg, 1909–11.

Pisarev, D. I. *Sochineniya.* 6 vols. St. Petersburg, 1909.

Plotkin, L. A. *Pisarev i Literaturni-Obshchestvennoe Dvizhenie shestidasyatykh Godov.* Leningrad and Moscow, 1945.

Bibliography

Stepniak (Kravchinskii). *The Career of a Nihilist.* New York, 1889.
————. *Underground Russia.* London, 1883.
Venturi. *Il Populismo Russo.*

CHAPTER IV

Akimov, Vladimir Petrovich. *Materialy Dlya Kharakeristiki Razvitiya Rossiiskoi Sotsial'-Demokraticheskoi Rabochei Partii.* Geneva, 1904.

Alekseyev, ed. *Protsess N. G. Chernyshevskogo.*

Annenskii, N. F. "N. G. Chernyshevskii i Krest'yanskaya Reforma," *Velikaya Reforma,* Vol. IV.

Breshkovskaya, Katerina. *Hidden Springs of the Russian Revolution.* Stanford, 1931.

Chernyshevskaia-Bystrova, N. M. *Letopis' Zhizni i Deyatel'nosti N. G. Chernyshevskogo.* Moscow and Leningrad, 1933.

Chernyshevskii. *Chto Delat'?* Moscow, 1947.

————. *What Is to Be Done?* Boston, 1886.

————. *Izbrannye Ekonomicheskie Proizvedeniia.*

————. *Izbrannye Sochineniia v Piati Tomakh.* 5 vols. Moscow and Leningrad, 1928–31.

————. *Kriticheskie Stat'i.* St. Petersburg, 1893.

————. *Literaturnoe Nasledie.* 3 vols. Moscow and Leningrad, 1928–30.

————. *Polnoe Sobranie Sochinenii.*

Dostoyevskii. *The Diary of a Writer.*

————. *Dnevnik Pisatelia.*

Druzhinin. *Gosudarstvennye Krest'yane i Reforma P. D. Kiseleva.*

Herzen. *Polnoe Sobranie Sochinenii i Pisem.*

Ivanov-Razumnik, R. V. *Istoriya russkoi obshchestvennoi mysli.* 2 vols. St. Petersburg, 1908.

Koz'min, B. P. "N. G. Chernyshevskii v III Otedelenie," *Krasnyi Arkhiv,* Fasc. xxix (1928).

Kropotkin, Peter. *Memoirs of a Revolutionist.* Boston and New York, 1930.

Labry. *Alexandre Ivanovic Herzen.*

Lavrov, Pierre. *Lettres Historiques.* Trans. by Mary Goldsmith. Paris, 1903.

Lebedev, V. I., ed. *Reformy Petra.* Moscow, 1937.

Lemke. *Politichiskie Protsessi v Rossii 1860–kh godov.*

255

The Russian Intelligentsia

Materialy Dlya Istorii Russkago Sotsial'no-Revolyutsionnogo Dvizheniya 1–16. 16 vols. 1893.

Mikhailovskii, N. K. *Geroi i Tolpa.* 5 vols. St. Petersburg, 1887–88.

Na Slavnom Postu: Posvyashchennyi N. K. Mikhailovskomu. St. Petersburg, 1905.

Novich, *Zhizn' Chernyshevskogo.*

Pazhitnov, K. A. *Razvitie Sotsialisticheskikh Idei v Rossii.* Petrograd, 1924.

Semevskii. *Krest'yanskii Vopros v Rossii v XVIII i Pervoi Polovine XIX Veka.*

Shchapov, A. P. *Sochineniya A. P. Shchapova.* 3 vols. St. Petersburg, 1906.

Shelgunov. *Vospominaniia.*

Shilov, A. "N. G. Chernyshevskii v Doneseniiakh Agentov Ill Otdeleniia," *Krasnyi Arkhiv,* Fasc. I (1926).

Tengoborski. *Études sur les Forces Productives de la Russie.*

Turgenev, Nikolai. *La Russie et les Russes.* 3 vols. Brussels, 1847.

Velikaya Reforma, 1861–19 Fevr. 1911. Sbornik Statei. 6 vols. Moscow, 1911.

Venturi. *Il Populismo Russo.*

Volgin, V. P. *Ocherki po Istorii Sotsializma. Izdanie 4–e. Dopolnennoe.* Moscow, 1935.

CHAPTER V

Censorship

Dzhanshiev, G. A. *Epokha velikikh reform; istoricheskiya spravki.* Moscow, 1898.

Engelhardt. *Ocherki Istorii Russkoi Tsenzury v Sviazi s Razvitiem Pechati, 1703–1903.*

Kennan, George. *Siberia and the Exile System.* 2 vols. New York, 1891.

Lemke. *Epokha Tsenzurnykh Reform.*

——. *Ocherki po Istorii Russkoi Tsensury i Zhurnalistiki XIX stolietiya.* St. Petersburg, 1904.

Nagradow, W. J. *Moderne Russische Zensur und Presse vor und Hinter den Coulissen.* Berlin, 1894.

Nikitenko, Aleksandr Vasil'evich. *Zapiski i Dnevnik, A. V. Nikitenko.* 3 vols. St. Petersburg, 1893.

Bibliography

[Shchebal'skii, Petr Karlovich, ed.]. *Istoricheskie Svyedeniya o Tsenzure v Rossii.* St. Petersburg, 1862.

Shchebal'skii, ed. "Materialy Dlya Istorii Russkoi Tsenzury," *Besyedy v Obshchestvye Lyubitelei Rossiiskoi Slovestnosti* (1871).

Skabichevskii, A. M. *Ocherki Istorii Russkoi Tsenzur'i.* St. Petersburg, 1892.

Sukhomlinov, M. I. "Materialy Dlya Istorii Russkoi Tsenzury," *Besyedy v Obshchestvye Lyubitelei Rossiiskoi Slovestnosti,* Vol. III, Nos. 8–9.

Press

Basilevskii, B., ed. *Revolyutsionnaya Zhurnalistika Semidesyatykh Godov.* Paris, 1905.

Dement'ev, A. G. *Ocherki po Istorii Russkoi Zhurnalistiki 1840–1850 gg.* Moscow, 1951.

Ershov, E. *Istorii Russkoi Zhurnalistiki i Obshchestvennosti.* Obrazovanie, 1906.

Evgen'ev-Maksimov. *Sovremennik pri Chernyshevskom i Dobrolyubovye.*

——. *Sovremennik v 40–e–50–e–gg.* Leningrad, 1934.

——., and G. Tizengauzen. *Poslyednie Gody "Sovremennika."* Leningrad, 1939.

Feoktistov, Evgenii Mikhailovich. *Vospominaniya.* Leningrad, 1929.

Greening, Irene. *Die Russische Öffentliche Meinung und Ihre Stellung zu den Groszmachten, 1878–1894.* Berlin, 1929.

Kallash, V. "Ocherki po Istorii Russkoi Zhurnalistiki," *Russkaya Mysl'* (1902).

Klevenskii, M. M., E. N. Kushevaya, and O. P. Markovaya, eds. *Russkaya Podpol'naya i Zarubezhnaya Pechat'.* Moscow, 1935.

Kluge, Ernfried Eduard. *Die Russische Revolutionäre Presse in der Zweiten Hälfte des Neunzehnten Jahrhunderts, 1855–1905.* Zurich, 1948.

Kuz'min, D. (E. E. Kolosov). *Narodovol'cheskaia Zhurnalistika, s Poslesloviem V. Figner.* Moscow, 1930.

Lanin, E. B. *Russian Characteristics.* London, 1892.

Lemke. *Ocherki Osvoboditel'nago Dvizheniya Shestidesyatykh Godov.* St. Petersburg, 1908.

Lenin, V. I., ed. *Iskra* (December, 1900 to October, 1905).

Nikitin, S. *Zhurnalistika, Pamyatniki Obshchestvenno-Politicheskoi Mysli.* Moscow, 1940.

Rosenberg, Vladimir Aleksandrovich. *Iz Istorii Russkoi Pechati, 1863–1918.* Prague, 1924.

"Revoliutsionnoe Sotsial'no-Politicheskoe Obrozrienie," *Vyestnik Narodnoi Voli*, Vol. V. (1885–86).

CHAPTER VI

Aptekman, O. V. *Obshchestvo "Zemlya i Volya" 70-kh godov.* Petrograd, 1924.

Bakunin, M. A. *Izbrannye Sochineniya.* 5 vols. St. Petersburg, 1920–22.

Berdyaev, N. A. *Sinn und Schichsal des russischen Kommunismus.* Luzern, 1937.

Breshkovskaya. *Hidden Springs of the Russian Revolution.*

Carr. *Michael Bakunin.*

Figner, Vera. *Memoirs of a Revolutionist.* London, 1927.

Georgievskii, A. N. *Kratkii Ocherk pravitel'stvennykh myer i prednachertanii protiv studenchiskikh bezporyadkov.* London and St. Petersburg, 1905.

Gol'denberg, L. B. "Vospominaniia," *Katorga i Ssylka*, Fasc. III, IV, V (1924).

Ivanov-Razumnik. *Istoriya russkoi obshchestvennoi mysli.*

Kantor, R. M. "Pis'ma Uchastnikov Protsessa 193," *Krasnyi arkhiv*, Fasc. II (1923).

Karpovich, Michael. "A Forerunner of Lenin: P. N. Tkachev," *Review of Politics*, Vol. VI.

Kluge. *Die Russische Revolutionäre Presse in der Zweiten Hälfte des Neunzehnten Jahrhunderts, 1855–1905.*

Kornilov. *Obshchestvennoe Dvizhenie pri Aleksandre II.* Moscow, 1909.

Koz'min. *P. N. Tkachev i Revolyutsionnoe Dvizhenie, 1860-kh godov.* Moscow, 1922.

Krupskaya, N. K. *Memories of Lenin.* 2 vols. New York, 1930.

Kulczycki, Ludwik. *Geschichte der Russischen Revolution. Einzig Autorisierte Übersetzung aus dem Polnischen von Anna Schapire-Neurath.* 3 vols. Gotha, 1910–11.

Lavrov. *Lettres Historiques.*

Bibliography

Lecky, W. E. H. *History of the Rise and Influence of Rationalism in Europe*. London and New York, 1914.

Nomad, Max. *Apostles of Revolution*. Boston, 1939.

Obshchestvennoe dvizhenie pri Aleksandre II. Paris, 1905.

Stepniak (Kravchinskii). *Underground Russia*.

Tatishchev. *Imperator Aleksandr Vtoroi*.

Titov, A. A. *Nikolai Vasil'evich Chaikovskii: Religioznyia i Obshchestvennyia Iskaniia*. Paris, 1929.

Tkachev, Petr Nikitich. *Izbrannye Sochineniya. red. vstp. Statia i Primechaniya V. P. Koz'min*. Moscow, 1919.

Venturi. *Il Populismo Russo*.

(Yakovlev, V. I.) *Revolyutsionnaya Zhurnalistika Semidesyatykh Godov*. Paris, 1905.

Zenkovskii, V. V. *A History of Russian Philosophy*. 2 vols. London, 1953.

CHAPTER VII

Ashenbrenner, N. Yu. *Voennaya organizatsiia "Narodnoi Voli" i drugie vospominaniia (1860–1904)*. Moscow, 1924.

Bakh, A. N. *Zapiski narodovol'tsa, Predislovie P. Anatol'eva*. Leningrad, 1931.

Bogucharskii, V. A. *Iz istorii politicheskoy borby v 70-kh i 80-kh gg. XX veka: Partiya "Narodnoi Voli," eya proiskhozhdenie, sud'ba i gibel'*. Moscow, 1912.

Buel, J. W. *Russian Nihilism and Exile Life in Siberia*. St. Louis, 1883.

Burtsev, V., ed. *Protsess shestnadtsatikh terroristov*. St. Petersburg, 1906.

Deutsch, Lev Grigorevich. "Pochemu ya stal revolyutsionnerom," *Golos minuvshago*, Fasc. V–XII (1919).

——. "Zagovor sredi krest'yan Chigirinskogo uezda," *Sbornik materialov i statey*, Fasc. I (1921).

DeWindt, Harry. *Siberia As It Is*. London, 1892.

Dragomanov. *K Biografii Zhelyabova*. Vol. II. Paris.

Figner. "Evgeniya Nikolaevna Figner," *Katorga i ssylka*, Fasc. II (1924).

——. *Narodovolets A. I. Barannikov v ego pis'makh*. Moscow, 1935.

——. *Polnoe sobranie sochinenii v semi tomakh*. Moscow, 1932.

Footman, David. *Red Prelude: Life of the Russian Terrorist Zhelyabov.* New Haven, 1945.

Ivanova-Boreytsa, Sof'ya. "Pervaya tipografiia 'Narodnoi Voli,' " *Byloe,* Fasc. IX (1906).

Ivantsin-Pisarev, A. I. "Pobeg P. A. Kropotkina," *Byloe,* Fasc. I.

Kantor. "Avtograficheskaya zapiska Stepana Shirayeva," *Krasnyi Arkhiv.* Fasc. VII (1924).

——. " 'Ispoved' Grigoriya Gol'denberga," *Krasnyi Arkhiv,* Fasc. V (1928).

Kennan. *Siberia and the Exile System.*

Koni, A. F. *Vospominaniia o dele Very Zasulich s predisloviem I. Teodorovicha.* Leningrad, 1933.

Koz'min. "K istorii 'Zemli i Voli' 70-kh godov," *Krasnyi Arkhiv,* Fasc. VI (1926).

Levitskii, V. (V. O. Tsederbaum). *Partiya "Narodnoi Voli" Vozniknovenie, bor'ba, gibel'.* Moscow and Leningrad, 1928.

Literatura partii "Narodnoi Voli." Moscow, 1907.

Lowe, Charles. *Alexander III of Russia.* New York, 1895.

Mikhailovskii. *Sochineniya,* SPB 1885, 1887–88. Vols. I–IV are "Izdanie 20e," Harvard Slav. 4347.4.1 (*Works,* 5 vols.).

Morozov, N. *Da zdrastvuet Narodnaya Volya: Istoricheskii sbornik.* Paris, 1907.

——. *Terroristicheskaya bor'ba.* London, 1880.

——. "Vozniknovenie 'Narodnoi Voli' (Iz vospominanii o Lipetskom i Voronezhskom s'ezdakh)," *Byloe,* Fasc. XII (1906).

"Moskva v marte 1881 goda," *Krasnyi Arkhiv.* Fasc. I (1926).

Nikolaevskii, B. I. "Ustav Ispolnitel'nogo Komiteta 'Narodnoi Voli,' " *Na chuzhoi storone,* Fasc. VII (1924).

Oshanina, Mariya Nikolaevna. "Pokazaniya: K istorii partii Narodnoi Voli," *Byloe,* Fasc. VI (1906).

Ovsyaniko-Kulikovskii. *Istoriya Russkoi Intelligentsii.*

Petrushevskii, I. I. "Iz zapisok obshchestvennogo deyatelia: Vospominaniya," *Arkhiv russkoy revolyutsii* (1934).

Pisnaya, V. N. "K biografii Zhelyabova (Materialy doznaniia po delu 193-kh)," *Katorga i ssylka,* Fasc. IV (1924).

——. "Studencheskie gody Zhelyabova," *Byloe,* Fasc. IV (1925).

"Protsess 20-ti narodovol'tsev v 1882 godu," *Byloe,* Fasc. I (1906).

Semenyuta, P. P. "Iz vospominanii ob A. I. Zhelyabova," *Byloe,* Fasc. IV (1906).

Bibliography

Shil'der, N. *Graf Eduard Ivanovich Totleben: Ego zhizn' i deya-tel'nost'*. St. Petersburg, 1882.
Solov'ev, A. K. "Pokushenie A. K. Solov'eva na tsareubiystvo 2 aprelya 1879 g., *Byloe*, Fasc. I–II (1918).
Tatishchev. *Imperator Aleksandr Vtoroi*.
Teodorovich, I. "Istoricheskoe znachenie partii 'Narodnoi Voli,' " *Katorga i ssylka*, Fasc. VII–IX (1929).
———. "K sporam o 'Narodnoi Voli,' " *Katorga i ssylka*, Fasc. I (1930).
———. "Pervoe marta 1881 goda," *Katorga i ssylka*, Fasc. III (1931).
Tikhomirov. *Russia: Political and Social*.
Yakovlev, Vasilii Yakovlevich, ed. *Literatura Partii Narodnoi Voli*. T^{ce} Pril. K Sv. Gosudarstvenniya prestupleniya v Rossii. Paris Société nouvelle de librairie et d'édition, 1905. No. 6 Russkaya Istoricheskaya Bibliotheka.
Zapiska o politicheskom sostoyanii Rossii vesnoy 1880 god. Berlin, 1881.

CHAPTER VIII

General

Alexinsky, Gregory. *Russia and Europe*. Trans. by Bernard Meal. London, 1917.
Baddeley, John F. *Russia in the Eighties*. London, 1921.
Brandt, B. F. *Inostrannye Kapitaly, ikh Vliianie na ekonomiches-koe Razvitie Strany*. 4 vols. St. Petersburg, 1898.
Breshkovskaya. *Hidden Springs of the Russian Revolution*.
Brutzkus, Boris. *Agrarentwicklung und Agrarrevolution in Russ-land*. Berlin, 1926.
Buel. *Russian Nihilism and Exile Life in Siberia*.
Byloe (monthly). St. Petersburg, 1906–1907. Suppressed, 1907. Superseded by *Minuvshie Gody*, published abroad.
Danilevsky, N. *Russland und Europa*. Stuttgart and Berlin, 1926.
DeWindt. *Siberia As It Is*.
Drage, Geoffrey. *Russian Affairs*. New York and London, 1904.
Finn–Enotaevskii, A. "Promyschlennyi Podem 1893–1899 Godov," *Sovremennoe Khoziaistvo Rossii* (1911), 45–50.
Gessen, I. V. *V Dvukh Vyekakh: Zhiznennyi Otchet*. Berlin, 1936.
Hedenstrom, Alfred von. *Geschichte Russlands von 1878 bis 1918*. Stuttgart and Berlin, 1922.

Human, Arthur. *Der Deutsch Russische Handelsverstrag vom 20, Marz, 1894.* Leipzig, 1900.

Istoriia Rossii v XIX Viekie. St. Petersburg.

Kennan. *Siberia and the Exile System.*

Kluge. *Die Russische Revolutionäre Presse in der Zweiten Hälfte des Neunzehnten Jahrhunderts, 1855–1905.*

Kornilov. *Ocherkii po Istorii Obschestvennago Dvizheniia i Krest'-ianshkago diela v Rossii.* St. Petersburg, 1905.

Korolenko, Vladimir. *Golodnyi God.* 5th edition. St. Petersburg, 1904.

Kovalevskii, Maxime. *La Russie à la Fin du XIX Siècle.* Paris, 1900.

Kulczycki. *Geschichte der Russischen Revolution. Einzig Autorisierte Übersetzung aus dem Polnischen von Anna Schapire-Neurath.*

Kulischer, Joseph. *Russische Wirtschaftgeschichte.* Jena, 1925.

Lamsdorf, V. N. *Dnevnik V. N. Lamsdorfa (1886–1890).* Ed. by F. A. Rothstein. Moscow, 1926.

Langer, William Leonard. *The Franco-Russian Alliance, 1890–1894.* Cambridge, 1929.

Lehmann, C., and Parvus. *Das Hungernde Russland.* Stuttgart, 1900.

Leroy-Beaulieu, Anatole. *L'Empire des Tsars et des Russes.* 3 vols. 3rd edition. Paris, 1893.

Martow, L. *Obshchestvennoe Dvizhenie i Umstvennye Techeniia v Period 1884–1905.* Istoriya Russkoi Literatury v XIX vieka, Izd. tov. Mir.

Mavor, James. *An Economic History of Russia.* 2 vols. 2nd edition, London, 1925.

Mendelieev, D. *K Poznaniiu Rossii.* München, Izdatel'stvo Milavida.

Migulin, P. P. *Russkii Gosudarstvennyi i Kredit (1769–1903).* 3 vols. Kharkov, 1904.

Milyukov, P. *Ocherki po Istorii Russkoi Kultury.* 3 vols. St. Petersburg, 1904.

Nikolai-On. *Histoire du Développement Economique de la Russie depuis l'affranchissement des serfs.* Paris, 1903.

Pobyedonostsev, K. P. *K. P. Pobyedonostsev i ego Korrespondenty.* Moscow, 1923.

———. *Moskovskii Sbornik.* 4th edition. Moscow, 1897.

Raffalovich, Arthur. *Russia: Its Trade and Commerce.* London, 1918.

Bibliography

Rosen, Baron. *Forty Years of Diplomacy.* 2 vols. London and New York, 1922.

Rozhkov, N. A. *Gorod i Derevnia v Russkoi Istorii.* 3rd edition. St. Petersburg, 1913.

Schlulze-Gävernitz, Gerhart O. *Volkswirtschäftliche Studien aus Ruszland.* Leipzig, 1899.

Spiridovich, General Alexandre. *Histoire du Terrorisme Russe, 1886–1917.* Paris, 1930.

Tengoborski. *Etudes sur les Forces Productives de la Russie.*

Tompkins, S. R. *Alaska.* Norman, 1945.

Tugan-Baranovsky, M. *Russkaya Fabrika v Proshlom i Nastoyashchem.* St. Petersburg, 1900.

Ular, Alexander. *Russia From Within.* New York, 1905.

Ulyanov, Vladimir (Lenin). *Razvitie Kapitalizma v. Rossii.* St. Petersburg, 1908.

Vestnik Narodnoi Voli, Sovremennoe Obozryenye. (1880–1886).

Vorontsev, V. P. *Sud'ba Kapitalizma v Rossii.* St. Petersburg, 1882.

Wallace, Sir Donald Mackenzie. *Russia.* 2 vols. New York, 1905.

Wittschewsky, Valentin. *Ruszlands Handels-Zoll-und Industriepolitik vom Peter dem Groszen auf die Gegenwart.* Berlin, 1905.

Ziv, V. S. *Inostrannye Kapitaly v Russkikh Aktionerykh Predpriyatyakh. Vypusk I, Germanskye Kapitaly.* Petrograd, 1915.

Zweig, Emil. *Die Russische Handelspolitik seit 1877.* Leipzig, 1906.

Peasant Agriculture, 1861 to 1917

Dietze, Constantin. *Stolypinsche Agrarreform und Feldgemeinschaft.* Leipzig and Berlin, 1920.

Fortunatov, A. *Itogi ekonomisheskago Izsledovaniia Rossiia.* Moscow, 1892.

Kovalevskii. *Obshchinnoe Zemlyevladenie prichiny, khodi i poslyedstviya ego Razlozheniya.*

Kuropatkin, A. A. *Zadachi Russkoi Armii.* 3 vols. St. Petersburg, 1910.

Lenin, V. I. *Razvitie Kapitalizma v. Rossii. Sochineniya.* Vol. III. 4th Edition. 1946.

Maslov, P. P., ed. *Obshchestvennoe Dvizhenie v Rossii v nachalye XX-go vyeka.* St. Petersburg, 1909–14.

263

Pavlovskii, Georgii. *Agricultural Russia on the Eve of the Revolution*. London, 1930.

Rozhkov, N. A. *Gorod i Derevnya v Russkoi Istorii*. 2nd edition. Moscow, 1904.

Sbornik Statisticheskikh Svyedenii po Moskovskom Gubernii: Otdyel Khozyaistvennoi Statistiki. Moscow, 1879.

Velikaya Reforma. 6 vols. Moscow, 1911. Contains articles by the following: Manuilov, "Reforma 19 Fevrala i obshchinnoe zemlevladenie"; Annenskii, "Chernyshevskii i krest'yanskaya Reforma"; Worms, "Polozhenie 19 Fevrala, 1861"; Kornilov, "Krest'yanskoe Samoupravlenie po polozheniyu"; Leont'ev, "Zakonodatel'stvo o krest'yankakh posle reformy"; Kranikhfel'd, "Poreformennoe krest'yanstvo v belletristike"; Pyeskokonov, "Ekonomicheskoe polozhenie v poreformennoe vremya"; Shakhovskii, "Vykupnye platezhy."

CHAPTER IX

Biographies of Lenin

Fox, Ralph Winston. *Lenin; A Biography*. London, 1933.

Hill, Christopher. *Lenin and the Russian Revolution*. New York, 1950.

Hollis, Christopher. *Lenin*. Milwaukee, 1938.

Kerzhentsev, Platon Mikhailovich. *Life of Lenin*. New York, 1939.

Krupskaya. *Memories of Lenin*.

Marcu, Valeriu. *Lenin*. Trans. by E. W. Dickes. New York, 1928.

Shub, David. *Lenin, A Biography*. Garden City, 1948.

Trotsky, Leon. *Lenin*. Authorized trans. New York and London, 1925.

Vernadsky, George. *Lenin, Red Dictator*. Trans. by Malcolm Waters Davis. New Haven and London, 1931.

Wolfe, Bertram David. *Three Who Made a Revolution*. New York, 1948.

General

Baron, Samuel H. "Plekhanov and the 'Emancipation of Labor' Group, 1883–1895," unpublished Ph.D. dissertation, Columbia University, 1952.

Dan, F. I. *Proiskhozhdenie Bol'shevizma, Izdatel'stvo "Novaya Demokratiya."* New York, 1946.

Bibliography

Bibliography

Garvi, P. A., *Vospominaniya Sotsial-demokrata*. New York, 1945.
Golder, F. A., *Documents of Russian History*. New York and London, 1927.
History of the Communist Party of the Soviet Union (Bolsheviks). The official English translation of *Istoriya Vsesoyuznoi Kommunisticheskoi Partii (Bol'sheviki)*.
Iskra. Organ of the Social Democratic party, 1900–1905.
Lenin. *Letters of Lenin*. Trans. and edited by Elizabeth Hill and Doris Mudie. New York, 1937.
——. *Selected Works*. 12 vols. Moscow and Leningrad, 1934.
——. *Sochineniya*. 34 vols. 4th edition. Moscow. (Deserving special attention are "Razvitie kapitalizma-v Rossii," Vol. III, and "Chto takoe druz'ya naroda?", Vol. I.)
Martow. *Geschichte der russischen Sozialdemokratie*. Trans. by Alexander Stern. Berlin, 1926.
Plekhanov, Georgii. *In Defense of Marxism*. Trans. by Andrew Rothstern. London, 1947.
——. *Nashi Raznoglasiya*. Geneva, 1884.
——. *Sochineniya*. 24 vols. St. Petersburg, 1920–27.
——. *Sotsializm i Politicheskaya Bor'ba*. Geneva, 1883.
Popov, N. N. *Ocherk istorii vsesoyuznoi kommunishicheskoi partii (Bolsheviki)*. Moscow and Leningrad, 1930.
Potresov and Nikolayevskii, eds. *Sotsial-demokratichiskoe dvizhenie v Rossii. Materialy*. 2 vols. Moscow and Leningrad, 1927.
Treadgold, Donald W. *Lenin and his Rivals: The Struggle for Russia's Future, 1898–1906*. New York, 1955.
Vpered. Organ of the Bolsheviks, founded after the second party congress in London in 1903.
Yaroslavskii, Yemilian, ed. *Istoriya V. K. P. (B)*. 3 vols. Moscow and Leningrad, 1939.
——. *Kratkaya Istoriya V. K. P. (B)*. 3rd edition. 1931.

CHAPTER X

Material on the history of the Social Revolutionary party is scarce. In the absence of an official history, the following contain some useful matter:
Chernov, V. M. *Rozhdenie revolyutsionnoi Rossii*. Paris, 1934.
——. *Pered Burei: Vospominaniya*. New York, 1953.
Gessen. *V Dvukh Vyekakh*.

265

Iskra. (Organ of Social Democrats.) 1900–1905.
Kulczycki. *Geschichte der Russischen Revolution.*
Mavor. *An Economic History of Russia.*
Nicolaevsky, Boris. *Azeff the Spy.* New York, 1934.
Protokoly I Syezda Partii Sotsialistov Revolyutsionerov. 1906.
Radkey, O. "The Party of the Socialist Revolutionaries and the Russian Revolution of 1917." Unpublished dissertation for Harvard University, 1939.
Spiridovich. *Histoire du terrorisme russe, 1886–1917.*
Treadgold. *Lenin and His Rivals.* New York, 1955.

CHAPTER XI

Astrov, N. I. *Vospominaniya.* Paris, 1940
Chernov. *Pered Burei.*
Chernyshevskii. *Polnoe Sobranie, Sochinenii.*
Dovnar-Zapol'skii, M. V. *Iz Istorii Obshchestvennykh Techenii v Rossii.* Kiev, 1905.
Gessen. *V Dvukh Vyekakh.*
Gurko, V. I. *Features and Figures of the Past: Government and Opinion in the Reign of Nicholas II.* Stanford, 1939.
Haxthausen. *The Russian Empire.* London, 1856.
Hedenstrom. *Geschichte Russlands von 1878 bis 1918.*
Hoetzsch, Otto. *Russland.* Berlin, 1917.
Ivanov-Razumnik. *Istoriya russkoi obshchestvennoi mysli.*
Kizevetter, A. A. *Na rubezhe dvukh stoletti* (Vospominaniya, 1881–1914). Prague, 1929.
Kornilov. *Obshchestvennoe Dvizhenie pri Aleksandre II, 1855–1881.*
Krupskaya. *Memories of Lenin.* New York, 1930.
Maklakov, V. A. *Iz Vospominanii.* New York, 1954.
———. *Vlast' i obshchestvemost' na zakatie staroi Rossii.* 3 vols. Paris, 1928.
Maslov, Potresov and Martow, eds. *Obshchestvennoe dvizhenie v. Rossii v nachalye XX-go vyeka.*
Milyukov. *Russia and Its Crisis.*
Ovsyaniko-Kulikovskii. *Istoriya Russkoi Intelligentsii.*
Semevskii. *Politicheskie i Obshchestvennye Idei Dekabristov.* St. Petersburg, 1909.

Bibliography

Tatishchev. *Imperator Aleksandr Vtoroi.*
Wallace. *Russia.*

CHAPTER XII

General

Badayev, A. E. *Bol'sheviki v gosudarstvennoi Dumye.* Moscow, 1932.
Bing, J., ed. *Letters of the Tsar Nicholas and the Empress Marie.* London, 1938.
Bok (Bock), M. P. *Vospominaniya o moem otsye P. A. Stolypinye.* New York, 1953.
Burtsev. *Borba za svobodnuyu Rossiyu.* Berlin, 1923.
Chermenskii, E. D. *Burzhuaziya i tsarizm v revolyutsii, 1905–1907.* Moscow, 1939.
Gessen. *V Dvukh Vyekakh.*
Golder, F. A. *Documents of Russian History, 1914–1917.* New York and London, 1927.
Gosudarstvennaya Duma. Stenograficheskie Otchety. St. Petersburg, 1906–16.
Gurko. *Features and Figures of the Past.*
Izvolsky, A. P. *The Memoirs of Alexander Izvolsky.* London, 1920.
Kaidanova. *Ocherki po Istorii Narodnogo Obrazovaniya v Rossii i S. S. S. R.*
Kokovtsov, V. N. *Iz Moego Proshlago: Vospominaniya, 1903–1919.* Paris, 1933.
———. *Out of My Past.* Stanford, 1933.
Kryzhanovskii. *Vospominaniya.*
Levin, A. *The Second Duma.* New Haven, 1940.
Maklakov. *Iz Vospominanii.*
———. *Vtoraya Gosudarstvennaya Duma.* Paris, 1946.
———. *Pervaya Gosudarstvennaya Duma (Vospominaniya Sovremennika).* Paris, 1939.
———. *Vlast i obshchestvennost'na zakatie staroi Rossii.*
Milyukov. *God bor'by.* St. Petersburg, 1907.
———. *Russia Today and Tomorrow.* New York, 1922.
———. *Vospominaniya (1859–1917),* 2 vols. New York, 1955.
Nicolaevsky, Boris. *Azeff the Spy.* New York, 1934.
Olgin, M. J. *The Soul of the Russian Revolution.* New York, 1917.

267

Padenie Tsarskogo Rezhima (*The Fall of the Tsarist Regime*). 7 vols. Leningrad, 1924–26.

Pares, Sir Bernard. "The Second Duma," *Slavonic Review*, Vol. II (1923–24), 36–55.

——. *My Russian Memoirs.* London, 1931.

——. *Russia and Reform.* London, 1907.

Shipov, D. N. *Vospominaniya i dumy: o perezhitom.* Moscow, 1918.

Spiridovich. *Histoire du terrorisme russe.*

Walsh, W. B. "Political Parties in the Russian Dumas." *Journal of Modern History*, Vol. XXII. (1951).

Whyte, Frederick. *The Life of W. T. Stead.* New York and Boston, 1925.

Witte. *The Memoirs of Count Witte.* New York and Toronto, 1921.

——. *Samoderzhavie i Zemstvo.*

——. *Vospominaniia.* Berlin, 1922–23.

——. *Zapiska po krest'yanskomu dyelu.* St. Petersburg, 1904.

Stolypin's Reforms

Dietze. *Stolypinsche Agrarreform und Feldgemeinschaft.*

Dorosch, Henry. *The Russian Agrarian Reform.* Philadelphia, 1927.

Lyashchenko. *History of the National Economy of Russia to the 1917 Revolution.*

Mavor. *An Economic History of Russia.*

Maynard. *The Russian Peasant and Other Studies.*

Owen, Launcelot A. *The Russian Peasant Movement, 1906–1917.* Westminster, 1937.

Pavlovskii. *Agricultural Russia on the Eve of the Revolution.*

CHAPTER XIII

Gershenzohn, M. O., ed. *Vyekhi; Sbornik Statei o russkoi intelligentsii.* Moscow, 1909.

Gessen. *V Dvukh Vyekakh.*

Intelligentsiya v Rossii. St. Petersburg, 1909.

Ivanov-Razumnik. *Istoriya russkoi obshchestvennoi mysli.*

Kaidanova. *Ocherki po Istorii Narodnogo Obrazovaniya v Rossii i S. S. S. R.*

Kitchin, George. *A Prisoner of the Ogpu.* New York, 1935.

Bibliography

Krupskaya. *Memories of Lenin.*
Lenin. *Sochineniya.*
Lossky, N. *History of Russian Philosophy.* New York. 1951.
Ovsyaniko-Kulikovskii. *Istoriya Russkoi Intelligentsii.*
Solov'ev, V. *Sobranie Sochinenii.* 10 vols. St. Petersburg, 1911.
———. *Pis'ma Vladimira Sergeyevicha Solov'eva.* 3 vols. St. Petersburg, 1908.
Struve, Petr. *Patriotca.* St. Petersburg, 1911.
Zenkovskii. *A History of Russian Philosophy.*

CHAPTER XIV

Since Chapter XIV constitutes largely a summary and an interpretation, I have drawn material from widely differing sources. I mention below only some of the material used.

Aldanov, M. "Tret'e Marta" in *P. N. Milyukov: Sbornik Materialov v chest' ego desyatilyetiya.* Paris. 1929.
Astrov. *Vospominaniya.*
Berdyaev. *The Origins of Russian Communism.* London, 1937.
———. *The Russian Idea.* New York, 1948.
Breshkovskaya. *Hidden Springs of the Russian Revolution.*
Chernyshevskii. *Izbrannye Ekonomicheskie Proizvedeniia.*
Dillon, E. J. (Lanin). *Russian Characteristics.* London, 1892.
———. *The Eclipse of Russia.* New York, 1918.
Dorovatskii and Chernuzhnikov. *Ocherki realisticheskago mirozryeniya.* St. Petersburg, 1905.
Dovnar-Zapol'skii. *Iz Istorii Obshchestvennykh Techenii v Rossii.*
Florinskii, M. T. *The End of the Russian Empire.* New Haven, 1931.
Kohn, Hans, ed. *The Mind of Modern Russia: Historical and Political Thought of Russia's Great Age.* New Brunswick, 1955.
Kokovtsev. *Out of My Past.*
Kucharzewski, J. *The Origins of Modern Russia.* New York, 1948.
Lednicki, Waclaw. *The New Europe.* n.p. n.d.
Lemke. *Ocherki Osvoboditel'nago Dvizheniya Shestidesyatykh Godov.*
Leroy-Beaulieu. *The Empire of the Tsars and the Russians.* 3 vols. New York and London, 1905.
Lyaschenko. *History of the National Economy of Russia to the 1917 Revolution.*

The Russian Intelligentsia

Maklakov. *Iz Vospominanii.*
Milyukov. *Russia and Its Crisis.* Chicago, 1905.
———. *Russia Today and Tomorrow.*
Obshchestvennoe dvizhenie pri Aleksandre II. Paris, 1905.
Pares. *The Fall of the Russian Monarchy.* London, 1939.
Pokrovskii, M. N. *Leninizm i Russkaya istoriya.* Moscow, 1930.
Popov, N. Tatishchev i ego vremya. Moscow, 1861.
Potresov, A. N. *Etudy o russkoi intelligentsii: Sbornik statei.* St.
    Petersburg, 1906.
Shulgin, V. *Dni.* Leningrad, 1925.
Sokolov, N. M. *Ob ideyakh i idealakh russkoi intelligentsii.* St.
    Petersburg, 1904.
Stalin, J. *Sochineniya.* 13 vols. Moscow, 1951.
Tikhomirov. *Pochemu ya perestal byt' revolyutsionerom.* Moscow,
    1895.
Venturi. *Il Populismo Russo.*
Wallace. *Russia.*
Walsh. *The Fall of the Russian Empire.* Boston, 1928.

Glossary of Russian Terms

Agent provocateur: an agent employed by the secret police to worm his way into the confidence of a person suspected of subversive designs and induce him to betray himself and his associates.

Artel: a form of co-operative enterprise.

Chernyi Peredyel: "Black Repartition," the name given to the moderate wing of the Populists (*narodniki*) in the eighties.

Chinovnichestvo: "officialdom," a collective noun derived from *chinovnik*, an official; the term is derogatory.

Decembrist revolt: an unsuccessful armed revolt led by army officers in 1825 to overthrow the Tsar and the existing government. The main events occurred on December 26.

Desyatin: a land measure, roughly equal to one hectare.

Golova: literally "a head," the name given to the chief official in a town; a mayor.

Guberniya: in tsarist times, a province.

Intelligentsia: A collective noun to include persons sometimes called "intelligenty" by the Russians. Although seeming to embrace a group of persons of superior education and intelligence, it actually designated only a small minority fanatically devoted to the cause of revolution.

Izpravnik: the head of the police in the county.

Knut: a whip consisting of a stock and a leather lash, used for punishing criminals.

271

Kolokol: a bell.

Myeshchanin (plural, *myeshchane*): a class of small craftsmen and traders, lowly regarded in Russia.

Myeshchanstvo: an abstract term derived from the above, to designate those characteristics which Russians thought to see in the *myeshchane;* an almost untranslatable term, the nearest English equivalent to which would appear to be Matthew Arnold's term "philistinism."

Nadyel: the allotment of land on an estate for one peasant family.

Narodnaya Volya: "People's Will," the extreme fanatical wing of of the revolutionary organization known as *Zemlya i Volya.*

Narodnichestvo: a general term for the movement involving the *narodniki.*

Narodniki: a term applied somewhat loosely to those revolutionary leaders who advocated various forms of peasant socialism; sometimes rendered "populists."

Nechayevshchina: a general term for the movement of which Nechayev was the center. It is formed on the analogy of the word *Pugachevshchina* (the Pugachev movement); used with a derogatory connotation.

Neglasnyi komitet: literally "secret committee," used in the sense of "privy" in privy council; describes the emperor's own private committee.

Obrok: payment in money or in kind from the peasant to his landlord for the use of his land.

Okhrana (more properly *Okhranoe Otdyelenie*): a name applied to the special police force created in 1881 to combat the revolutionaries and to protect the person of the emperor.

Osvobozhdenie: "Emancipation," the name adopted by Peter Struve for his periodical started in Stuttgart in 1902.

Osvobozhdenie Truda: "emancipation of labor," the name adopted by Plekhanov for his group operating among the industrial workers in Russia after 1893.

Osvobozhdentsy: persons associated with Struve in his enterprise.

Otnoshenie: a document sent by one department or official in the government to another.

Pansions (French, *pensions*): boarding schools.

Pomyest'e: a system of land tenure in which the holder was required to perform certain services.

Glossary

Pugachevshchina: the Pugachev peasant and Cossack revolt in the reign of Catherine.

Raskol'niki: "dissidents," the name applied to those who withdrew from the Orthodox church in the great schism of 1667.

Raznochintsy: originally, a member of the intelligentsia of other than noble origin; he might belong to the clergy, the merchant class, or even the peasantry.

Redemption dues: yearly dues rendered by the peasant to the government for his land, under a long-term purchase contract.

Slavophile: one belonging to a school of writers at the middle of the nineteenth century which wished Russia to return to an earlier tradition in which religious faith would play a greater role in her culture.

Sovremennik: "Contemporary," the name given to a periodical founded by Alexander Pushkin.

Starosta: the head man of the village.

Sudebnye Palaty: a court of the second instance; a court of appeal for the district.

Third Section (of the Imperial Chancery): a special force of police that came into existence in 1826 just after the Decembrist revolt. It came under the monarch's direct control. It was replaced in 1881 by the *Okhrana.*

Tsenzura karatel'naya: "punitive censorship," a system which allowed editors and writers to publish without preliminary approval, but at the risk of committing an offense under the law.

Tsenzura predvaritel'naya: "preliminary censorship," a system of censorship which required editors and writers to submit a manuscript for the permission of the board of censorship before publication.

Usadba: the peasant's cottage, together with outhouses, garden, and orchard; awarded to the peasant as his personal property under the emancipation of 1861.

Uyezd: county.

Vyekhi: Signposts.

Zemlya i Volya: a revolutionary group formed in 1876 which favored peasant socialism.

Zemskii Sobor: an assembly of various orders that existed during the sixteenth and seventeenth centuries.

273

Zemstvo (plural, *zemstva*): an institution for local government that came into existence in 1864. *Zemstva* were either county or provincial.

Index

Index

194; decree of dissolution, 196; in budget control, 201; manifesto of June 3, 1907, 202; Third Duma opened, 202; Fourth Duma, 207; leaders blamed, 207; revolutionary spirit of First and Second Dumas comes to an end, 223
Dzhaparidze: proposes political education instead of food, 200

Economic development: slow in post-reform period, 21; conflict between the government and revolutionary beliefs, 146
"Editing commission": 7
Education: ban on private schools and *pensions* raised, 24; Sunday schools, 241f.
Electoral law: of December 11, 1905, 191; of June 3, 1907, 204
Emancipation: proclamation, 8; compromise, 15; contradiction, 16; change of attitude on, 52ff.; unsettled questions, 62
English Revolution of 1688: 178
Estonia: peasant reform, 1816, 5

Famine of 1891–92: 161; revolutionary tempo quickens, 153; attitude of revolutionaries towards, 174
Fighting Organization: 164; stage a bank robbery, 169f.; fresh plots against the Tsar, Stolypin, Grand Duke Nikolai Nikolayevich, 170
First Duma: 169
Flerovskii (Bervy-Flerovskii), D. I.: contributes to the "To the people" movement, 110
Frank, S. L.: contributor to *Vyekhi*, 214; indicts revolutionists in "Etika Nigilizma," 219; defines intelligentsia member as "warrior monk," 220
Free Word (organ of liberals): 180
Fulon, General (chief of police): 187

Gapon, Father: and national minority groups of socialists, 167; induces workers to march on the Winter Palace, 187
Geikin, Baron (captain of gendarmes): killed at Kiev, 123

General Committee on peasant question: formed from nonofficial committee, 7
Gershenzon, M. O.: editor of *Vyekhi*, 213f.
Gessen: resents efforts to discredit revolutionary movement, 223
Gogol, Nikolai: 42
Goldenberg, G. D.: deserts *Narodnaya Volya*, 136
Gold Standard: 21
Goremykin (president of council of ministers): 197
Gredeskul, N. A.: writes in *Intelligentsiya v Rossii*, 224

Hague, The, Peace Conference of 1898: 147
Haxthausen, Baron: report on Russian agriculture, 54; visited Russia in 1841, 177
Herzen, Alexander: critical of government, 27; offers to publish *Sovremennik* in London, 28; "Very Dangerous," 30; effect of support of Poles, 37; denounces nihilists, 49; contributes to nihilism, 50; views on the peasant question, 56f.; disillusionment with emancipation, 64; works diluted by Kavelin, 184f.; considers relation of individual to society, 215; Kolokol appeals to discontent, 232

Ignatov (member of *Osvobozhdenie Truda*): 148
Illegal press: underground publications, 94; *émigré* journals, 94
Incendiary fires: in St. Petersburg, 1862, 28; lead to arrest of Chernyshevskii, 34
Industrial boom: effect on revolutionary ideas, 161
Industrial Revolution: 176
Intellectual life of the nineties: 162
Intelligentsia: against the government, 97f.; attitude towards the famine, 145; characterization of new Marxist revolutionaries, 155f.; Berdyaev's views on, 220
Iron and steel industry: suffers as a result of emancipation, 21

277

Index

126f.; becomes minister of interior, 127
Lossky, N.: 222f.

Mad Summer (of 1873): 110f.
Maklakov, V. A.: on negotiations between Milyukov and Trepov, 195; negotiations for Kadet cabinet, 196; on a parliamentary system, 242
Manchester School: 176
Manifesto of October 17: 188, 202
Manuilov: on the retention of the commune, 63n.
Marxism, converts from: votaries of, 180; fitted into discipline of Social Democratic party, 216; expression of apostasy in view of government, 217; ignore personal responsibility, 219
Marx, Karl: *Das Kapital*, 149
Massacre of Jan. 9.: 187
Mass trials: trial of the 50, trial of the 193, 114
Meshcherskii, Prince: influence on the press, 82
Mikhail, Grand Duke: refuses the crown, 249
Mikhailov, A.: brings back proclamation "To the Younger Generation," 29
Mikhailovskii, Nikolai: spokesman for *Narodnaya Volya*, 129; insists on communal labor, 129; and direction of human affairs, 129f.; and orthodox marxism of Plekhanov, 180; works diluted by Kareyev, 185; and relation of individual to society, 215; criticized by Berdyaev, 217; attitude toward securing privileges guaranteed by law, 243
Military service: compulsory in 1874 for all, 13
Milyukov, P. N.: *Russia and its Crisis*, 183; objective of, 184; Clemenceau urges government to appoint as head, 195; negotiates with Trepov, 195; insists cabinet be entirely of Kadets, 196; supports intelligentsia, 224; on relations between sovereign and people, 231; urges Grand Duke Mikhail to take throne, 249

Milyutin: deputy to Lanskoy, 6; removed, 8
"Movement of liberation": 181, 217
Mozentsov, General-Adjutant: killed by terrorists, 124
Mukden: battle before, 188
Municipal self-government, 1870: amplification of Catherine's reform of 1785, 13
Muraviev, Count: suppresses Polish revolt, 36
Mutinies in the fleet: Sveaborg, Cronstadt, Black Sea, 169
"*Myeshchanstvo*": 177

Narodnaya Volya: blows up wing of Winter Palace, 126; blows up imperial train, 126; espouses cause of complete political freedom, 133f.; suspends activity until after the coronation of Alexander II, 138; hardly survives famine of 1891–92, 142; carries on agitation among workers, 149
Narodnichestvo: 52; origin of, 67; liberalism last flowering of, 184
Narodniki: 52; ignore backwardness of peasant agriculture, 98; do not distinguish between worker and peasant, 149
Natanson, M. A. (leader of the *Chaikovtsy*): 106
Nechayev, Sergei G.: relations with Bakunin, 104; *Catechism of the Revolutionist*, 104; *Narodnaya Rasprava*, 105f.; falls into hands of Tsarist police, 106
Nekrasov: poem on censorship, 26
Nicholas I: denounces serfdom, 5
Nicholas II: reply to address from the *Zemstva* in 1895, 179
Nihilism: popularized by Turgenev, 39; term applied loosely to revolutionary terrorists, 39; repudiation of artistic and ethical standards, 40; effects of, 40; contributions to, 43; forerunner of, in Europe, 44; characteristic sayings of nihilists, 45; anti-estheticism, 45; explanations from Russian society, 46f.; the *raznochintsy* as explanation, 48;

Index